The Dance of Opposites

Ancient wisdom for promoting health and happiness in the here and now.

By
Rudy Scarfalloto

Introduction by Robert Anton Wilson

Bookman LLC
Publishing & Marketing
**Providing Quality, Professional
Author Services**
www.bookmanmarketing.com

The first edition of this book was published in 1998, under the title *The Alchemy of Opposites*.

READERS' COMMENTS

"A very important work."
—Margaret Hiller, Unity Minister, co-author of *Dare to Dream*

"For those who hunger for truth, but are confused by the many conflicting ideas in the literary market, *The Dance of Opposites* is a breath of fresh air."
—Constance C. Pettigrew, Author, Humorist, Recovery Counselor

"This book gives us profound insight into one of the most fundamental features of life within the physical body—the interaction of opposites."
—William Richards, Author of *Pearls of Wisdom*

"Dr. Scarfalloto's work breaks free from the restrictions and assumptions of other models. His work has exceeded my expectations."
—Joel Rachelson, Ph.D., Psychotherapist

"What Dr. Scarfalloto has done is AMAZING! There is more insight in one page of this book than in 100 pages of most other books I have read. I found myself re-reading some chapters two or three or even four times."
—Elizabeth Sundby, Teacher

"A poignant, courageous and, at times, quite humorous work."
—Jim Gabriel, Director of The Academy of Somatic Healing Arts.

CONTENTS

ACKNOWLEDGEMENTS

I would like to thank the following individuals whose teachings and insights helped me in writing this book:

Dr. Camden Clay, for putting into application the idea, "The only way out is way in."

Joseph Collins and Dr. Jerry Epps, for those spontaneous and enlightening discussions.

Lee and Suzanne Harris, for teaching me the key idea that opposites are two sides of the same coin.

Robert Stephens, for his excellent work in Mastery of Words.

Justin Sterling, for his insights into the interaction of men and women.

Special thanks to my beloved former wife, Angelia Wicker, whose magical presence was instrumental in bringing this book to life.

INTRODUCTION
by Robert Anton Wilson

Every month I receive a pile of books the publishers want me to read and to comment upon. Very, very rarely do I receive one that arouses my enthusiasm as much as the present work, which manages to bring some of the most advanced concepts of Oriental and Occidental mysticism into a framework so down-to-earth that even the allegedly esoteric "unity underlying all opposites" seems so obvious that you wonder how anyone could ever have overlooked it.

Indeed, the singular achievement of this book consists in making you understand why the human mind must overlook unity once we begin thinking at all, and why we must re-discover it if we continue thinking clearly enough and long enough. Only one other book explains so clearly why we always begin by positing polar opposites and why we must end by reconciling the opposites: G. Spencer Brown's *Laws of Form*. And, alas, you need some background in mathematical logic and cybernetics to understand Spencer Brown. You just need common sense and an open mind to understand Dr. Scarfalloto.

Dr. Scarfalloto begins with an enlarged **Y** to illustrate the bifurcation of the nervous system when the brain stem splits into the right and left brain hemispheres. This hauntingly resembles Dr. Wilhelm Reich's famous diagram for the big-energetic unity underlying biology and psychology:

And that, in turn, suggests the bottom, or root, of the well-known emblem of medicine, the staff with two intertwined serpents (which appeared in the dream that inspired this book), as Dr. Scarfalloto explains in the introduction.

In China, the same symbolism appears in the philosophy of the Tao, the cosmic energy that always manifests as the opposing forces of yin and yang.

A symbolism that appears in so many places and times does not belong in the category of "beliefs" or "concepts." It pre-exists such front-brain abstraction. It comes, rather, from that timeless abyss which Carl Jung called the "collective unconscious," or from Sheldrake's "morphic field," or the "akashic records" of Theosophy —i.e., from a level so deep that we cannot profitably consider its symbols as ideas but only as the preconditioning forms (or archetypes) out of which all of our less primitive images, and eventually abstract ideas, can grow.

Dr. Scarfalloto's method of reducing all opposites to their underlying unities uses only everyday examples from ordinary human life so that anybody can understand this book. (Few can understand Jung, Sheldrake, Leary, etc.) Consider by contrast the shock tactics of Aleister Crowley:

Nothing is.
Nothing becomes.
Nothing is not.

The mind whirls. If one has the taste for this kind of meta-logic, one struggles with Crowley for a long time before understanding what these Strange Loops communicate. Most people lack that taste and give up quickly. Nobody will give up on *The Dance Opposites,* I suspect. It deals immediately and urgently with our most intimate and painful conflicts and shows us with great clarity how we got into them and how we can work our way out of them again.

A last word: this book seems too good for simple "reading." Rather, you should keep it handy and re-read a chapter a day for a few years, until you begin to *feel deeply* the simple path that Dr. Scarfalloto presents.

Robert Anton Wilson

FOREWORD

The Snake

This book was born early one morning when I awoke from a startling dream. The main feature of the dream was a snake. Snakes in dreams are not that unusual. This creature, however, was thousands of feet long and proportionately wide, and had *two* extremely ferocious looking heads.

In the dream, I was flying close to the snake's heads, high in the air among the clouds. The beast undulated in a most menacing manner. Its tail was far below on the ground. The two heads had intense, ravenous eyes. Each mouth was wide open, revealing dagger-like teeth and a sharply forked tongue.

The serpent was also extremely venomous. It was obviously capable of annihilating me with no effort at all. In addition, I saw that its power was so great that it could easily swoop down and destroy all of humanity.

Even though I was afraid, I prepared myself to fight. I did so by climbing into a two-headed snake costume, which was going to act as my "battleship." And so, we squared off, ready to do battle, high in the air among the clouds. At that point, I awoke.

For a while, I remained motionless in bed with my eyes closed. Behind my closed eyelids, I still saw the gigantic snake, and I continued sensing its horrific destructive power, as if the dream was still in progress.

Even after I opened my eyes, I continued feeling its deadly presence. I stared at the sky through the open window in my room, watching the clouds drift by.

For me, the dream was, to say the least, unprecedented. Still seeing the snake clearly in my mind, I said to myself, "This probably means something."

As the emotional impact of the dream gradually wore off, I took note of my initial impressions as to the meaning of the dream. The first impressions upon awakening tend to be the most accurate, because the door to the subconscious mind is still wide open, and the uncensored information is readily available.

In this particular dream, I had several strong impressions. I remained in bed and allowed them to crystallize in my mind.

Later that day, I consulted books and experts to get additional information as to the possible meaning of the symbols in the dream. Not surprisingly, I found no reference to extremely ferocious two-headed snakes of monstrous proportions. So, I went back to my strong initial impressions, which were as follows:

- The two-headed snake symbolized *duality* – the dance of opposites. This idea was reinforced by the appearance of the second snake (me in the costume).

- The humongous size of the snake suggested that the duality in question wasn't merely one particular pair of opposites. It was the granddaddy of dualities, containing within it all other pair of opposites.

- The foreboding feeling that the snake was extremely powerful and dangerous suggested that I would either master it or be devoured by it – devoured by the conflicting opposing forces within me.

- The dreaded fear that the snake could destroy me and all people on Earth suggested that the snake not only symbolized duality within me personally, but also touched into the collective consciousness of humanity. This impression was reinforced by the snake's tremendous size and extremely high altitude above the earth – its two heads ready to swoop down on the population below.

- The final impression was that if I tried to overpower and destroy the snake, I would surely lose. The message was, *Don't kill it, just understand it.* If this had been an actual snake in the outer world, I would have laughed at such an idea; however, since the snake was a symbol of the opposing forces within my own mind, the idea that I could master it through understanding was reasonable.

Duality Is Fun...Except When It Isn't

In the days that followed the dream, my mind was flooded with a variety of opposing qualities and concepts. As I watched each pair of opposites parade through my mind, I had the notion that duality is beautiful, and that it does not have to be synonymous with conflict. I saw a man and woman dancing, rejoicing in their differences; the strength of him delighting in the grace of her, and the grace of her embracing the strength of him. I then had the frightening and exciting notion that *all opposites* can be experienced in this manner.

When inner duality is *not* fun, it shows up as neurosis – a condition in which opposing forces are at war within the individual. We set them at war with each other by judging one as good and the other as bad. We then identify ourselves with the one that is judged as good and pretend the other doesn't exist – except maybe in someone else.

External forms of duality are generally well tolerated. Most of us do not experience neurosis because *up* is the opposite of *down*. We are not emotionally tortured by the fact that *hot* is the opposite of *cold*. We do not lose sleep over the oppositeness of *night* and *day*. However, when the opposing forces consist of our own emotions and thoughts, we find it more difficult to just observe them without taking the whole thing personally.

This book addresses those interesting forms of *internal* duality – inner opposites – such as truth/lie, hold on/let go, pleasure/pain, forgiveness/revenge, birth/death, etc.

The Big Joke

The big joke is this: *With any pair of opposites, the side we have judged as inferior is the one that rules us.* Likewise, when we see both sides and recognize them as partners in the dance of creation, the inner conflict or neurosis dies. It does not die, however, as a soldier on a battlefield. It dies as a seed dies when it breaks its outer shell and becomes a sprout. The sprout is the awareness of life beyond the war of opposing forces.

In other words, when we see the harmonious dance of opposites in the world of duality, we awaken within us the remembrance of singularity or unity. We start to see such harmony by first understanding what opposites really are. So, we will begin by asking a simple question: What is it that makes two things opposites? That question is answered in chapter one.

CHAPTER 1

Not Just Apples and Oranges

"What about apples and oranges?" asked the young lady, sitting in the first row.

I was teaching my usual anatomy and physiology class to a lively group of budding massage therapists. When the young lady asked her question, I stopped in my tracks, at first, not knowing what to say. You see, up to that moment, the class was not actually focused on anatomy and physiology – not in the usual sense, anyway. We had sort of gone off on a tangent, and somehow found ourselves talking about the interaction opposites. Massage students are like that. On the surface, they may look like average citizens, but in reality, they tend to be renaissance thinkers – interested in just about everything.

We were talking about how the very life within our bodies is a dance of opposites. "When the dance is harmonious," I declared, "life renews itself."

The class had been happily rambling on about the dance of opposites within us and around us, when that young lady asked about apples and oranges. Apparently, in her mind, apples and oranges were opposites. They aren't, but she didn't know that because I had not bothered to explain what constitutes "opposites". There I was, trying to get the students to understand that creation is a dance of opposites, when I had not even bothered to define "opposites". *Opposites are partners in the dance of creation.* Sounds rather cosmic, but it has no meaning if you think that opposites are just "apples and oranges". We might nod our heads in philosophical agreement as we say: *when opposites are balanced and integrated, life renews itself,* but the statement doesn't really mean anything if we do not first understand what makes two things opposites.

So, the class went off on yet another tangent as we endeavored to clearly define opposites. We were neglecting our regular class work;

but that was okay because they were a bright group and we were ahead of schedule anyway.

If Two Things Are Opposites…

If two things are opposites, they define each other. Each side has meaning only in the presence of the other. If we eliminate one, the other loses it identity. For example, night defines day, up defines down, hot defines cold, young defines old, darkness defines light, etc. On the other hand, "apple" and "orange" do not define each other. We can certainly recognize an apple without comparing it to an orange.

In other words, opposites are *relative* terms. Life is about *relationship,* and the interaction of opposites is the most fundamental way of *relating* things. When we take the time to understand the simple dance of opposites in the created universe, the complexity that follows makes more sense.

For example, once we understand that opposites are simply two things that define each other, we would not say that two people are opposites. The term, opposite, specifically refers to a pair of *qualities, ideas* or *choices* that define each other. You cannot completely know yourself by just comparing yourself to others. The wholeness of who you are, ultimately, is beyond comparison, therefore, you can't be someone's "opposite".

Granted, you can get some understanding of yourself by comparing *some* of your qualities with the "opposing" qualities exhibited by others. For example, one person defines himself as a male by comparing himself to a female. There is nothing wrong with this, provided we recognize that such knowledge is limited; each individual has qualities that go beyond gender and beyond duality – qualities that cannot be understood or appreciated through comparison.

Each Carries the Seed of the Other

It is fairly easy to understand that opposites are two qualities, ideas or choices that define each other. Opposites, however, have another calling card: *If two things are opposites, each side bears the seed of the other.* If we look deeply enough into one side, we see the seed or essence of the other. When each side expresses itself in fullness, it brings forth the pure essence of the other. In one sense, each side *becomes* the other. And so, the dance of opposites is, among other things, a dance of transformation. This is the dance of transformation that makes life possible.

In other words, true polar opposites are not static. They may be likened to the roots and the fruit of a single plant. The root gives rise to the fruit, whose seed brings forth new roots. Simplicity swells into complexity, which then returns to simplicity. Energy condenses into matter, which then returns to energy. Spirit condenses into flesh, which returns to spirit. The child becomes an adult, and the adult must, once again, become a child.

When this dance of transformation is allowed to unfold naturally, life goes on with ease and grace. When we resist or disrupt the flow of this dance, we suffer.

The life of the body consists of many pairs of opposing functions and qualities interacting harmoniously – hot and cold, rigidity and flexibility, acid and alkaline, emptiness and fullness, wetness and dryness, slow and fast, cyclical motion and linear motion, and numerous other opposing "energies" and tendencies.

The mind also consists of many opposites – thoughts, emotions and choices – in a perpetual dance of transformation. The dance occurs whether we are aware of it or not. However, as conscious beings, we have the choice of cooperating or not cooperating with it. Cooperating doesn't mean that we have to identify the many pairs of opposites in the body and mind so we can figure out how to make them fit together. They tend to integrate silently and automatically, especially when we recognize that life *is* a dance of opposites. The more deeply we understand this dance, the more we tend to flow with it. The more we flow with it, the more we invite vibrant health, mental clarity and emotional serenity.

The purpose of this book is to allow the reader to gently cultivate a basic recognition of the dance. From a practical standpoint, this book touches on a broad range of topics that impact our health and being – love, forgiveness, self-worth, sexuality, creativity, intimacy, freedom, responsibility, addiction, depression, fear, anger, the resolution of paradoxes, religion, birth, death, choice, destiny, etc. All of these can be deeply understood when seen from a perspective that recognizes the dance of opposites within us.

The Rest of This Book

With a few exceptions, each of the remaining chapters in this book addresses one pair of opposites. Most of them are true polar opposites that fit the description given above. In other words, *each side defines the other and bears the seed of the other.* Such opposites include *Pleasure & Pain, Birth & Death, Pride & Humility, Giving & Receiving, Rebel & Conformist.*

I must confess, however, that some of the dichotomies presented in this book may not fit the above definition of hard and true polar opposites. They are, nonetheless, emotionally charged issues or troublesome choices that tend to behave somewhat like opposites in our minds. We often wrestle with these issues consciously or unconsciously, and that is why they are addressed in this book. These quasi-opposites or "opposoids" include *Individuality & Community, Christian & Pagan, Evil Spirits & Troubled Mind.*

Furthermore, we often establish dichotomies by comparing something to the absence of that something. These opposites include *Sane & Insane, Conscious & Unconscious, Known & Unknown, Powerful & Powerless, Light & Darkness.* Some individuals may argue that these are not true polar opposites because technically, only one side really exists. However, whether or not we consider these to be true opposites, we still make these distinctions in our minds, even when we think we don't – *especially* when we think we don't.

In summary, if two things are opposites, they define one another. In addition, if we examine any pair of opposites closely enough, we see that each side bears the seed of the other. The next chapter describes the two basic ways that opposites interact with one another.

CHAPTER 2

Understanding the Dance

Opposites interact in two ways: they *compete* and they *complement.* Both are essential to life.

When the many opposing functions and energies of the body "compete," each side restrains or subdues the other, so as to avoid harmful excess. Therefore, the body doesn't get too hot or too cold, too wet or too dry, too acidic or too alkaline, too relaxed or too agitated, etc.

The same holds true for the workings of the mind. Mental clarity and emotional serenity are made possible by the many opposing thoughts, ideas, emotions, desires and choices that test, prune and temper each other.

When opposites complement one another, they enhance and exalt each other. One side "fits" into the other. Each derives its identity from the other. Each reaches the fullness of its potential in the presence of the other, thus creating a "wholeness' that otherwise would not be possible. For example, the normal posture and alignment of the body is the result of *rigid* bones connected to *flexible* tendons, ligaments and muscles. We can move because of *active* muscles pulling on *passive* bones.

With regard to the workings of the mind, intellect and intuition reach the fullness of their potential when they allowed to complement one another. Our capacity to give is enhanced by our capacity to receive, and vise versa. Work supports play, and play supports work.

We are alive and healthy because the many opposing functions and qualities interacting harmoniously within us – they compete and complement in appropriate ways.

People Are Not Opposites

Before we apply this dance of competition and complementing to human relationships, we must, again, emphasize that people are not opposites. True opposites define one another. On the other hand, the wholeness of an individual cannot be understood though comparison with others. The individual's personality is rich and totally unique. Every person has qualities that, ultimately, transcend duality and therefore, cannot be comprehended through comparison.

Two people, however, can have some opposing *qualities.* In fact, any two individuals will have a few or many opposing qualities. To the extent that they do, they will recognize one another, as if looking into a mirror. Their awareness might be a nonverbal or emotional recognition, sometimes called "chemistry". This simply means the individuals have the potential to compete and complement one another.

In a true complementary relationship, the two individuals enhance one another but cannot replace one another. If one party belittles the other or tries to usurp the power of the other, both sides lose. This does not mean that the competitive part of the relationship must be eliminated. It is simply integrated. The two sides can truly complement each other because the competitive part is ever present to question, confront and challenge the two individuals, so as to promote stability and balance.

Such harmony is possible to the extent that each individual is in touch with a sense of self that is beyond duality – beyond comparison. When we are in touch with our silent essence, competing and complementing find their rightful place. We can compare ourselves to others and even compete, without becoming nasty or insecure. We can form healthy relationships because we sense that our wholeness resides within, not in finding another person who fits (complements) us perfectly. Neither do we frantically try to change ourselves or the other person so as to create a better "fit". We can just relax and delight in our differences, allowing our many opposing qualities and energies to dance the dance of life.

Synergy and Intimacy

A complementary relationship has the quality of *synergy*. Synergy is a condition wherein the whole is greater than the sum of the parts. Synergy doesn't just happen between two individuals. Any two or more people or things can synergize. When there is synergy, there is wholeness. All the parts integrate in such a way as to create something new.

With regard to two people in relationship, the capacity to complement one another goes hand in hand with the capacity to be intimate with one another. Intimacy simply means the individuals share a high level of honesty and trust.

When we say that two individuals *complement* one another, we are describing how they function or work together. When we say they are *intimate*, we are describing how they relate emotionally.

In other words, when we speak of opposites in general, we say the two sides interact by competing or complementing. With regard to two individuals in a relationship, we can also say the two parties can interact through *competition or intimacy*.

Competition and intimacy are not mutually exclusive. The two tendencies flow and ebb organically in any relationship. In general, when the competitive instinct is allowed to express honestly, its natural tendency is to evolve into intimacy.

The Evolution of Intimacy

The year was 1891. The cold wind blew briskly, and the rain fell steadily, as six men carried the coffin out of the church. Inside the coffin was the body of General William T. Sherman, who, twenty-six years earlier, had captured Atlanta, thus crippling the confederate army to end the Civil War.

One pallbearer was a sickly old man who was warned by his doctors not to attend the funeral because, in his condition, he ran the risk of contracting pneumonia and dying.

He attended anyway. Standing outside in the inclement weather, he even refused to wear a hat, out of respect for General Sherman. As the doctors predicted, he caught pneumonia and eventually died. He

7

had no regrets, however. As he lay on his bed, he was asked why he had risked his life like that. He simply said, "General Sherman would have done the same for me."

Who was that man? A fellow Union soldier? No. He was General Joseph E. Johnston, Sherman's confederate counterpart in the Atlanta campaign. These two men, who had once tried to annihilate each other, had developed a deep respect for one another.

Almost exactly one hundred years later, I found myself in a wooded area, northwest of Atlanta, not too far from the place where General Sherman and General Johnston had met in battle. I was holding an air-powered rifle that fired paint-filled plastic pellets that splattered on impact. I stood with a group of thirty or so goofy-looking men wearing helmets, goggles and heavily padded ponchos. I said to myself, "This is dumb; I don't want to do this."

I soon realized, however, that my reluctance to play paintball had nothing to do with the dumbness of the game but rather my fear of engaging in competition and losing. So, I decided to participate, figuring it was good for me.

Eventually, I found myself running through the forest, sweating, growling, crawling on my belly and diving for cover to avoid the dreaded barrage of paintball bullets. Sometimes my team won and sometimes we lost. Either way, I thoroughly enjoyed the game as I participated in the hasty planning of strategies and attacks on the enemy fort. I even felt the thrill of personally capturing the enemy flag, racing with it through a volley of paintballs and diving over the wall, into the safety of our fort. I was very pleased with myself.

Later, both teams sat around a huge campfire and had dinner. I soon forgot who was on what team, and the act of capturing the flag shrank into insignificance.

My experience with paintball showed me that underneath my fear and judgment of competition was a love of competition. This is not surprising. We often judge and fear what we secretly desire. Likewise, once we fully recognize how we enjoy competition, we discover the genuine desire to relate to others beyond competition. When the competitive instinct is expressed honestly, it *wants* to evolve into intimacy.

In other words, the element that creates intimacy (the "seed" of intimacy) is already present in the competitive nature. That element is passion.

Competition & Passion

I once listened to a speaker who stated that men are driven by the desire to compete, while women are driven by the desire to form intimate relationships and are, therefore, spiritually more highly evolved than men. Many of the people in the room objected to such a sexist idea. They became rebellious and angry, which, apparently, was the intention of the speaker. He also stated that one of the ways men form deep friendships is by first engaging in competition, especially physical competition. This, according to him, is why women are superior; they have the remarkable ability to bond with one another without having to kill each other first.

The above generalization about men and women is just that – a generalization. It is a useful generalization that highlights an important point. If we (men and women) reject or suppress our desire to compete, we block the road to intimacy. If we try to create intimacy by denying our competitive tendencies, we sabotage intimacy.

Competition is one way of expressing our vitality and individuality. In attempting to purge ourselves of competition because we have judged it as inferior to intimacy, we also cut off the flow of our lively self-expression. The result is that intimacy goes out the window.

We are often quick to discard the fighter within us, unaware that the combative spirit has within it the potential for genuine acts of caring and affection. It's like a chunk of metal ore that we might overlook because it looks rough and dirty, and so, we do not see that it contains gold. In our quest for love and intimacy, we – especially men – have performed a funny dance. We discard the fighter, wash our hands, make ourselves look pretty, and then approach the goddess of love, and ask, "Where do I find intimacy?" And, she serenely responds, "It is in the ground, exactly where you buried it."

To be intimate means we bring into the relationship all aspects of ourselves, including the part that likes to compete. If we keep that part secret, it competes in secret. If we hide that part in shame, it manifests in a way that brings shame. If it is rejected, it expresses itself in a way that creates rejection. If we think it to be destructive and malicious, it manifests in a destructive and malicious way. If we think that it is useless, it manifests in a way that causes us to feel useless. If we express it cleanly and honestly, it evolves into intimacy.

Competition & Self-knowledge

The hidden motivation for competition is the desire for self-knowledge. In everyday life, we define ourselves by comparing ourselves to others. Competition provides us with the opportunity to experience ourselves in contrast to others. Once we experience ourselves in this manner, the natural progression is to know ourselves within the context of intimate relationship.

A major reason we might linger too long in the competitive mode is that we judge it harshly. On the other hand, if we simply recognize the competitive drive and allow it to unfold naturally, it evolves into the passion for self-knowledge and a desire to bring that knowledge into intimate relationship.

Compromise

Compromise is the middle ground between competition and complementarity. In a compromise, each side accepts less than full satisfaction in order to co-exist with or otherwise accommodate the other.

Compromise works best when each side has values that cannot be compromised. In everyday life, this looks like the willingness to compromise by first refusing to compromise one's personal truth. Compromising truth generally means we are truthful only if it makes us look good or somehow gives us power over others. When we do this, our efforts to compromise break down. We might experience short-term success, but we eventually become unsettled on the inside, and things tend to fall apart on the outside.

When we are mindful of our deeper values, compromise tends to work. Though we make concessions, there is no feeling of having been cheated or deprived. We can happily haggle over prices and logistics, but regardless of the outcome, there is peace because we have not compromised or otherwise sacrificed the pearl of great price. In fact, when we refuse to compromise the pearl of great price, it seems to shine more brightly, emitting a powerful and inexhaustible energy that galvanizes our thinking and enlivens our relationships.

Covert Competition

It is important to emphasize that accepting the competitive instinct does not mean that we merely tolerate its presence, as we might tolerate a naughty child. We are speaking here of a gut-level knowing that we really enjoy it.

If such integration of competition does not occur, we invariably try to get rid of it. However, since there is no place to put it outside of ourselves, "getting rid of it" translates into putting it somewhere within ourselves where it can't be seen. In other words, it becomes covert or unconscious.

When competition becomes unconscious, its power multiplies. It silently takes dominion. It frequently shows up as passive aggressive behavior. We smile sweetly and compete silently; disguising it as service, religious piety, altruism and other forms of spiritual one-upmanship.

Redirecting Competition

Just as covert competition is insidiously destructive, excessive competition has the obvious disadvantage of destroying both parties. Or, they might just replay the scene again and again until they finally catch on.

When we begin to allow competition to evolve into intimacy, we find clever ways of expressing our competitive instinct, so that, rather than leaving a legacy of death, we leave a legacy of relationship. Rather than having gladiators fight to the death, we have football games and pie eating contests. Rather than having feudal wars among power-hungry dukes who plunder each other's treasure, we have colleges competing for trophies and stealing each other's mascots. Rather than having a duel to the death, we have philosophical debates and games of ping-pong. These are all ingenious methods of recognizing the competitive spirit and allowing ourselves to experience it free of harsh judgment, so that its power and potency can evolve into genuine expressions of intimacy.

Beyond Competition

Though most of us have some degree of competitiveness, it is possible to virtually transcend it. In the presence of such a rare individual, the competitive nature within us can do what it secretly yearns to do; it relaxes, for it does not feel diminished or harshly judged by such a master. There is no hidden message of "I'm better than you because you're competitive and I'm not." Obviously, such a hidden message can only be sent by someone who is very competitive and is in denial of it. One who is genuinely non-competitive sends a different non-verbal message: *we are equal.*

CHAPTER 3

Duality & Singularity

To be in *duality* is to perceive opposites. To be in *singularity*[1] is to experience unity. The two perspectives dance together in our minds, giving us our everyday experience of life.

Duality gives us the ability to compete, complement, analyze, describe, dissect, discern, categorize, document, set goals and experience achievement as well as failure. Singularity, in and of itself, cannot do any of these, for it does not recognize anything outside of self. There is nowhere to go because all is here. There is nothing to do because everything simply *is*. Singularity does not say, "There is duality and here am I, singularity."

In other words, a mind that is having a profound awareness of singularity does not say, "I am in singularity, and that poor idiot out there is stuck in duality." Only the mind that is firmly planted in duality can say that singularity is better than duality, or vice versa. We must be duality to even speak of duality.

Unity Within Diversity

The mind in duality still retains a memory of singularity. In everyday terms, the awareness of singularity translates into a sense of equality. The memory of singularity flavors our perception of diversity with curiosity, acceptance, affection and thankfulness. These echoes of singularity reverberate through the mind, allowing us to con-

---

[1] The term *singularity* is borrowed from astronomy. It is the mathematical expression for a point in space where there is no space in the usual sense. In astronomy, a singularity, has no *here* and no *there*, no *now* and no *then*. It is a singular point where time and space have merged into something beyond time and space as we know them.

template the many forms of humanity – the rich, the poor, the hero and the villain – with understanding and a sense of kinship.

Singularity lives in our deep appreciation for the things we do in the world of duality. The memory of singularity is silent, but if it could speak, it might say something like, *I love being alive, and I love life in its diversity!*

"Shifting" From Duality Into Singularity

The perception that we are moving along a continuum from duality into singularity has meaning only for the mind in duality. Once we "shift" into the full-blown awareness of singularity, we perceive that we really haven't gone anywhere. There was no race, and no one came in first.

Be that as it may, the mind in duality wants to know, *How do I increase my awareness of singularity?* As suggested above, we move toward singularity just by experiencing it here and now as the capacity to appreciate who we are and what we do in everyday life. When singularity is experienced in the world of duality, the bus driver has as much intrinsic value as the king; the prostitute is as holy as the priest; doing the laundry feels equally important to the experience of timeless bliss. In fact, the reason we cannot sustain the state of timeless bliss is the lingering perception that it is better or more important than doing laundry, driving to work or telling your friend that you feel sad or angry. In other words, we get pulled into the drama of duality by our tendency to devalue it.

The Question and the Answer

To live in duality is to question. To be aware of singularity is to experience the answer. To give singularity more importance than duality is to place the question at war with the answer. To ask a pure question is simply to desire an answer. If the question is devalued, there can be no answer.

There are many accounts of near-death experiences in which the almost-departed soul experiences the overwhelming presence of cosmic love and peace beyond duality. When they are told to go back to

Earth, they become disappointed or even angry. Why did they have to return? In so many words, they are told they have work to do back on Earth. The nature of the work, if we strip it down to its essence, is to move beyond the judgment that the grandness of there is better than the smallness of here.

Neutrality

Experiencing the oneness beyond duality does not mean we become neutral. Neutrality is just another way of being in duality. Neutrality is literally in the middle of opposing forces. Neutral is zero; singularity is infinity. Neutrality is neither; singularity is both. Neutrality sees the two opposing forces as mutually exclusive; singularity sees them as inseparable. Neutrality sees incompatibility; singularity sees that one side contains the other. Neutrality perceives that one side can defeat the other; singularity recognizes that whatever is done to one is done to both. Neutrality is the impartial judge; singularity does not judge for it sees no separation. Neutrality says, "I don't care who wins;" singularity says, "I care about both, for I am both." Neutrality might show up as the earnest attempt to forgive sins; singularity is the awareness that there never was any sin. Neutrality is dispassionate; singularity is passionate beyond measure. Neutrality is lukewarm; singularity is both hot and cold. Neutrality is androgynous; singularity is simultaneously male and female. Neutrality is indecision; singularity is a quiet certainty that needs no validation.

Neutrality is reached by being disengaged, propped squarely between two polarities. Singularity is reached by being fully engaged and going all the way to one side with deep sincerity, which allows us to discover the seed of the other.

The inner call to go beyond duality compels us to move beyond neutrality. As long as we remain neutral on any two opposing views, we cannot discover that one is contained within the other; we do not experience the birth of one in the heart of the other. Perhaps this explains the wisdom of the biblical passage that advises us to be hot or cold but not lukewarm.

The Value of Neutrality

At the risk of being at odds with the Bible, there is value in being lukewarm or neutral. In fact, if we wish to move beyond neutrality, we must first know and appreciate its value.

As long as we honestly perceive duality, neutrality has value. Neutrality is a discipline; it is an exercise in objectivity. If we sincerely do not know the solution to a given issue, the honest thing to do is to gather data so we can be fair to both sides, as any honest judge or true scientist would do.

To be consciously neutral is a fine art. It is different from being unconsciously neutral. To be unconsciously neutral means we are stuck in neutral. We do it, not out of choice, but out of fear and self-doubt.

Neutrality is a skill that requires attention, thoughtfulness and humility. For example, while I was in my office, I happened to overhear a phone conversation in the adjacent room. My friend and colleague was acting as the mediator in a fight between a husband and wife. Let's call them "Jane" and "Bob". My friend, while speaking to one of the warring parties, declared that he was perfectly neutral and was not interested in taking sides. He spoke for quite a while on this, making a strong point of his neutral stance. Later that day he spoke with another close friend to whom he passingly said, "Bob is having a problem with Jane."

Interesting choice of words. "Bob is having a problem with Jane," instead of, "Bob and Jane are having a problem." I brought this to my friend's attention. He looked inside himself and discovered that he did have a hidden emotional leaning toward Bob. After a moment of embarrassment, he laughed about it.

Having acknowledged the value of neutrality and the mindfulness that is required to be neutral, we are then free to acknowledge our genuine bias. This eventually compels us to *feel* the truth of the other side. To feel the truth of both sides simultaneously is to perceive *duality* while experiencing *singularity.*

CHAPTER 4

Old Brain and New Brain

(The Integrated Brain)

We perceive duality by thinking. We experience singularity by feeling. Thinking allows us to separate things. Feeling allows us to bring things together. Normal waking consciousness is a blend of thinking and feeling.

The correlation of duality with thinking and of singularity with feeling is crudely reflected in the anatomy of the brain. The cerebrum, or new brain, houses the capacity to think, discern, dissect, analyze and compare. The brainstem, or old brain, contains centers for our animal desires and instincts.

The cerebrum consists of two well-defined hemispheres that seem to grow out of the brainstem. The two-pronged cerebrum and the singular brainstem may be visualized as the letter Y. The cerebral hemispheres are like the upper branches of the letter Y, and the brainstem is like the base.

The lower end of the brainstem, often called the old reptilian brain, integrates and unifies our vital body functions. The upper end of the brainstem interfaces with the cerebrum to generate the full spectrum of our everyday human emotions.

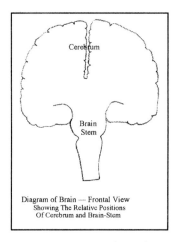

Diagram of Brain — Frontal View
Showing The Relative Positions
Of Cerebrum and Brain-Stem

By virtue of the numerous connections between the cerebrum and brain stem, the two are functionally united. Our logical thoughts are influenced by the impulses that emerge from the brainstem. Likewise, our animal urges are influenced by every thought generated within the cerebrum. The smooth operation of the cerebrum is dependent on the smooth operation of the brainstem, and vice versa. The two interact in a seemingly infinite variety of ways to create the unique tapestry of physical and psychological qualities of the individual.

Cut Off

As in other dualities, if we value the thinking of the new brain over the feelings and instincts of the old brain, or vice versa, the one that is regarded as inferior becomes the secret ruler. In this case, the separation is often described as a "cutting off" of our rational thinking from our feelings. In reality, this is impossible without seriously endangering physical survival. However, the two can become somewhat dissociated. This happens when the thinking of the new brain represses or censors the instincts and urges of the old brain. As a result, the discerning power of the cerebrum becomes cold, calculating, intellectual tyranny and harsh judgment, while the instincts and urges of the brainstem translate into hysteria, chaos, seduction and addiction. *These two conditions can exist only in the presence of each other.* Each is the result of lack of harmony between the animal (feeling) experience of the brainstem from the human (thinking) experience of the cerebrum.

In Western cultures, this inner split is personified as *Satan,* often shown as a two-horned beast. The two horns represent duality, and the ferocious animal/human face represents the primordial impulses that have become monstrous because they were rejected, subjugated and exploited by the human intellect.

Reunited

The two parts of the brain are reintegrated when the cerebrum recognizes the feelings rising out of the brainstem. The cerebrum uses its power of discernment to simply report the truth of those feelings.

The harmonious blending of human discernment of the new brain with the primordial impulses of the old brain results in the everyday experiences of kindness, respect and integrity. The integration deepens as the new brain cultivates the ability to be still, so that it can listen more deeply to the echoes of singularity rising up as feelings from the old brain. Such a deeper integration of the new and old brain may translate into religious ecstasy, transpersonal bliss, timeless peace and a sense of connection with the rest of life.

The Three Healers

In everyday life, there are three ways of promoting inner integration: *truthfulness, stillness and loving touch.* These three activities support the brain in integrating itself and integrating all opposing functions within. This is how we create wholeness of the body and mind. Wholeness shows up tangibly as vibrant health, mental clarity and emotional serenity.

In other words, the inner integration of opposites and eventual transcending of opposites do not require mystical knowledge. We quietly promote inner integration through the daily practice of truthfulness, stillness and loving touch. These three activities are instinctual. We are drawn to them whenever we feel a need for healing of the body or mind.

Staying in Touch

Most of us can recognize the importance of truthfulness and stillness for health and well-being. Loving touch, however, is often neglected. The importance of loving touch reflects the fact that we are mammals – like dogs, cats and horses. The mammalian brain needs sensory input in the form of frequent touch. Without that sensory input, the brain's integrative ability declines.

For infants, touching is critically important. Inner integration, especially integration of the new and old brain activities, depends on physical touch. This is especially true in the first precious hours following birth. The quality of those first stimuli to the uninitiated nervous system of the infant are of prime importance.

Animal studies have shown that, with many mammals, if the mother does not lick the infants, they die. Likewise, if human babies are not touched sufficiently, they experience physical and psychological disturbance.

Loving touch remains important throughout life, not only in interpersonal relationships but also in the relationship of the thinking self to the feeling self. Depression, sexual abuse, self-destructive behavior, addiction and brutality have been linked to touch deprivation.

The Oral Instinct

Though the human mamma relies on her hands to touch the baby, the older instinct to use her mouth is apparently still intact. This was dramatically illustrated by a woman who gave birth while she did not have full use of her arms and hands. The attendant in the delivery room was going to take the baby away since the mother obviously could not hold it. However, the mother still wanted her baby, and she screamed bloody murder until the attendant complied.

As per the mother's demand, the attendant placed the baby – still covered with birth slime – against the mother's chest. The woman then proceeded to lick the infant all over.

With our civilized sensibilities, we might conclude that the woman was being abhorrent, however, my own conversations with women patients over the years – mothers and non-mothers – suggest that if the

20

new mom is being spontaneous, she is likely to taste, lick and bite her baby. She is likely to place her mouth on the baby's bare tummy and play motorboat. She might even stick the baby's entire hand or foot in her mouth and give it a thorough massage with her teeth and tongue. And, the baby loves it, of course. I suspect that for every mother who yields to this old oral instinct, there are many others who have a notion to do so but ignore it, perhaps feeling quietly embarrassed for having such animal impulses.

The Changing Face of Health Care

Since civilized society emphasizes rational thinking over feeling, our health care and education have conspicuously ignored touching. Traditionally, hospital births tend to separate mother and child almost immediately following birth. Pediatricians had, at one time, instructed parents to avoid picking up the baby when it cries. Some pediatricians even instructed the parents to tie the baby's hands to the crib to prevent it from sucking its fingers. Years ago, kindergarten and first-grade teachers were encouraged to "hug every child, every day." As of this writing, one of my patients, a public school teacher, informed me that she and her colleagues are advised against touching the children.

With increased awareness of the importance of touch, we find that health care practices are changing. Many hospitals are becoming more respectful of mother/child bonding during birth. Some pediatricians have broken with tradition by advocating home births and telling parents to touch the child as much as possible. Some even advocate allowing the little one to sleep with the parents – a practice that had been considered perverse by other medical authorities in the United States. Likewise, in recent years, we have seen a dramatic increase in the demand for health care practitioners that emphasize hands-on-body procedures.

Physical touch is one way of making emotional contact. To maintain inner health and outer harmony, we must touch each other emotionally as well as physically. Lack of physical and emotional contact contributes to a split in the personality; thoughts are at odds with emotions, and logic is at odds with instinct. This split gets projected into many areas of our lives and typically shows up as interpersonal conflict.

The dissociation of the old brain from the new brain may also be looked upon as a defense mechanism of sorts. When feelings are too painful to bear, the cerebrum simply unplugs itself from the source of those feelings. Touching the body is a way of reconnecting the two. When this happens, the traumatic memories and feelings that compelled the separation to occur in the first place may be re-experienced or remembered. This is why deep massage, even if it is not painfully deep, may trigger the spontaneous release of emotions and the remembrance of long forgotten events.

Truthfulness and Stillness

Physical touch is intimately connected to the ability to tell the truth and to be still and quiet. In order for the whole brain to stay in touch with itself, the body must be touched, lovingly and frequently. This establishes inner harmony, allowing the hard-driving cerebrum to be still so that it can listen respectfully and express truthfully the deep feelings rising up from the brainstem.

Again, most of us recognize the importance of truthfulness and stillness for health and well-being, especially on the mental and emotional levels. We can also see how truthfulness and stillness go hand in hand. Telling the truth helps us to quiet the mind. Likewise, stillness helps us to get more deeply in touch with our truth and to express it honestly. Sometimes, however, inner turmoil remains no matter how earnestly we try to practice truthfulness and stillness. Quite possibly, what is missing is an adequate amount of loving touch.

The synergistic blend of touching, stillness and speaking the truth allows the many warring or neglected parts of the individual to come together into wholeness. Truthfulness, stillness and loving touch allow the new brain and old brain to function as one brain.

CHAPTER 5

Pleasure & Pain

(A New Look at Old Addictions)

Deep inside the brain, in the upper region of the brainstem, is an area known as the hypothalamus. The hypothalamus is a major meeting ground where nerve cells from the old brain reach up to be embraced by cells reaching down from the new brain, thus allowing our purely biological functions to become part of our overall awareness. Also, within the hypothalamus, we find a tiny gray lump of tissue called the *pleasure center.*

The pleasure center is composed of a cluster of nerve cells that communicate freely with other parts of the brain involved in eye-sight, hearing, touch, taste and smell. In addition, areas of the brain that are involved in problem solving, creativity and emotional expression are also plugged into the pleasure center. Any given activity feels good because it results in stimulation of the pleasure center.

Mother Nature wired the brain so that whatever feels good is also good for us. We are motivated to carry out life-sustaining functions because these same activities stimulate the pleasure center. Therefore, even if we had no intelligence at all, we would still be innately driven to do things that keep us alive and healthy. We eat just enough, drink just enough, get just enough sleep, exercise and have sex to adequately stimulate the pleasure center. When these activities no longer stimulate the pleasure center, we stop doing them. The saturation point – when a given activity no longer stimulates the pleasure center – coincides with the point when the same activity is no longer beneficial to the individual.

In other words, in the absence of interference, we don't have to think about how much and what kind of food to eat, when to sleep, how long to sleep, when to have sex, when to be sociable, when to be alone, when to go out and play and when to stay home and read a book. The pleasure center takes care of it all.

If our life-sustaining activities do not result in the experience of pleasure, we might simply stop doing them and die. This has been demonstrated experimentally. An electrode was implanted into the pleasure center of a male rat. The electrode was also connected to a lever in the cage so that the rat could stimulate its own pleasure center at will. The result: The rat stopped eating, drinking and sleeping and refused the company of receptive female rats. The animal died. We might argue that the rat died happy, but the point is that it died because its pleasure center was not allowed to fulfill its natural function.

Humans seem to respond in a similar manner. Individuals addicted to certain drugs stop taking care of their basic needs because the pathways to the pleasure center have been disrupted.

It is important to emphasize that the pleasure center is stimulated, not only by routine life-sustaining functions like eating and drinking, but also by a vast variety of other activities, such as smelling a flower, sitting under a tree in the middle of a peaceful meadow, painting a picture, reading a poem, watching a baby smile, taking a walk with a friend, admiring the motion of a ballet dancer, etc. In addition, the emotional areas of the brain (the limbic system) are intimately connected with the pleasure center. This is why telling the truth and "getting it all out" feels good. Furthermore, the expression of truth opens the door to intimacy with others, which also stimulates the pleasure center.

If we close the door to certain avenues of pleasure, we automatically try to compensate by overusing the remaining pathways. We might do this to the point that the activity in question is no longer a source of health for the body and mind. For example, if we deprive ourselves of emotional expression, we might try to compensate by having sex more often. If sexual pleasure is inaccessible, we might compensate by eating more. If the existing avenues of pleasure are insufficient, we might come up with artificial methods such as smoking, drinking alcohol and taking drugs. On the other hand, when all naturally occurring avenues of pleasure are open and accessible, each one is likely to be used in a way that promotes physical and emotional well-being.

Pain

The pleasure center has a next door neighbor – the pain center. Stimulation of the pain center causes us to feel physical pain or emotional distress. Any activity is experienced as painful only if it results in stimulation of the pain center.

Physical pain is a marvelous invention of Mother Nature. It is a system of alarms designed to motivate us to resolve whatever is threatening our physical well-being. Physical pain is the smoke detector, burglar alarm and watchdog that stand guard over the body.

Emotional Pain

If we touch a hot stove, the pain that immediately follows is obviously triggered by excessive heat on the body. In the case of emotional pain, the cause might be more difficult to define and is subject to the unique history of the individual. There is an underlying simplicity, however. A major cause of emotional pain is suppression of those activities that produce emotional pleasure.

As mentioned earlier, a major source of pleasure is the expression of genuine emotions, especially when it is associated with intimacy with others. It follows that a major source of emotional pain is failure to express oneself genuinely.

Failure to express the genuine self has the same effect on our emotional well-being as lack of food on the physical body. Emotionally, we are fed by the expression of personal truth. When we deprive ourselves of this soul food, we feel "empty". Chronic emotional pain is a gnawing and aching feeling that often bears a resemblance to physical hunger. Perhaps that is why we often try to fill the emotional hunger by eating more. Likewise, when we express ourselves genuinely, we experience emotional pleasure, which is often described as a feeling of being *fulfilled*.

The Pleasure of No Pain

While I was driving with a friend, she commented that the seatbelt in my car felt very pleasant against her. At first, I thought her comment was rather strange; I was unaware of my own seatbelt pressing against by body. She went on to say that the seatbelt in her own car pushed against her neck and was therefore very annoying. In comparison, the seatbelt in my car was a delight to her.

My friend's comment underscores the fact that the experience of pleasure or pain is ultimately subjective, involving a delicate balance between the pleasure and pain centers in the brain. Functionally, the pain and pleasure centers are closely related. Like other pairs of opposites, pleasure and pain define each other. Each derives its identity from the other. How we experience pleasure is defined by how we experience pain. Every experience of pleasure is defined by a background of accumulated experience of pain, and vice versa. In fact, if an individual were in constant pain (physical or emotional), the sudden removal of the pain would be experienced as "pleasure". As one former drug user once pointed out to me, what felt so good in taking the drug was "not feeling pain". The "fix" is the blessed relief of not feeling the pain or anxiety.

The Agony & Ecstasy of Painting the Fence

There are instances where the pleasantness and unpleasantness of a given activity are clearly a matter of choice or attitude. Painting a house can be a pleasing experience today and very unpleasant tomorrow. In other words, the sensory input is exactly the same, but is handled differently in the brain.

In Mark Twain's novel, *Tom Sawyer,* our hero was convinced that the act of white-washing the fence was a dreary experience, and he was unwilling to convince himself otherwise. So, he did the next best thing. Through his artistry as a con-man, he convinced his friends that white-washing the fence was a glorious experience that any healthy boy would gladly pay for – which they did.

To Feel or Not to Feel

Toning down the pain response results in a similar dampening of the pleasure response. Individuals who seem to feel very little pain also seem to feel very little pleasure. Such an individual doesn't appear to be bothered very much by the little upsets of life but, at the same time, seems to have a decreased ability to take pleasure in a beautiful sunset or the touch of a loved one. Even the pleasure of sexual intercourse is decreased and becomes restricted to a small region of the body. Once the pleasure center has been toned down through the blocking of the pain center, we then try to compensate by over-stimulating the pleasure center with food, sex, loud music, alcohol, etc.

Getting the Wires Crossed

Because pleasure and pain are highly subjective, they can be conditioned. If the nervous system is allowed to develop naturally, it learns to direct harmful stimuli to the pain center and beneficial stimuli to the pleasure center. Therefore, harmful activities are experienced as unpleasant, while beneficial activities are experienced as pleasurable.

This process can apparently be reversed. Activities that harm the body can be experienced as pleasurable, while activities that promote well-being, such as expression of genuine emotions and loving touch, are equated with pain and therefore avoided.

If a small child, whose neural circuits are still very malleable, is repeatedly punished for self-expression, the result is that the child learns to associate self-expression with pain. Thus, the very activity that promotes emotional well-being and intimacy is regarded as painful and scary, and is therefore avoided.

Addiction

When this reversal of the functions of pleasure and pain is severe enough, the individual is said to have an addiction. When an addiction is present, activities that harm the body can be experienced as pleasurable, while activities that promote health and well being are avoided. The same substance that brings short-term comfort also causes long-term damage. This is not surprising. When we hide the truth, we tend to harm the body. The addictive behavior is designed to hide truth.

The Pleasure of Pain

The blurring of pleasure and pain in their respective functions can be so deep that the individual may appear to be addicted to pain. In one sense, the pain becomes pleasure. This can show up in a number a hidden ways. For example:

- Addiction to suffering and tragedy.
- Addiction to personal struggle.
- Taking pleasure in watching others suffer and struggle.
- Addiction to being hurt or victimized.
- Addiction to martyrdom.
- Addiction to yearning.
- The romantic lure of not having what you want.
- The sweet ache of *almost* getting what you want.
- The pleasurable agony of unrealized potential.
- Preoccupation with death and dying.

These conditions are more common than we might think. To the extent we repress the genuine self, pleasure and pain drift away from their natural functions. When we block the natural portals of pleasure, we are likely to develop addiction to pain. When our lively self-expression is so severely repressed that we feel trapped by life, we are likely to secretly yearn for death.

I Am Alive

We can untangle the relationship of pleasure and pain by under-standing their commonality. The common ground of pleasure and pain is *aliveness*. Aliveness is a quality of self-awareness that includes, but is not limited to, our emotions and body sensations. If we close the door on the aliveness that we experience through the pleasure of par-ticipating in life-enhancing activities, then we will experience our aliveness through pain.

We might harm ourselves, doing anything that produces physical pain and emotional turmoil, so we can have the experience of *I am alive*. There is nothing stupid or deranged about this behavior. To desire the experience of *aliveness* is fundamental to our well-being. If denied, it causes us to override common sense and even our basic survival needs.

The primordial feeling of aliveness is separated into pleasure and pain by judgment – a gut level sort of judgment that is designed to support the health and well-being of the individual. However, even when pleasure and pain appear to have strayed from their ideal function, we must be respectful of their unique expression in the individual. If we criticize our "taste" with regard to what we find pleasurable and painful, we are, in effect, judging the judgment, which, typically, causes us to become even more emotionally twisted.

On the other hand, we can use our judgment judiciously by simply being honest with regard to what we find pleasurable and painful, which sets the stage for healthy choices. Such honesty results in a gradual transmutation of the pleasure and pain response. We become more appreciative of their equally brilliant and complementary functions. When we do this, we walk that straight and narrow path that leads to a door, beyond which is the freedom to know *I am alive* beyond the fear of pain and pursuit of pleasure. This is the peace that is said to be beyond human understanding, for it is beyond duality.

CHAPTER 6

Fear & Desire

(Restoring Them to Their Natural Functions)

Fear is a protective emotion that compels us to move away from something. Desire compels us to move *toward* something. On a purely biological-survival level, fear and desire serve the same functions as pain and pleasure. Basically, fear is the anticipation of pain, and desire is the anticipation of pleasure. Fear directs us away from the potential source of pain, protecting us from whatever might endanger our health and survival. Desire directs us toward the source of pleasure and promotes health and well-being.

Like other true opposites, fear and desire define one another. Each derives its meaning from the other. The obvious presence of one suggests the hidden presence of the other.

As is true for pain and pleasure, fear and desire have a complementary relationship. The healthy expression of fear supports us in fulfilling our desires. Likewise, when we are respectful of our desires, fear finds its proper place as well. They might take turns on center stage, but, at any given time, the visible one is silently supported by the invisible one.

Excessive Fear

The fear response can be overlaid with programming that is contrary to the health and well-being of the individual. Rather than protecting us from things that could hurt us, fear prevents us from doing things that could bring us greater health and happiness. The guardian of our well-being becomes a ball and chain that we drag around.

One of the ways fear becomes counterproductive is by making us afraid of confrontation, conflict or competition. We learn to engage in confrontation only if we do not have to risk personal discomfort, rejection or failure. We don't play unless we are sure we will win.

Excessive fear causes us to value safety more than truthfulness, which means that relationships become shallow and dull. Furthermore, since we do not value truth, we also do not value justice. If we are so concerned about safety that we neglect truth, we also become blind or indifferent to the rights of others. We speak the truth and show respect for others only if doing so allows us to control the situation. We also tend to avoid situations where our weaknesses might be exposed. We associate only with those whom we can control or who do not push us beyond our comfort zone.

When we become skillful at avoiding our fears, our talents and social skills become tools for keeping our fears and anxieties hidden. For example, if I'm very articulate but afraid of emotional closeness, I might use my gift-of-gab to avoid emotional closeness. As a result, fear and anxiety silently grow. This is the reverse of the biblical wisdom that says, *Your biggest weakness shall become your greatest strength.* In other words, our talents and abilities, when ruled by hidden fears, become crippling weaknesses.

When the fear response is thus adulterated, we not only avoid potentially fulfilling excursions into the unknown, but we also blindly stumble into situations that are damaging. In other words, when the fear response is no longer a reliable part of common sense and discernment, we are likely to be too careful or not careful enough.

If we are lucky, we will fail in our fearful attempts to stay in the safety of the known. When we experience enough of these failed attempts at staying in safety, we clean up our fear response so that it can stand side by side with pain, as a trusted sentinel of our health and well-being.

Problematical Desires

Under Mother Nature's design, desire moves us toward activities that enhance our health and well-being. For animals living in the wild, controlling desires is irrelevant. A desire dissolves on its own when it is simply allowed to fulfill its function. Its function is to motivate the animal to do something beneficial.

For humans, things are a bit more interesting. Besides survival, a number of other factors determine whether or a not we are drawn to something. For example:

- It is a novelty. Newness tends to evoke curiosity.
- It is scary. We are naturally curious about anything that evokes fear.
- It is forbidden or socially unacceptable. When something is forbidden, it entices us. In fact, one of the easiest ways to create desire for a particular thing is to make it taboo. Our innate desire for freedom stimulates curiosity for any forbidden thing.

Many other subtle factors can influence which way our desires draw us. Some of them do not necessarily promote health and well-being. In an addiction, fear and desire have reversed their roles. The addict is drawn to something that is harmful, while fearfully avoiding things that promote health and well-being. Much can be said about the mechanism by which this reversal occurs. In general, our desires tend to become problematical when they are habitually suppressed or harshly judged.

Perverse Psychology

Because fear and desire are so closely related, we can artificially generate desire in a given area simply by creating fear. A benign application of this principle is the roller coaster at the amusement park. We desire to go on the ride because it's "scary". The fear, when openly expressed, produces hormonal secretions similar to those occurring during strong desire and emotional expectancy. In other words, openly expressed fear can easily become excitement.

Another application of this principle is "reverse psychology," in which we trick someone into desiring something, by artificially erecting a wall of fear around it. This is commonly done unintentionally by authority figures that instigate an unwanted behavior by rigidly suppressing it or otherwise judging it. This is the case of the teenage daughter who develops a strong desire to date a certain boy because her parents said "no." On the other hand, if the parents simply offered their insight and then set clear and respectful boundaries, the daughter would, more than likely, access her own inner discernment. Since she isn't blinded by the thrill of doing something forbidden, she can more effectively assess the young man's attributes.

For example, when I was a teenager, I received some unexpected support in my first attempt at dating. The support came in the form of my girl friend's overprotective mother. I met the girl – whom I will call "Debby" – while we were both counselors at a day camp. Debby's mother preferred that her daughter date Jewish boys, and frowned upon her dating an Italian boy. Furthermore, when Debby's mother found out that I was not merely of Italian ancestry, but a *native born Sicilian*, she absolutely drew a hard line – which her daughter absolutely had to cross. My new-found sweetie found me that much more appealing. I had it made! Debby was an attractive girl with no shortage of boys who were interested in dating her. But, she wanted only me – the one boy who caused her mother to throw a royal conniption fit!

Our Fears Lead Us to Our Desires

"Since, finally, the armored animal, man, is utterly incapable of reaching his most ardent longed-for goal, namely, freedom of his organism from rigidity, dullness, immobility and the rest of the biophysical straitjacket, he must of necessity fear and hate it; and the less he is capable of reaching it, the more he must hate it... Man's cruelty is directed mainly against what he most longs for..."

—Wilhelm Reich, 1950

The above passage is great news. It tells us that we judge, fear, hate and deny those things we secretly want but believe we cannot have. The more unreachable a thing seems, the more we fear and hate it. The hidden frustration of *I cannot have this,* becomes the judgment, *I should not have this,* and therefore, *no one else should have this.*

So, why is Dr. Reich's insight great news? It is great news because it offers an important clue for determining what we really want.

If we are afraid of something, we are probably curious about it and perhaps secretly desire to experience it – or something related to it. Therefore, if we wish to discover our deepest desires, we need only look into our deepest fears. This does not have to be as scary as it might seem. A practical and gentle application of this principle is to simply approach every fear by asking, W*hat is the desire behind this fear?*

Desire is like a vacuum, an empty vessel waiting to be filled. Fear may be seen as the door or seal upon that empty vessel. If our desires become totally repressed and forgotten, the only clue to their existence is the fear that covers them. That fear is a valuable landmark, for it shows us where our desires are buried.

The big joke is that once we remove the lid of fear that covers the great vacuum, we discover that the vacuum, quite often, cannot be filled from the outside – though we try. That which fills the vacuum is already in the vacuum. In other words, we do not fill the vacuum by stealing from life. To do so only deepens the hunger. The fulfilling of our deepest personal desires is the gift that each of us *gives* to life.

Of course, we do receive energy and nourishment from those around us, but we are not fully satisfied until we have given back more than we have taken. The seed receives nourishment from the earth and sky, becoming a tree that brings forth more seeds and enriches the rest of life. When we are fully alive, we want to bring forth new life. In fact, the yearning to bring forth new life is one of our most fundamental desires. And, not surprisingly, the inability to do so is one of our deepest fears...which brings us to the next chapter.

CHAPTER 7

Creativity

(Not Just for Artists)

As mentioned in the previous chapter, when we encounter our fears, we discover hidden desires. Desire often takes the form of creative urges. Whether we feel like singing, dancing, painting, building a shelf, planting a garden, giving birth or making pizza, creativity is a way of expressing the genuine self. Therefore, creativity tends to be pleasurable.

Anything that is pleasurable also has the potential to be painful. The greater the potential for pleasure, the greater the potential for pain. This is why we might avoid our creative impulses. Instead, we engage in repetitive and habitual behavior, staying in the safety of familiar territory. We might repeat the same thing over and over because the thought of doing otherwise evokes fear – the threat of pain.

One of the recognized characteristics of neurosis is unconscious repetitive behavior. This is obvious in the case of someone who gets drunk every Saturday night to avoid boredom. More commonly, millions of people get up every morning and do repetitive work they do not enjoy because if they failed to do so, they would have to face the fear of having no money, or perhaps the fear of losing the emotional security of familiar ground.

This is not to imply that creative activity is better than repetitive activity. There is wisdom in repetitive behavior. It protects us from being overwhelmed by trying to do too much too soon. The repetitive behavior keeps us functional until we receive the signal to go into the new and unknown. That signal comes from within.

When creativity sleeps in the arms of repetitive or known behavior, it does not sleep as a bear in the winter but as a caterpillar in its cocoon. The repetitive behavior paves the way for creative expression.

During that time of staying in the known, the hidden forces of creativity are incubating in stillness and darkness, gathering strength in the domain of the subconscious mind.

Not surprisingly, when we receive the inner signal (or simply are forced by circumstances) to face our hidden fears and pain, and break away from old habits, we often experience a wave of creativity. This is the basis for the myth that all true artists must suffer. However, it is not the suffering that stimulates creativity, but the removal of old patterns of pretence and superficiality, and the moving away from the safety of familiar but confining behavior.

The Bipolar Gift

In one sense, creativity is the ability to dip into the formless realm of singularity, and then giving it form in the world of duality. If we tap into singularity and cannot express it harmoniously in the world of duality, the result is dissatisfaction, hostility, depression or confusion.

Throughout history, prayer, meditation, breathing techniques and psychotropic drugs have been used to tap into the deep well of creative inspiration within. Quite often, however, the experience is not integrated into everyday reality. It does not take form as a tangible and sharable creation. In such an event, the awareness usually doesn't just go away. It remains and turns into a poison in the body and mind. The pleasurable energy that courses through the body may become a searing fire that burns out the nervous system and disrupts the vital organs. The awareness of limitless potential becomes grandiosity. The awareness of one's uniqueness becomes arrogance. The blissful merging with others becomes a loss of personal boundaries. The grandness of the universe becomes a feeling of personal worthlessness and pessimism that can spill over into suicidal thoughts. The boundless energy that makes sleep almost unnecessary becomes a nagging insomnia. The sense of, "I can have anything I want," becomes fits of rage and tantrums when the desired outcome is not forthcoming. The sense of transcendental peace becomes lethargy and boredom. The awareness of the *One Life* becomes unbearable loneliness and isolation. The heightened awareness of one's surroundings becomes sensory overload and overwhelm. The feeling of freedom becomes a terrifying sense of disorientation. Any or all of these conditions may appear when we tap into singularity but are unable to integrate it into the world of duality.

Interestingly enough, similar symptoms are experienced by individuals diagnosed with *bipolar disorder,* previously called *manic depressive disorder.* "Bipolar" refers to the mood swings associated with this condition. The individual can fluctuate randomly from elation to suicidal depression. The high or manic periods include grandiose thoughts, a sense of great power and perhaps a tendency to sleep very little. There is a lack of discernment or disregard for the limitations of time, space and money. This can show up as uncontrolled spending, a frenzy of activity, and jumping from one new project to another, leaving most of them incomplete. These manic episodes may then be followed by a time of deep depression that might include headaches, chronic pain, and digestive disorders that don't respond to any treatment.

The bipolar individual may exhibit a lack of personal boundaries, which can show up in a number of ways. For example, there might be a feeling of "taking on" the thoughts and feelings of others. The absence of boundaries may also express itself in more aggressive ways. The individual might be very invasive and disrespectful of the free will of others. There might be a lack of respect for someone else's domain, whether it be money, property or a spouse. Such an individual, though behaving like an outright thief, is also expressing – in a twisted sort of way – the knowing that life is singular. In this case however, the instinctual knowing that says, *I am the One Life* translates into, *All things belong to me.* Such individuals are as little children in a candy store, taking what they want and thinking nothing of it. Not surprisingly, such an individual can also be fiercely territorial one moment and very generous the next.

If you find yourself identifying with some of the above-mentioned symptoms, relax. Most individuals have some degree of difficulty integrating the boundless realm of singularity into tangible reality. This difficulty is given the medical diagnosis of "bipolar disorder" only when it has reached a level that significantly disrupts the individual's ability to function. Furthermore, such difficulty doesn't necessarily mean there is something biochemically or psychologically wrong with the person. The "difficulty" could very well be that the individual's antenna is just very sensitive. They see and feel more than they can comfortably handle. The situation can certainly get more complicated if the heightened awareness is combined with other factors such as a troubled childhood.

The apparent connection between bipolar disorder and creativity is further supported by the observation that bipolar individuals are often quite articulate and witty. They can spontaneously pull out a clever phrase. In addition, they are often keenly perceptive, having a heightened awareness of their environment that may seem to border on the supernatural.

Like the person who intentionally taps into the infinite, the bipolar individual can routinely experiences both sides of everything. To do so in an integrated way translates into great creativity, because creation is a dance of opposites. However, to do so chaotically translates into a sense of overwhelm, confusion, and the supreme frustration of feeling "something" and not being able to translate it into a tangible form. The frustration of the bipolar individual is not unlike that of the artist who is unable to place on canvas what is felt deeply within.

Many psychologists are understandably cautious about equating creativity with mental instability. They are concerned that some individuals will use this correlation to justify irresponsible and erratic behavior, rather than honestly facing their personal issues. The individual might use this information to place a badge of nobility on their condition. Psychologists who work with this condition emphasize that most creative individuals are not mad, and most individuals diagnosed with bipolar illness are not creative geniuses. However, the correlation is strong enough to suggest that many individuals who suffer from bipolar disorder and related conditions might benefit if they are given the time and space to see the hidden gift in their "delusions". They might be helped if their wild flights of thought and emotions are allowed to run their course and then land safely, rather than having them prematurely shot out of the sky and shot up with suppressive drugs.

When the troubling ability to identify with both sides of any issue is fully integrated in the world of form, it becomes a valuable asset.

Such ability includes the desire to bring the sides together. To see beyond boundaries is to develop a genuine respect for boundaries. This is how the golden rule becomes a living reality. We cannot steal from others or do harm to others, because we will feel it directly and personally. Such a feeling has nothing to do with externally imposed guilt; it is the natural outgrowth of a quiet feeling – the silent knowing that life is singular.

CHAPTER 8

Doing & Being

(Understanding Self-Worth)

Creativity (previous chapter) is a blend of *doing* and *being*. *Doing* refers to the performance of a task to achieve a specific outcome. *Being* is a state wherein we spontaneously interact with life.

Doing is the vehicle for expressing our *being*. Likewise, *being* includes a deep appreciation for what we are *doing*. In other words, to *be* is to enjoy what we *do*. The harmonious blending of doing and being means that we give equal value to both. We recognize that both are important ways of experiencing self-worth.

Self-Worth

Self-worth based on doing is earned. Self-worth based on being cannot be earned. Self-worth based on doing is tangible. Self-worth based on being is intangible; we may not even recognize it as self-worth; it's just a silent sense of serenity; a sense of being at peace with oneself. Self-worth based on doing typically involves connecting with others. Self-worth based on being involves connecting with oneself. The two are obviously related. Connection with oneself supports us in connecting harmoniously with others. The reverse is also true: connecting with others properly supports us in connecting with self.

There is a place within us where we want to do. We want to create and achieve. This drive is usually linked to the desire to receive acknowledgment from others. Such a desire is sometimes regarded as a form of vanity, a sin or a weakness that has to be purged. In truth, it is a simple and natural thing. It is a voice that says, "Look at what I have accomplished –I have put my heart into it and I'm really proud of it." We might be afraid of allowing this voice to be heard, unaware that the desire to be recognized for what we do goes hand in hand with the sharing of what we do.

When we reject or conceal our desire to be acknowledged for what we do, two things happen. Firstly, the suppressed desire for external validation becomes the silent ruler of our doings. Like any desire, this one becomes stronger through suppression. Secondly, by holding back or devaluing our desire to be recognized for what we do, we close the door to the intrinsic sense of self-worth that is beyond doing and beyond external recognition.

Likewise, if we are not in touch with the desire to know that we are loved regardless of what we do, nothing we do can truly satisfy us, and no amount of external acknowledgment will fill our cup; we simply won't let it in. In fact, we might sabotage what we do.

That "sabotage" is simply our own inner wisdom setting us free from the outer ambitions that have become as chains. In other words, when we lose touch with our being, we tend to sabotage our doing, which forces to get back in touch with our being.

The unconscious need to know that we are loved regardless of what we do is the basis for the common religious declaration: "I'm not worthy of God's love." It is the recognition that there is nothing we can *do* to win God's Love. Receiving God's love simply means that we know ourselves as God knows us. In secular terms, this translates into remembering who we are, which is say, we have contacted our *beingness.*

The declaration of "I'm not worthy to receive God's Love," might seem silly or, at the very least, technically inaccurate. However, there is hidden wisdom here. When the individual really *feels* his/her inability to *do* anything to win or earn God's love, the declaration of "I'm not worthy," might pack a bigger emotional wallop than a more moderate and technically more accurate statement, like, "God loves me regardless of my actions."

The Goal & The Path

When we are goal-oriented, we are in the *doing* mode. When we are in the doing mode, we put all distractions and temptations aside and focus on a task. To be goal-oriented is to be in a frame of mind wherein we commit ourselves to a certain outcome and (whether we admit it or not) invest a certain portion of our happiness on its achievement. This means we will feel the thrill of victory or the agony of defeat. Either way, we *feel,* which might be the hidden motivation for emotionally committing ourselves to a goal; it allows us to feel something — one way of another.

When we are path-oriented, we are in the *being* mode, which means we allow ourselves to enjoy the journey; to run the race for the thrill of feeling the wind and the surge of adrenaline as we race for the finish line, and the joy of being in relationship with the other runners. In the path mode, the journey is a delight regardless of who comes in first.

If the goal and the path appear to be in conflict, we have judged one as more important than the other, and thus, we have lost sight of the complementary relationship of the two. Having a goal simply means we acknowledge what we want. The goal gives us a clear purpose — a direction for the outpouring of energy. When we are emotionally aligned with a specific goal or purpose, we feel a*live.* The goal, whether or not it is stated, gives us an opportunity to feel the aliveness of knowing what we want and going for it. This is so intrinsically fulfilling that the actual achievement of the goal is reduced from a life-and-death situation to the icing on the cake.

Devaluing the Goal

As with other opposites, when we judge the goal or the path as better than the other, the one that is devalued is driven underground and, from there, it runs us. For example, if we declare that the path is more important than the goal, we might convince ourselves that we don't care if we win or lose. This means the part of us that really wants to win is judged as inferior and shoved into the cellar. In effect, we are saying to this aspect of ourselves, "You are worthless; go away." Having rejected and suppressed the part that wants to win, we run the race half-heartedly, because if we put too much passion into it, we will reveal the competitor that we are trying to run away from. If we win, we act nonchalant, denying the barbaric thrill of victory. If we lose, we act nonchalant, denying the disappointment of defeat. The bottom line is that by denying the goal-oriented competitor that wants to win, we suppress the very passion that makes the race thrilling. Furthermore, the suppressed competitive tendency is likely to express secretly as passive-aggressive behavior and covert competition wearing the mask of benevolence.

Devaluing the Path

When the goal is valued more than the path, there is an unspoken assumption that the end justifies the means. This frequently translates into the justification of injustice, killing in the name of God, tyranny in the name of law and order, and deception to keep the peace. We see this in the politician who lies or uses other unethical practices to get elected. We see this in war, where the killing of children is justified as a necessary evil for achieving the "greater good." What is not generally recognized is that the "necessary evil" tends to create a result that is like itself. We often perpetuate conflict, injustice, unhappiness or simply fail to *really* achieve our goals because we have gone too far in invoking the concept of "necessary evil" − which means that we value the goal more than the path.

Therefore, if our goal becomes so important that we are tempted to disregard the path, we would do well to stop and think. We must bear in mind that, ultimately, the goal *will* resemble the path.

If the game is valued more than the player, people become pawns, craftsmen become cogs, and friends become allies whose only worth is their ability to help us achieve our goals. On the other hand, when we walk the path with dignity and honesty, the goal is achieved, and the path is a joy.

CHAPTER 9

Purity & Fullness

(Two Primal Urges)

Some of the pairs of opposites described in this book may be understood more deeply by first understanding the dance of *purity* and *fullness*.

Purity

Purity, in the physical sense, refers to uniformity, consistency or sameness. Purity often translates into the presence of just one thing. For example, in the language of chemistry, a substance is said to be pure when it is singular in its consistency. To a chemist, a chunk of matter is "pure" when it is composed of just one specific chemical or element.

In a broader sense, *pure* can also refer to emptiness, nothingness, silence and stillness. On the human level, the term *purity* is often used to describe a very high level of personal integrity. It is an absence of pretense or hypocrisy, virtually synonymous with innocence. Purity can also refer to being in touch with what is basic and fundamentally important to us. In other words, purity is about being in touch with our essential nature.

Purity is not just a philosophical ideal. The desire for purity is one of our basic in-born instincts. It compels us to be authentic and congruent. We feel driven to empty ourselves of whatever is false or inconsistent with the genuine. All our perceptions, beliefs and behaviors are exposed to the purifying fire that burns off the deception and superficialities that hide who we really are.

To be in touch with our fundamental desire for know our purity implies that we do not "use it" as means to an end. If we use it for show it is no longer purity.

Fullness

Fullness refers to abundance and variety. In the physical sense, fullness is abundance and variety of *things*. On the human level, fullness translates into a state of *wholeness,* wherein no part of oneself is neglected, cast out or otherwise denied. Every part of oneself is recognized and allowed its natural place.

Fullness can also translate into *fulfillment.* Our experience is full when there are no unfulfilled desires. Our understanding is full when all the separate bits of information are well integrated in the mind. When our understanding is full, we are at peace with ourselves and the life around us. We feel whole. When we have that sublime sense of fullness, we relax, for the journey has been completed, and something new and pure can be born.

The Dance of Purity and Fullness

At any given time, we might feel called to experience purity or fullness. Sometimes we want to experience the richness and fullness of life, and sometimes we just want to retreat to the purity and simplicity of the essential self. Each side, however, must give birth to the other. When we have fullness of experience and fullness of understanding, the many small parts of self seem to spontaneously merge into a larger and singular self. The many voices merge into the purity of a single voice that cries out, *I Am.* Likewise, when we feel the purity of the singular self, we cannot help but reach out to create fullness and richness.

Purity and Fullness in Everyday Life

In everyday life, the dance of purity and fullness, though ever present, is seldom expressed in its generic form. We usually don't say, *I feel pure today* or *I feel full today.* Neither do we say, *I want to feel purity* or *I want to feel fullness.* Our experience of purity and fullness usually takes the form of other pairs of opposites, such as laughing & crying, humility & pride, giving & receiving, will & feeling, fasting & feasting, austerity & wild abandonment, responsibility & freedom, clean & dirty, darkness & light. Each of these pairs is addressed in later chapters of this book.

The play of purity and fullness is also seen in the experience of pain and pleasure, addressed in chapter five. Pleasure, when it is allowed to carry out its natural function, may be described as a sense of fullness or fulfillment. Pain, when it is allowed to carry out it natural function, compels us to purify ourselves of things that are harmful or otherwise obstructive to our health and well-being. Pain has the capacity to empty us of all frivolities and self-deception. Pain makes us focus. It preempts whatever we are involved with at a given time, simplifies our goals and wipes the slate clean so we can make room for what really brings us fulfillment.

Are there ways of contacting our inner purity without creating pain? Certainly. It is not the pain that purifies us, but our capacity to focus our attention. We can cultivate the capacity to focus through solitude, introspection and the daily practice of honest self-expression.

Whether we do it through pain or conscious effort, we are instinctively driven to contact that deep place of purity. Like breathing, we can stop that quest temporarily, but eventually, nature takes over. Sooner or later, the desire to experience inner purity asserts itself. The desire to know our purity, if neglected, eventually overrides all other desires and all other influences, including common sense and logic. Instinctively, we seem to know that the doorway to fulfillment is purity.

If we contact inner purity through pain, the fulfillment that follows will probably take the form of some kind of pleasure. The pleasure will, more than likely, take form in a way that is "symmetrical" to the pain we endured.

If we manage to contact inner purity through a method other than pain or discomfort, we are likely to experience fullness in a way that cannot be adequately described as "pleasure". The purity that is beyond pain, and the fullness that is beyond pleasure are often described as the state of *Isness*.

If, however, the attempt to contact Isness translates into a rejection of pleasure or pain, we will repeatedly stumble into alternating experiences of pain and pleasure, purging and binging, fasting and feasting. This pattern tends to dissolve when we allow pain and pleasure, and other expressions of purity and fullness to each have their moment on center stage.

CHAPTER 10

Laughing & Crying

(Two Ways of Feeling Alive)

Laughing and crying are two common ways of spontaneously expressing aliveness. They are closely related physiologically. The movements of the abdomen, chest and face associated with laughing and crying are strikingly similar. Even the respective sounds are somewhat similar. And of course, if we laugh really hard enough, we will, more than likely, shed tears.

Laughing and crying are also closely related psychologically. When we laugh or cry, the places inside us that may have been emotionally shut down are awakened. Places that had been in conflict or incommunicado are making peace. In both activities, emotions flow freely because we feel connected to ourselves.

Reconnecting with oneself is not unlike reconnecting with a loved one; we are likely to laugh or cry. The connection might also take the form of a new insight that is deeply meaningful to us. We suddenly become aware of something that we have never been aware of before, so we spontaneously laugh or cry.

In addition, when we laugh or cry we stimulate ourselves physiologically. Many joints and muscles are worked, the internal organs and glands are massaged and capillaries dilate, sending life-giving blood to the deep tissues that previously may have been deprived.

Laughter is often used as a means of releasing emotional tension. Comedy is a way of spoofing our own suffering, weaknesses or inconsistencies. We create cartoons and caricatures of our inconsistencies and perceived weaknesses, so we won't try to hide them or take them so seriously. Laughter softens the hard angles and smoothes out the rough edges.

The great medicinal quality of laughter is fully realized when we recognize that crying is equally great as a healer. Both are important methods of releasing tension and moving emotional energy. To say that one is better than the other is the same as regarding pleasure as more important than pain. When we don't try to exalt one over the other, each finds its natural expression; surging forward and then yielding to the other with ease and grace.

Purity of Tears and Fullness of Laughter

Though laughing and crying tend to have their healthiest expression when they are given equal importance, the truth is that most of us would prefer to laugh rather than cry. This is normal and healthy. It is part of the overall instinct to seek well-being and happiness. However, when we cling to laughter and hide the tears, the result is that we limit our capacity to laugh fully.

To laugh fully, we have to feel deeply. When we suppress tears, we cannot feel deeply. The more we suppress our tears, the more we limit our laughter. Specifically, we laugh only when things go wrong. When suppression of our tears is severe enough, laughter becomes a toned down version of satanic laughter, which can only experience pleasure in watching the stumbling and suffering of others. Likewise, the more honest we are about our own pain or sorrow, the higher we can soar in laughter, until we reach the fullness of laughter.

Fullness of laughter is laughter that laughs at no one. It is like a fire that burns clean. Fullness of laughter transmutes everything without consuming anyone, leaving no ashes or charred remains.

Fullness of laughter does not think itself to be better than the purity of crying. Both are expressions of genuineness. The two are intimately related. That is why it is possible to respond to overwhelming happiness by crying.

If we go deep enough into the feeling nature, we discover that fullness of laughter and purity of crying are separated by an exceedingly fine line that can be crossed again and again without skipping a beat or loss of continuity of expression; each one yielding to the other with the fluidity of two beloved partners in a dance.

49

Rudy Scarfalloto

We might even reach a place where we seem to laugh and cry simultaneously, unable to distinguish whether we are expressing one or
the other at any given moment. In such a place, there are no words to
describe what we feel. We might, however, imagine that if the feeling
could talk, it might say, *"Here I am...all of me...and I am so thankful
to be all here."*

CHAPTER 11

Pride & Humility

(Two Ways of Feeling Self-Worth)

When we feel proud, there is a sense of "fullness". We "swell" with pride. We feel there is more substance to our existence. We spontaneously stand at attention in response to the substance filling us and radiating from us.

While healthy pride is a sense of fullness, genuine humility may be said to be a state of purity. The experience of humility may be described as one of emptiness or simplicity. The presence of humility means we are, on some level, aware of our inner emptiness and are at peace with it; neither rejecting it nor flaunting it as a spiritual badge of honor. If we try to take credit for it, it vanishes.

Pride, Humility and Self-worth

Both pride and humility give us a sense of self worth. Pride is a sense of self-worth based on doing. Humility is a sense of self-worth based on being. Pride is healthy when it is a celebration of what we do. Humility is healthy when it translates into serenity with the perceived limitations of what we can do. We are at peace with the limitations of our doing because we have silently contacted our being.

Since pride is based on the things we create or accomplish, it is a tangible way of feeling self-worth. Healthy pride is based on work done with care and attention. Pride in our own accomplishments emerges naturally when we do our best. Any show of humility here is false humility.

Interestingly enough, we can also feel pride in the accomplishments of an individual or group to whom we feel emotional closeness. For example, we can be proud of the accomplishments of our parents, children, brothers or sisters. There is no logical reason why we would feel pride in someone else's accomplishments, unless we consider the possibility that, on a deep feeling level, we regard that person as a part of us.

While pride is based on tangible work, humility is based on the wordless sense of who we are beyond our work and beyond outer appearance. Humility is based on contact with the genuine self, pure and simple. Any show of pride here is false pride, since the deep awareness of who we are includes a sense that we are all basically passengers on the same bus.

Pride has to do with our unique self-expression as individuals, while humility is based on a quiet realization of our commonality, our primordial kinship and oneness. Pride is a feeling that celebrates our tangible and measurable achievements, while humility is a feeling of gratitude based on qualities within us that are intangible and beyond our capacity to measure.

Complementary

Healthy pride goes hand in hand with healthy humility. Pride is the mountain; humility is the valley. The fullness of pride radiates spontaneously and unashamedly from the emptiness of pure humility. When we are in touch with our beingness (the genuine self), we take pride in what we do. Such pride does not fall because it is quietly supported and stabilized by humility.

Pride without humility shows up as arrogance, vanity and over-concern with social customs and superficialities. Excessive or inappropriate pride is an unconscious attempt to hide inner feelings of emptiness that have become too frightening to face due to years of denial and pretence.

Humility without pride is not humility. It is strained piety, false modesty, ceremonial self-defacement and ritualized self-mutilation. Such pseudo-humility is an attempt to hide frozen pride; it is arrogance or vanity that we secretly cling to.

The Keeper of Pride

The keeper of pride is truth. Humility empowers our pride, and truth is what connects pride to humility. In everyday life, we maintain pride in what we do by cultivating truthfulness. We are honest with regard to what is important and what is not important to us. We claim what is truly ours and let go of what is not ours. Genuine pride can rise and swell on the wings of truth. Such pride has no need to restrain or censor itself, for it has done no wrong and told no lie.

The Keeper of Humility

The keeper of humility is humor. It is a special kind of humor. It is the kind of humor that can laugh at oneself without degrading oneself. Humility is about contacting the genuine self (beingness). As mentioned in the previous chapter, when we make contact with who we really are, and accept who we really are, we are likely to laugh (or cry). Humility that is grim and grave conceals a secret pride that takes itself very seriously.

One major reason that we might find it difficult to laugh at ourselves is that we have not allowed ourselves to cry. The reverse is also true; we might be secretly afraid to relax and allow ourselves to gently laugh at ourselves if doing so might expose hidden tears.

Without humor there is no humility. Without real humility there is no humor – except for biting sarcasm or taunting ridicule.

Union

The union of pride and humility is experienced as thankfulness. We are thankful for what we do and who we are. We are thankful for what we have and for what we don't have. We are thankful for our substance and our emptiness. We are thankful for being able to rise up and express the fullness of who we are, and we are thankful that we can relax and gently float down to the purity of who we are.

Under the common roof of thankfulness, pride is a strong tower of truth, while humility is a free and easy flowing stream of humor and warmth. They might interact as the lover and the beloved in an embrace so deep, they may be experienced as one and the same.

CHAPTER 12

Clean & Dirty

Mother Nature wires our nervous system so that we instinctively want to maintain a certain level of cleanliness. This is understandable since cleanliness promotes health and safety. Many animals living in the wild clean and groom themselves and each other, and they refrain from defecating or urinating in their living space.

For us humans, cleanliness has an additional meaning. Our instinctual leaning toward physical cleanliness reflects a deeper desire for purity on the consciousness level. The tendency to drift into dishonesty might show up as neglect of one physical body. As we allow deception, hidden anger and hurts to accumulate in our relationships, we might notice an accumulation of clutter around us. Or, we might go the other way. The deep-seated feelings of being emotionally or spiritually "dirty" might show up as hyperbolic cleanliness on the physical level. Either way, the degree of "purity" on the consciousness level greatly influences how we handle our physical cleanliness.

Down and Dirty

Though we instinctively seek cleanliness, phrases such as, "Let's get down and dirty," indicate that we secretly equate dirtiness with pleasure. Magazines and movies that are aimed at arousing sexual desire are often referred to as "dirty". This is not surprising. As mentioned earlier, the things we harshly judge or otherwise reject are often the same things we secretly desire.

We can more fully understand the dance of clean and dirty in the mind by looking at one particular version of this duality – sterile and septic. From a purely biological standpoint, there is nothing good or bad about sterile or septic. To a microbiologist, these two words simply indicate the absence or presence of microbial life. When these two words are used in non-scientific ways, however, they are charged with whatever emotional bias and inner conflict that we happen to carry.

As an expression of cleanliness, sterile is considered good, respectable and safe. On other levels, it can also imply lifelessness, dullness, lack of creativity and the inability to procreate. The soil on which we grow flowers, fruits and vegetables is very septic. It is teaming with a rich assortment of bacteria, fungi, bugs and worms – and their copious bodily secretions and excrements. This is fertile earth. The blacker the better! The septic tank and compost heap are very dirty and disgusting places, but the revolting biological activity converts the garbage into something useful.

On the social level, the double emotional meaning of the word "sterile" often sets up an unconscious conflict. We want to be clean and sterile because it is sensible, hygienic and socially acceptable, but we also equate cleanliness with the absence of vitality. Such inner conflict says, "I want to live life to the fullest, but if I'm full of life, I'm dirty. I want to be clean, but if I'm clean, I'm lifeless."

Unity Beyond Opposites

The healthy expression of clean and dirty ultimately depends on the harmonious dance of purity and fullness within our minds. The desire to experience the purity of the genuine self goes hand in hand with the desire to live life to the fullest. When the purity of the genuine self is allowed to blossom into fullness of who we are, we typically allow clean and dirty their rightful place without obsessing about them.

Obsession is about guilt and shame. When we harbor a cesspool of guilt and shame, we often protect ourselves by becoming overly logical, while toning down our feelings. Quite often, the only red flag that marks the presence of the hidden emotional burden is obsession – about cleanliness, etc.

The inner conflict is resolved when we get in touch with the inner purity of who we really are, beyond pretense and deception. This is the purity that has remained unchanged all the years of our lives, regardless of how dirty we think we are. This is the purity that transforms the emotional debris of the past into the rich and fertile soil on which we grow our personal gift of life that we give to life.

By thus reclaiming our inner purity and allowing ourselves to live life to the fullest, the duality of clean and dirty can dance harmoniously in the mind. We take proper care of the body and the home and we realize there is a time to be clean and a time to be dirty.

CHAPTER 13

Giving & Receiving

(Two Ways of Relating)

The dance of giving and receiving appears to be a fairly benign topic of discussion. It's the sort of thing people might discuss at a party, a philosophy class, or a church service. In reality, the dance of giving and receiving is linked to our most intimate and private beliefs about ourselves. How we give and receive has roots that reach down to our infantile needs and into the places of deepest fear.

Relationship

Relationship is about giving and receiving. Giving and receiving is how life relates to life. The two are always present, whether the giving and receiving are visible or invisible, tangible or intangible. Out relationships are harmonious to the extent that giving and receiving are balanced.

The serious inability to give and receive is like the two edges of the same inner dagger that silently rips the emotional nature. As emotional beings, we want to relate to one another. We relate primarily by giving and receiving. The inability to give and receive is quite painful. If this condition is not resolved, it forces us to escape into isolation and addiction. We will do anything to numb the pain of not being able to give and receive.

The ability to give purely and receive in fullness results in the feeling of physiological and emotional pleasure that spills over into a sense of wholeness beyond the usual experience of pleasure and pain. It is the laughter of a child; it is like the tree receiving freely from the earth and sky, and giving freely to the earth and sky; it is two lovers, one penetrating the other, while, on a deeper level, each penetrates and is penetrated by the other; it is the mother giving, and the infant receiving, both unobstructed by the notion of indebtedness; it is the command, "Let there be light…and let that light take form as the laughter of a child, the fruitful tree, the embracing lovers, the mother nursing the infant … for that is who I Am."

Pure Giving & Full Receiving

To be human is to want to receive. We express this desire overtly or covertly. When we do it covertly, we become a bottomless pit that can never be filled. When we do it overtly, the bottomless pit becomes an inexhaustible fountainhead of vitality from which we give. We find that we are simultaneously giving in a way that does not diminish us, while receiving in a way that does not diminish others.

Pure giving can only happen in the presence of full receiving. The two are ever united, and regardless of appearance, they are symmetrical. If person *A* gives, but person *B* does not receive it gracefully, the giving probably was not as pure as person *A* believed it to be.

Doing Harm With Giving & Receiving

We do harm to ourselves and others when we try to give with the hand that really wants to receive or receive with the hand that really wants to give. To attempt to receive when the real desire is to give, is to harm oneself through self-indulgence and frantic pleasure-seeking. These are simply attempts to cover the pain of withholding the gifts we are yearning to give. It is like withholding the birth of a baby in the womb. The withheld energy becomes toxic in the system, causing degeneration of the body and mind.

To attempt to give when the real desire is to receive is to give from lack. The act of giving from the place that really wants to receive usually translates into interference. We try to give something to someone who does not wish to receive what is being offered.

Things of Value

Things of value may be placed into two categories: Things that can be stolen, and things that cannot be stolen

Things that can be stolen are tangible items like cars, money, watches, television sets, ships, airplanes, etc. In other words, they are possessions that occupy space and exist in linear time therefore, they can only be in one place at one time. If we give some of these items away, they are no longer available to us. Therefore, we are mindful of how much of this stuff we give away. When we do this, we are not merely looking after our self-interest. By being skillful and honest in managing our perishable treasures, we open the door to the pure experience of treasures that cannot be stolen.

Things that cannot be stolen include joy, laughter, kindness and truth. Since these treasures don't take up space and are not subject to the limitations of matter, they can be shared freely without being diminished. In fact, they appear to *increase* every time they are given away.

We might argue that these intangible treasures *can* be taken away, but this can happen only to the extent that our giving has hidden strings attached to it. Those strings may be so well hidden that the giver may not be aware of them.

Giving With Strings Attached

Hidden strings are created when we give from the place that really wants to receive (giving from lack). This is when our giving translates into interference. This is when we become heavily invested in having people respond a certain way.

Even when we are not involved in tangible forms of giving and receiving, hidden strings can still be present in the form of emotional expectations. In essence, we invest our happiness in someone else's behavior. If they behave one way, we are happy, if they behave another way, we are unhappy. The more of these strings we have, the more easily our happiness can be "stolen" by others. The fewer strings we have, the less likely that anyone can rob our intangible treasures.

However, even if someone does manage to maliciously or accidentally "steal our joy," the thief can't have it either, because the only way to steal such a treasure is to destroy it. The good news is that such a theft is only temporary. Inner joy is like a plant whose roots are exceedingly deep. Cutting the flowers and stems simply makes the roots grow deeper.

I'm not implying here that all such emotional strings are unhealthy. When we have affection for others and trust them with our feelings, they, in essence, hold the "strings" to our heart. Therefore, their scorn or indifference can leave us feeling crushed or betrayed. On the other hand, the vibration of those same strings creates the sweet and tender music of deep intimacy. What we *can* do is exercise some discernment with regard to who we allow to hold our emotional strings.

Unity of Giving and Receiving

By being responsible for our own emotional strings, we can give freely of our truth, kindness and laughter. Every time we give them, we notice that we also receive them. This is how we come to know that giving and receiving are one. The more we do this, the more deeply we sense their unity. When the unity of giving and receiving is experienced strongly enough with our intangible treasures, the experience carries over into the material world as well.

CHAPTER 14

Holding On & Letting Go

(Understanding How Energy Flows)

To understand the dance of holding on and letting go, let's ponder electricity. Electricity may be simplistically seen as the flow of electrons from one place to another. They flow because there is an excess of electrons in one place relative to another. The place that has an excess of electrons is said to be electrically negative, and the place that is deficient is electrically positive. The flow of electrons is called the current.

The operation of electrical appliances depends on the current of electrons, made possible by the excess of electrons on one end of the wire relative to the other end. This difference in the density of electrons is called the voltage or charge. The greater the voltage, the more intense the subsequent current.

In other words, to establish an effective flow of electrons, there must be a *holding on* so that a charge can be built up. This is how electrical transformers work. A step-up transformer is an electrical dam of sorts. It absorbs an electric current, holds on to it to build up charge, and then releases the current of electrons at a greater voltage to do work that could not be done at the lower voltage.

Emotional Charge

On the emotional level, *letting go* is important to our health and well-being. If, however, we assert that letting go is better than holding on, we are setting ourselves up for internal conflict (neurosis).

Whether we know it or not, we routinely hold on and let go throughout the day. There is no formula that tells us when it is appropriate to hold on or let go; when to express and when to hold back;

when to speak and when to be silent. We might hold on because of fear or because it seems like the more intelligent choice. Sometimes we don't know why we hold on or let go. We just do so instinctively. Perhaps our silent inner wisdom has decided that it would be useful to build up emotional charge by holding on to the emotion for a while, so we can build up a charge.

She Tried To Make Herself Let Go

In my office, I once employed the services of a registered nurse/massage therapist. One afternoon, we were standing outside the office chatting, as we waited for the next patient. At one point, she mentioned that she was feeling persistent stiffness and tension in her neck. After she treated the condition with various physical modalities, it still bothered her. So she asked me, "What else can I do for it? I can't seem to make it let go."

Rather than addressing her question from a structural standpoint, I found myself intrigued by her statement, "I can't seem to make it let go." I had the impression that her choice of words gave a clue as to why the tension was persisting.

She had already pondered the idea that her physical tension was related to something that was bothering her emotionally, but again, her statement was, "I can't figure it out."

I suggested that she change her strategy from, *making it let go* to *letting it let go.* I suggested that she might get to the emotional cause by shifting from trying to figure it out, to just relaxing and allowing the answer to emerge from within.

The following morning, we met at the office again. This time, she was radiant. The answer to her dilemma had come to her gradually on the preceding day. Not only had the tension totally released, but she was on an emotional high, feeling as playful as a child. She reported that her neck felt great and her entire body felt energized and limber.

She indicated that the tension in her neck was a resentment she had been unknowingly holding for five months – since her last birthday. At that time, her fiancé was not feeling well, and both of them were rather busy. As a result, they were unable to celebrate her birthday.

Like many of us, she had a tendency to refrain from mentioning her birthday, while secretly hoping that someone would take charge and organize a party. She had felt very disappointed. However, she judged her emotional reaction as childish and inappropriate, so she kept it to herself and forgot about it.

Shortly after she had that realization, her neck problem cleared up completely and she felt wonderful. In her giddy and playful state, she called her fiancé and said, "I want to celebrate my birthday!"

She not only acknowledged her own birthday, but she had the audacity to ask for a celebration *five months after the fact.* This behavior was very out of character for her.

By holding on to her emotions for five months, they silently built up a charge. When she finally let go, the released emotional energy resulted in a healing that, apparently, went far beyond the neglected birthday. She used the emotional charge that had built up over a five-month period to break through a wall of fear and inhibition that had been in place for years.

Was this just a temporary high? Apparently not. She remained visibly changed. Weeks later, she stopped what she was doing, and, in amazement, she declared, "I just realized, I love my patients!"

CHAPTER 15

Speaking & Silence

(Two Ways of Cultivating Personal Power)

We hold on or let go every time we make the choice to speak or be silent. As with other opposites, speaking and silence have the capacity to complement one another. When we discipline ourselves to speak words that are honest, the mind can more easily go to the place of deep silence. Likewise, in silence we tend to bring forth words that are honest.

The absence of speech is one level of silence. A deeper level is stillness of all thoughts. Such silence is golden, for it brings forth mental clarity. In stillness and silence, we are rejuvenated; we bring forth a sense of newness and a zest for life, as if we are seeing a sunrise for the first time. That sense of renewal is expressed as newfound power and clarity in our communication.

Things Held In Silence Increase In Power

Thoughts and emotions that are kept secret become the powerful rulers of our reality. This is the reason for the everyday practice of tending to our own psychological health by expressing troublesome thoughts and feelings.

Sometimes, it is wise to keep a secret for a while, provided it is done out of respect rather than fear or the need to control others. When a secret remains a secret beyond its time, it becomes a breeding ground for hurtful actions. This applies to all secrets, whether they are deeply personal, social or political.

I Knew It, Until I Opened My Mouth

When silence is used intelligently and respectfully, it allows precious personal truths to rise naturally into the conscious mind. We may experience this during deep meditation, prayer, or a quiet walk in the woods. We might awaken one morning with a clear sense of what God means to us. We may have a dream or vision that wordlessly reveals our purpose in life. Yet, if we try to express the vision in words, it often becomes meaningless. This is especially true if our intent is to use the vision to glorify ourselves in the eyes of others, or to belittle someone else.

Even if our intentions are sincere, speaking a truth prematurely can cause it to wither away. Truth, in its primordial form, is boundless and therefore wordless. The moment we speak it, we impose boundaries on it. This is why personal truth might require a period of silence, during which it can gather strength and take shape as words and actions that reflect the purity of that truth.

Quietly Listening and Boldly Speaking

I was once acquainted with two counselors whom I will call "Jack" and "Bill". Jack had this philosophy: We will not assume to know what you are thinking or feeling, and we will not assume to know what is running you or what is best for you. We will simply listen so that you may use us as a witness to help you discover your own truth.

Bill had this philosophy: Everyone has permission to say whatever they want to whomever they want, uncensored, uninhibited.

One might assume that my two friends were sometimes at odds with each other. One appeared to be sage-like and unobtrusive, and the other, wild and bombastic. Yet, the two strategies can achieve similar results.

How can these two divergent philosophies achieve the same result? The answer is that they are not really divergent—they are convergent. Each one, done in fullness gives birth to the pure essence of the other.

Jack's strategy was to create a neutral space where each person could feel safe to go deeply into their personal truth without risk of being attacked, manipulated or brainwashed by others. The emphasis is on *listening*.

Bill's strategy was to maximize honest and uncensored interpersonal communication, challenging people to express things they wouldn't dare say in normal conversation. There was just one stipulation to Bill's strategy: whatever anyone says about anyone is a clear reflection of the person making the statement. In other words, the more emotional charge I have when I tell someone my perception of them, the more I am exposing myself. And, that's okay. It's more than okay. Rather than censoring our tendency to find fault in others, it is given free expression, and is thus transformed into a powerful tool for self-discovery. With this self-discovery comes the ability to really *listen*.

When Jack and Bill apply their respective principles with skill and heart, each recognizes and gives birth to the other. On the other hand, if either principle is held rigidly, it will regard the other as a threat. Furthermore, each one becomes a tool of manipulation and exploitation. For example, if someone tells me that I am too inhibited and that I should speak up more, I can use Jack's hands-off philosophy as a wonderful shield, by telling my accuser, "You cannot know what is best for me." My assertion could very well be true, but in the moment, I'm using that truth as a smokescreen to direct attention away from me.

Another way of misusing Jack's philosophy is to withhold our genuine perceptions and feelings about someone else, which leads to a secret, holier-than-thou attitude that silently says, "I know what's going on with you; but in my wisdom, I will refrain from speaking up because I am letting you muck through the mistakes I know you are going to make before you arrive at the enlightened place where I am now." By thus withholding our honest perception, our relationship with the other person has changed from friend/friend to teacher/student, parent/child, sage/idiot.

Likewise, Bill's philosophy of, *Say what you want to whomever you want,* can easily degenerate into wholesale blaming to hide deeper feelings of insecurity. The overt expression of "truth" is used to hide other truths. When this happens, arguments tend to spiral out of control. There is no resolution, just an ever-mounting pile of accusations, misunderstandings and hurt feelings.

Each of the two principles can become a trap if held rigidly. Each defeats its own purpose when it rejects the other. Each one done in fullness gives birth to the pure essence of the other. Honest speaking promotes empathic listening, and vice versa.

CHAPTER 16

Conscious & Unconscious

(The Day and Night of the Mind)

"There's no such thing as an unconscious mind," said my friend, 'George,' as we sat in an outdoor restaurant having lunch. "There's only one mind," he said, "and it's entirely conscious; there are simply elements that we choose to temporarily forget."

He stated that the distinction between conscious and unconscious is artificial. I agreed with him in principle, but I was feeling competitive, so I challenged him. I said, "George, if the distinction between of conscious/unconscious is artificial, why did we make it up, and why do we use it so much?"

The obvious answer is that we find it useful. Even when we don't use the words, *conscious* and *unconscious*, we still silently make that distinction every time we use terms like, remember/forget, awake/asleep, aware/unaware, intentional/unintentional, known/unknown. I pointed this out to my friend, and then, feeling a bit mischievous, I added, "Since we obviously find it useful to make the artificial distinction between conscious and unconscious, let's do it *consciously* rather than unconsciously."

Making the Distinction

The conscious mind holds the thoughts and emotions that we are aware of at any moment. The unconscious mind contains everything else. The conscious mind is in charge of deliberate action, making the distinction between oneself and others, what is ours and what is not ours; keeping track of time; making choices and judgments.

The unconscious mind – on the deepest levels – makes no judgment with regard to what is right and wrong, good/bad, friend/enemy.

It has no concept of time and space, no sense of separation, and is, therefore, in full communication with other minds. Making no clear distinction between oneself and others, it has no sense of territory. It has virtually limitless knowledge that it sends to the conscious mind as inspiration, insight and intuition.

The unconscious mind also stores all the memories and feelings that the conscious mind is unwilling to handle. When the conscious mind tries to get rid of an unpleasant memory or disagreeable emotion, it simply stores the data in the unconscious mind.

The price for keeping a tight lid on the unwanted memories and emotions is that we also shut the door on empathy, joy, genuine kindness and intuition. Furthermore, the unwanted memories and emotions exert a powerful influence on us. They become the authors of our physical reality. Therefore, the answer to the question, "How do I really know what I hold in my 'unconscious' mind?" is simple: we just look around at the physical world we have created for ourselves: we look at our bodies, our work and our relationships. Each is a reflection of what really runs us, regardless of who we think we are, and what we profess to believe.

In one sense, the physical reality we create may be looked upon as an attempt by the unconscious mind to become conscious. When the conscious mind judges the creations as "bad," learning is blocked. In its harsh judgment of the creation, the conscious mind says, "I do not wish to know this part of myself right now." The unconscious mind simply replies, "Okay," and tries again later.

My Kindly Intentions

While writing this section of the book, I, coincidentally, had a confrontation with one of the students in my anatomy and physiology class. The issue was a question on a test that the class had taken the previous week. The student did not agree with my interpretation of her answer. We spoke privately about the matter for several minutes. I felt that I was right in my interpretation, so I held my ground, though I did acknowledge her for being forthright.

When the class reconvened, the student was still visibly unhappy. There was also a subtle tension in the room. The rest of the class was aware of the little debate between that particular student and myself. I wondered if other students had taken issue with my interpretation of the question, but were too shy to speak up.

So, I asked the student to express to the class why she was unhappy with her test. I reasoned that her candor would encourage other students to speak up. She felt embarrassed about doing so, but with a little cheering-on from the class, she expressed herself openly.

I told myself that my intention was to communicate to her and the rest of the class that their opinions were welcomed. However, that was not the result of my efforts. Later that day, the student called me on the telephone and stated that she felt terribly upset. She said the experience triggered childhood memories of Catholic School, where she was sometimes humiliated in front of the class for being "stupid".

My conscious intention was certainly not to punish or humiliate her. Yet, that *was* the result. I then looked back and remembered other instances where I (through good and honorable intentions) did things that resulted in someone feeling invalidated. Then, I recalled my own childhood and remembered the times I felt belittled and humiliated.

My interaction with that student reminded me that the *results* of our actions are a reflection of what we hold the subconscious mind. My conscious intention to be a supportive teacher was mixed with my unconscious programming to hurt another human being in the same manner that I had been hurt. And, by a remarkable coincidence, I had picked the one student in the class who was the most vulnerable.

A word of caution: If we become aware of these subconscious motives while we carry a lot of self-condemnation, the effect can be quite demoralizing. Therefore, if we choose to examine the subconscious programming that underlies our daily interactions, we must remind ourselves to be as objective as we can, and to have a measure of respect for all those who are involved.

Synergy of Conscious and Unconscious

In order for the average person to maintain physical, mental and emotional health, the conscious mind must be allowed to have a time of rest. The other deeper parts of the mind don't need such rest. The cognitive part of the brain needs to rest in order to maintain clarity of thought. The part of the brain that governs the deeper awareness and visceral functions does not need such rest; in fact it is most active when the cognitive brain is sleeping.

One of the assumptions often made by individuals interested in metaphysical pursuits is that conscious is better than unconscious. For sure, the evolution into greater conscious awareness of ourselves is natural. It occurs spontaneously when our conscious and unconscious aspects are allowed to dance harmoniously with one another. In one sense, we might say that the unconscious parts of ourselves "want to" become conscious. Such evolution is simply the result of living the life we want to live. Such evolution has its own timing and rhythm. We really cannot "speed it up." When it looks like we have successfully accelerated the evolution of unconscious into conscious, we have simply dissolved the "blockages" that had been slowing us down. Quite often those blockages take the form of trying too hard to speed ourselves us. When we do so, we are generally reacting to external pressures and neglecting our own inner rhythm and timing.

To complicate matters, having convinced ourselves that conscious is better than unconscious, we can then plug in our own notion of what specifically constitutes being "conscious" or "unconscious". We define what it means to be awake, aware, illumined or enlightened. Essentially, those who agree with our own beliefs are considered more conscious or enlightened, and all others are unconscious, deceived or just evil.

In order to maintain health and well-being, the conscious and unconscious aspects of the mind must be balanced and integrated. As with other opposites, these two are mutually supportive. On a physiological level, such balance is reflected in the complementary relationship between wakefulness and sleep. There is a complementary relationship between those parts of the brain that need to rest and those that don't. The more thoroughly we are able to rest the cognitive mind (through sleep, deep relaxation, mediation, etc.), the more fully we can access the deeper intuitive nature. Likewise, the serenity and inspiration that emerges from the deep part of the brain (the part that doesn't sleep) allows the cognitive mind to be at ease, to sleep more deeply and, therefore, function more effectively.

CHAPTER 17

Judgment

Judgment is how we perceive opposites. When we judge, we perceive greater and lesser, right and wrong, desirable and undesirable, pleasant and unpleasant, smart and stupid, innocent and guilty.

We cannot express judgment in one direction without the other. Every time we consciously say "this is good," we unconsciously affirm that the opposite is bad. If we regard one thing as superior, we must regard something else as inferior.

When we suppress overt judgment, we do it covertly. When we judge consciously, we compel the judgment to evolve into a deeper awareness that ultimately transcends the perception of opposites. Judging consciously means that we honestly admit that we perceive a difference and that we recognize our genuine emotional bias.

The biblical injunction to refrain from judging can be a great stepping-stone to freedom when it sets us free from the thinking that robs us of our peace. It is a stepping-stone when it translates into the removal of excessively harsh judgment that we might place on ourselves or others. It is a blessing when it sets us free from the judgments that cause us to assume that our way of thinking is superior to those who see things differently. On the other hand, if we flatly say, "Don't judge" under any circumstance, we have set a splendid trap for ourselves. To stop judging – in the broadest sense – we have to stop thinking altogether. Even if we understand that "don't judge" means that we simply avoid harsh criticism and assumed superiority, we must be careful: We could seduce ourselves into believing that we are free of harsh judgment, but have merely suppressed it and driven it underground. And so, we might silently strut about, secretly judging others, as we beam them a benevolent smile. The funniest version of this when we harshly judge others for being "judgmental."

One way to free ourselves of excessive or inappropriate judgment is to be aware of it. This becomes easier when we recognize the many ways that we can express judgment.

The Many Faces of Judgment

When opposites interact harmoniously in the mind, the result is mental clarity and emotional serenity. In order for opposites to interact harmoniously, judgment must have its proper place.

Judgment finds its proper place when we regard it as an ability rather than as a disability. We allow it to express appropriately so that it doesn't express inappropriately. Judgment tends to find its proper place when we recognize its many facets, described below.

Judgment is Not Just a Thought

Judgment has a mental component: "In my opinion, General Custer made a poor decision..." and it has an emotional component: "Green snot! How gross!" The mental and emotional components of judgment are inseparable, though one might be more obvious than the other. Regardless of how detached we appear to be with our perceptions, they are always accompanied by a subtle emotional charge.

Judgment finds its proper place when we regard it as a cognitive skill that we cultivate, as well as an emotional bias that is simply allowed to be. We cultivate the mental aspect of judgment by questioning our perceptions for accuracy. When we do so, the emotional component also finds its proper place.

The Mental Component of Judgment

The mental component of judgment allows us to make sense of the world around us. It is the ability to properly separate things, set clear boundaries and exercise discernment. It is our capacity to be objective. It is the impartial judge who weighs the evidence, or the methodical scientist who gathers data.

The Emotional Component of Judgment

We read novels and watch movies because we are emotionally drawn in by the interaction of opposing forces. In a similar manner, we judge ourselves and others, thus setting up the drama of opposing forces in our minds. Such drama generates a sense of purpose, a mission, or just keeps us engaged and entertained.

As we recognize the emotional part of our judgments, we tend to become more objective since the emotional component no longer gets tangled with the cognitive component. In fact, when we simply let the emotional component be, without rejecting or trying to justify it, we might discover that it contains subtle intuitive hunches that support our mental awareness.

One hidden reason why the emotional component of judgment might seem problematical is that we have cut off other sources of aliveness, such as creativity and intimacy. When we are able to reopen these other portals of aliveness, we find a proportionate decrease in the tendency to harshly judge ourselves and others, and less tendency to seek out drama and conflict.

Judgment Has an Element of Projection
We tend to judge others in accordance with our own past experiences. This is especially true when we harbor hidden guilt. We punish others for our sins. Therefore, when Jesus said to the crowd, "Let he who is without sin cast the first stone," we might wonder if he was aware of the hidden joke in his statement – only a sinner would cast a stone at another sinner.

A slightly more benign expression of projection is when we try to correct our weaknesses in others. We tend to teach others the lessons *we* need to learn. For sure, there is a certain wisdom in this. The ideal doctor to treat diabetes is one who has (or better yet, *had*) diabetes. Such a doctor has probably studied the disease in great detail and has an intimate emotional understanding of it. On the other hand, we would not want to go to a diabetic doctor who treats all patients as if they have diabetes.

Judgment is Incomplete Knowing
Our judgment of any situation is typically based on partial knowledge. When we judge a thing, we know something about it, but only in part. Discarding the judgment is like throwing away a piece of a

puzzle. Likewise, to regard our particular judgment as the whole truth is to remain incomplete in our knowing. Judgment is transcended, not by stamping it out, but by using it as a step in fully understanding the thing being judged.

Judgment as Self-Fulfilling Prophecy

Our judgments tend to be self-fulfilling. They tend to change reality so as to conform with the judgment. The person making the judgment might, therefore, feel even more self-righteous than before: "You see, I was right, he's behaving just like I said he would!"

The power of judgment to produce change is more noticeable in situations where the person making the judgment is in a position of authority or is adept at projecting his or her intentions or beliefs on others. This is especially true when the person on the receiving end happens to be emotionally vulnerable and open to suggestion.

Again, judgment is partial information. By rigidly holding on to that information as if it were the whole truth, we cause it to blow out of proportion. We then create our external reality in such a way as to validate our judgment. This is how we deepen self-deception and escalate conflict.

Judgment by Any Other Name

Anger is judgment with a strong emotional component. When we are angry at someone, we are saying, "What you did was bad, and I want you to feel guilty about it."

The expression of genuine anger can be beneficial for all parties involved. However, since the expression of anger is often difficult, we try to beautify it by denying that anger includes judgment, blaming and guilt-pushing. As a result, anger becomes easier to express, but is not experienced in fullness. Experiencing it in fullness means we recognize the judgment, the blaming, the feeling of having been victimized, the desire to make the other person feel guilty. In recognizing the anger in fullness, its energy is released in fullness, and is therefore free to change into passion and caring.

The Need to be Angry

Anger might persist because we are not seeing the whole picture. We only see the parts that make one person the villain and the other the victim. If we expand our perception of the situation, we see that our anger can linger for a number of hidden reasons. For example, when we feel justified in our anger, we don't want anything to dampen it because we feel energized by it. We feel energized by the sense of righteous indignation. If our self-esteem is low, we jump at any chance to feel justifiable anger, and we resist any change in perception that might deflate our anger.

Jealousy Cloaked as Judgment

We might think we are judging someone harshly because the other person is doing something that goes against our sense of ethics. However, closer examination may reveal that our judgment stems from an underlying resentment that the other person is doing something that we secretly want to do.

Judgment and Non-judgment

One of the most subtle forms of judgment is the one that says, "Non-judgment is better than judgment." This is the last one to fall away before we "shift" from the awareness of duality to the profound awareness of singularity or unity. As we approach this point, we are greeted by the realization that judgment and non-judgment have equal value.

Beyond Judgment

One evening my, then, future wife and I were sitting at the kitchen table talking about unconditional love, which is to say, love beyond judgment. At one point in our conversation, she began experiencing something akin to a full-body orgasm (I wasn't touching her). This was followed by some amazing words that flowed from her mouth: "We do love ourselves, completely, and unconditionally, right now. So, in learning how to love ourselves, we are simply remembering that we already love ourselves, and our very presence here on Earth is an expression of that great love... In the beginning, we were filled with love, and that can't ever change... Every breath I take has purpose. Every word I speak, every deed I perform, everything I see and hear and feel has purpose. This is way beyond not judging. This is a gut-level knowing that everything I think and speak and do, or witness others think and speak and do is sacred."

After speaking for while, she fell silent. I didn't say anything, because I was busy writing down her last words. The only sound in the room was the ticking of the clock. Then she resumed.

"Every tick of the clock is sacred," she declared. "Every judgment is sacred! Non-judgment is sacred! We loved ourselves so deeply from the beginning, that we gave ourselves the great gift of this life and every detail in it. When we fully realize what a great gift of love this life is, we are then complete with it, and we move on to the next life which is also a great gift of love..."

I frantically tried to write down her words, as she paced around the kitchen in a semi-trance. I didn't dare ask her to slow down.

"...And the whole evolution of life is love," she continued, "which was at the beginning as it always will be, while, simultaneously, it is ever changing and unfolding moment by moment. This is the paradox of love. It is as it has always been, and always will be, even as it unfolds and changes with every breath we take. This knowledge, this amazing awareness, has always been in me. I'm simply recognizing it again right now, in a way that I have never recognized it before."

Just when I thought she was done, she cranked up again. So I grabbed my pen and resumed writing like a mad man:

"We are simultaneously unique individuals and exactly the same, unfolding and discovering exactly the same thing, each in our own way. This is not a truth that we grasp with the logical mind. It is a feeling that we surrender to, moment by moment. Every thought, feeling, action, inaction is just the truth of God I Am. And this is why we don't really have to eat or drink. All energy and all life emanates from within us, from every cell. We are forever self-sustaining. When we remember this fully while we are within physical bodies, our bodies too will be self-sustaining, needing nothing from the outside to keep it going. Our apparent need for food and water is a creation of our beliefs. And this, too, is sacred...it was from love that we chose our human experience."

CHAPTER 18

Justify & Condemn

(Two Ways of Judging)

Judgment often takes the form of *justification* or *condemnation.* Justification literally means that we try to make ourselves or others appear right. It often shows up as excuses, defensiveness or denial. Condemnation, when directed at oneself, typically shows up as guilt or shame. Condemnation directed at others shows up overtly as accusation or covertly as resentment.

Self-justification is typically a shield that hides self-condemnation. Both justification and condemnation are ways of saying, "I don't like myself." Self-justification is an indirect way of hating oneself, while self-condemnation has the dubious virtue of being more to the point.

Defending the Weakness

When we are ready to break the protective shell of denial, the funny relationship between condemnation and justification becomes all too clear. We see that in the very act of justifying or making excuses for the perceived weakness, we cause the weakness to persist or even amplify. In fact, the defense of a perceived weakness will amplify the weakness more readily than the overt condemnation of it. Overt condemnation is visible and, therefore, more manageable, while justification conceals the condemnation and, therefore, prolongs and deepens its corrosive effect.

Individuals who consciously attempt to overcome an addiction quite often seem to belittle themselves or lament their weakness. This, however, is often a step up, for it is not nearly as crippling as the hardcore addict who denies, rationalizes, minimizes or defends to the death the addictive behavior.

Why We Condemn Others

There are mental and emotional reasons to account for the chronic tendency to condemn others. On the mental level, we condemn others because we perceive them as guilty. On the emotional level, we condemn others because it gives us a feeling of aliveness.

Mental

Any sort of condemnation is about guilt. We condemn ourselves because we perceive ourselves as guilty. We condemn others because we perceive them as guilty.

The perception of guilt is one way that we justify separation. If we are in favor of the separation, the perception of guilt might be called "discernment." If we are not in favor of separation, the perception of guilt is called "being judgmental."

We might deny there is a link between separation and guilt because we do not wish to be seen as the accusers of our brethren. So, we attempt to make a "clean break" from those we dislike, but we deny that we see them as guilty of misconduct. The result is that the perception of guilt lingers in the subconscious mind.

We can certainly want to separate from others without necessarily perceiving them as guilty. We might simply feel incompatible with them. If, however, we do feel violated or otherwise mistreated, a clean separation means we recognize those feelings. Thus recognized, the wound is able to heal, and the perception of guilt can change. We do not *make* it change. We simply *allow* it to change. As part of this change, we might eventually realize that the guilt we perceived in the other is a reflection of our own.

Emotional

On the emotional level, condemnation is one way that we feel "aliveness". When we are at peace with ourselves, we generate feelings of aliveness through emotional closeness with others, creative expression, loving touch and spiritual contact (contact with one's genuine self). If these portals of aliveness are lacking, we will probably stimulate ourselves in other ways, such as condemnation and fault-finding. Even if we honestly admit that our perception of guilt is erroneous, we might still drift in the direction of condemnation if it happens to be a major source of aliveness for us.

Hate Groups

Every hate group in society feeds on the energy of condemnation. In that regard, they are not much different from the rest of us. It's just a matter of degree. It does not matter whether the condemnation is generated by the group or directed at the group. Either way, the organization is sustained by the energy of condemnation.

We condemn the hate groups by actively trying to eradicate them or reform them, or passively assume there is no truth in them. Any sort of condemnation guarantees their continued existence. We can terminate the hate groups in the same manner that we terminate most other problems: by allowing them to complete their function. The function of the hate groups in society is complete when two things happen:

- We realize that their gross misconduct reflects a subtle misconduct present in the rest of society.
- We realize they are simply playing out a caricature of some basic wisdom that the rest of us are holding in denial. For example, certain hate groups speak of a "purity" or "perfection" in humanity. The perversion of this truth says that only certain people are destined to experience this purity or that some groups have it more than others. Therefore, the ones who have it can wipe out, subjugate or "guide" the inferior ones who don't have it. The purity beyond the perversion can be experienced as a simple feeling. It is a feeling we get when we look at others and see ourselves. The perversion tries to force its image of beauty upon all of humanity. The purity beyond the perversion looks at all of humanity and perceives beauty. This is the purity we are all evolving to.

CHAPTER 19

Why We Argue

In order for conflict to persist, both parties must be in denial about something. This is true for interpersonal conflict as well as social conflict. As an example, let's consider the abortion issue.

For all of my adult life and for as far back as I can remember into my childhood, the abortion issue has been a focal point of political and religious debate. As a young man of about nineteen years, well indoctrinated in traditional Christian values, I was definitely opposed to legalized abortion. As far as I was concerned, those who were in favor of legalized abortion were just flat-out wrong. As I became older and became exposed to other viewpoints, I become definitely in favor of legalized abortion. As far as I was concerned, those who wanted to make abortion illegal were just flat-out wrong.

When I was definitely against legalized abortion, I was operating under the belief that human life is *sacred*. When I was definitely in favor of legalized abortion, I was operating under the belief that all individuals have the natural right to *choose* what they will do with their own bodies.

If we see this issue only from a mental standpoint, the two sides are forever at odds with each other. When we include a strong element of feeling, an amazing thing happens. The two issues (sacredness and choice) are not only quite compatible, they are *inseparable*. The sacredness of life is meaningless if choice is denied. Likewise, freedom of choice quickly loses meaning if it is exercised in such a way that denies the sacredness of life.

Each Bears the Seed of the Other

In the pro-life/pro-choice debate, each side does not fully comprehend the meaning of its own teaching as long as it denies the truth of other side. To place the sanctity of life and freedom of choice at odds with each other is to instigate subtle inner conflict, because, deep inside, we know the two to be inseparable. Such inner conflict is typically suppressed and, therefore, projected out as conflict with those who have suppressed it in the opposite manner.

The same relationship exists between any two opposing forces or ideas. When we reject one side, we render the other incomplete. The recognition of this relationship can produce anxiety in us if we have a strong vested interest in one side. That is why we tend to deny that such a relationship exists. Thus, we can happily argue for one side or the other and be totally convinced that we are right and the other is wrong. This is one of many hidden factors that perpetuate conflict and controversy. Some others factors are described below.

The Hidden Motives for Controversy

- **Relationship.** By joining a cause, we create relationship with those who hold the same belief.
- **Purpose.** Controversy creates a sense of purpose. By getting involved in a cause greater than myself, I become greater than myself. This factor, though subtle, is quite powerful because the need to feel connected to something bigger than oneself is fundamental to our well-being.
- **Identity.** For someone who is struggling for a sense of identity, joining a cause or any organization provides an answer. Who am I? I am a democrat, a republican, a communist, etc. The group gives each member an identity that is tied to the organization. Each member is sustained emotionally by the identity provided by the "greater presence." To leave the organization is to risk losing one's identity.
- **Nobility.** By contrasting ourselves against "darkness," we perceive ourselves as being "enlightened". By calling attention to the inferiority of the other, we are, by implication, proclaiming our superiority. We point to their foolishness so we can appear wise. We point to their guilt, so

we can look innocent. We point to their lies, so can appear to be honest.

- **Certainty.** There is a feeling of power that comes with the illusion of certainty. The appearance of certainty is achieved by denying there is any truth in the opponent or any lie within oneself.
- **Political Power.** Controversy is an easy way to call attention to oneself. Similarly, the presence of an enemy, tangible or otherwise, is an ideal magnet to gather together followers and collect money.
- **Entertainment.** Conflict of any kind engages our attention. Without it, we might become bored. Can you imagine a movie or novel without conflicting forces?
- **Aliveness.** Relationship, purpose, identity, nobility, certainty, political power and entertainment all create a sense of aliveness. One way or another, we must generate that sense of aliveness, for this is how we maintain the will to live. Conflict of any kind is a potential source of aliveness.
- **Seeing Oneself in the Opponent.** When the above-mentioned motives for creating an enemy are recognized, we see the deepest one. We realize that we encounter the enemy and remain in their presence so as to encounter that hidden part of ourselves reflected by the enemy. Regardless of how many reasons we uncover for the conflict, the bottom line is that each party in a dispute is unconsciously attempting to recognize in the other a truth that is denied within oneself. Aliveness is what we want. The purest and most potent form of aliveness is the act of looking upon another person and seeing oneself.

Does This Mean We Shouldn't Argue?

Seeing truth in the opposition doesn't mean we talk ourselves into adopting a neutral position. If we do not value our own truth we cannot value the truth of the other party.

Neutrality has value. It is often an important step in conflict resolution. Full resolution, however, does not happen entirely through middle-of-the road neutrality. In fact, resolution is hindered if we are neutral because we are simply too timid to stray one way or the other. The ability to see truth and beauty in the opponent is born out of our willingness to stand cleanly in our truth as we experience it moment by moment. If we genuinely believe in our viewpoint, we argue the point fiercely and sincerely, without censorship, patronizing diplomacy, or placating smiles. This creates the emotional openness that eventually allows us to see the truth presented by the other.

The process doesn't stop there. Consistent honesty causes that same emotional openness to become ever deeper. Consequently, not only do we see the truth presented by our opponent, we eventually see *ourselves* in the opponent.

CHAPTER 20

Will & Feeling

(The Two Sides of Our Humanity)

The will and feeling nature are the two sides of our human awareness. Their interaction creates the unique personality of every individual. The two are often placed at war with each other by the judgment that makes one more important than the other, or the belief that one side should overpower the other. This is a major cause of inner conflict. In other words, conflict within the mind (neurosis) typically translates into some sort of silent battle between the will and feeling nature. We can resolve that inner conflict by understanding the dance between the will and feeling nature. Such understanding begins by first defining what we mean by "the will" and "the feeling nature."

The Will

The will is our capacity for sustained attention. It is our ability to make choices. The will is firm, directed, linear and consistent. The will can show up as courage, persistence and self-discipline.

Courage is the swimmer who stands at the edge of the water and jumps in, not knowing how deep it is, or what might be swimming around just under the surface. Beyond the raw courage to jump in, the will shows up as the capacity to keep swimming until the destination is reached. The water is cold, the salt stings the eyes, the muscles get tired and achy, but the will keeps the swimmer moving.

The will expresses most commonly as our everyday thoughts, perceptions and beliefs. The will includes our intellect – our capacity to learn from the past and plan for the future. The will is our capacity to set boundaries and exercise discernment. The will is about doing, setting goals, working and building.

One very important quality of the will is that it can be developed. Cultivating the will is a process of reminding ourselves that we are at choice. We remind ourselves over and over again of what we really want, though faced with intimidation, or tempted by immediate gratification.

Quite often, the will shows up as the capacity to perform a given activity even though we don't "feel like it." This is why the will can appear to be at odds with the feeling nature.

The Feeling Nature

Whereas the will is directed and linear, our feelings are expansive. The feeling nature is easy, melting and free. The will exerts effort, while the feeling nature is effortless. The will allows us to be ever at attention and vigilant, while the feeling nature allows us to relax, let go and trust. The will is about doing, while the feeling nature is about being.

Whereas the will can be trained and developed, our ability to *feel* is not something that we "learn" how to do. Expressing feelings is like sneezing. We can't make ourselves sneeze; we simply relax and sneeze. The feeling nature expresses most commonly as our physical sensations, emotions and desires. We can feel hot or cold, pleasure or pain anywhere on the body. We can feel emotions such as happiness, sadness or anger throughout the day. Our everyday desires can be physical, emotional or both.

We also have other expressions of the feeling nature that are more subtle and ethereal than sensations, emotions and desires. These include intuition, instinct, empathy, compassion and conscience. Though we can identify each of these expressions of the feeling nature, there is an underlying unity. If we try to suppress or deny one aspect of the feeling nature, the others suffer as well. If we suppress our animal instincts and desires, our capacity for genuine compassion is decreased. To the extent that we lose touch with our everyday emotions, we also tend to lose touch with our intuition.

Another important distinction between the will and feeling nature has to do with time. The will keeps track of time. The feeling nature doesn't. The will learns from the past and contemplates the future, while the feeling nature is ever in the present. The feeling nature is, therefore, our well-spring of innocence and spontaneity. On a feeling level, every experience is a new experience. Feelings can seemingly come from nowhere and then disappear into nothing.

Having no existence in the future, the feeling nature does not plan or plot. Having no past, it is incapable of holding a grudge. It is also incapable of learning. The modification of our feelings through learning is made possible by the will. For example, our everyday emotions are greatly influenced by our memories, perceptions and beliefs that are gathered over time.

The Inner Dance

As with other opposites, the will and feeling nature are inseparable. Each is meaningless without the other to define it. The will is like the banks of a river that allow the water to flow to its destination. The banks contain the water, while allowing it to flow in the direction that it naturally wants to flow. Without the boundaries provided by the will, the feeling nature becomes hysterical; it is water flowing chaotically, with little force and no direction, until it dissipates its energy, stagnates and sinks into the soil of unconsciousness. Likewise, genuine feelings, honestly expressed, constitute a potent driving force that purifies and deepens the will, as rushing water cleans and maintains the banks of a river. In everyday life, the harmonious union of the will and feeling nature shows up as mental clarity and emotional serenity.

In other words, when the will and feeling nature are in harmony, they complement one another; each one gives shape and substance to the other. The will gives our feelings force, direction and fullness of expression, while the expression of genuine feelings has the effect of purifying and sharpening the will.

The harmonious union of the will and feeling nature occurs when the will disciplines itself to be still and listen to the feeling nature. The more deeply the will listens, the more precisely it can choose. For example, two people might feel sexually aroused by each other and even feel a nice little emotional fluttering in the heart. However, there might also be a deeper feeling – an instinct – that says, *no, not this one,* or perhaps, *go slow, real slow.* We may not hear the deeper feelings very clearly if we have habitually ignored them. The result is that we feel "split". One part of us seems to say yes, while another part seems to say no.

In truth, all expressions of the feeling nature – no matter how different they are – tend to coexist peacefully. They are born from the same womb, grow up in the same house and are very much at ease around each other. The "split" occurs when the will judges some feelings as good, some as bad, some as useful and some as useless or inferior.

The split is healed when the will listens deeply and respectfully to *all* feelings emerging from within. This is how the will learns how to make intelligent choices. This is when the will makes choices that *feel* right.

Brother Passion & Sister Grace

When pure will is married to the fullness of feeling, they give birth to a son called Passion and a daughter called Grace. Passion is forged though intent and attention, while Grace seems to emerge from nowhere in particular, independent of individual effort.

Grace is typically less visible then Passion, but no less powerful. The two are inseparable. Passion is born when the will is purified of pretence and feelings are allowed to be as they are. When driving Passion is exhausted, Grace steps in to help her brother. She may or may not actually remove the obstacles, but, either way, she allows the drama to unfold more gracefully. Regardless of the situation, she magically appears when needed, often in unexpected ways. This is why Grace is, by her very nature, *amazing.*

Damning The Flow

Self-condemnation obstructs the flow of feelings. Total obstruction of feelings results in a loss of will, including the will to live. Partial obstruction of feelings causes the will to become obscured and shallow; which is to say, wishy-washy, wimpy, spineless, spaced out and apathetic. The individual has no clear boundaries – no clear sense of self. The mind is cluttered and bogged down with ideas, beliefs and disapproving voices accumulated over time. This is the making of the addict. Or, the individual might overcompensate for self-condemnation by erecting a wall of rigidified will, which relates to life with a dictatorial certainty.

Whether we have a poorly developed will (as in the addict), or a rigidified will (as in the dictator), the result is the same – feelings do not flow freely and life becomes meaningless.

Addiction

When an addiction is present, the individual finds pleasure in activities that harm the body, while avoiding activities that promote health and well-being. The same substance that brings short-term comfort also causes long-term damage. This is not surprising. When we conceal the truth, we harm the body. The addictive behavior is, among other things, a way of hiding truth.

Just as the will and feeling nature go together, so do addiction and harsh judgment. We might hide one and display the other, but both are always present within the same person. An individual who displays an obvious addiction is ruled by hidden judgment in the form of self-condemnation, self-hatred and unexpressed harsh judgment of others. Likewise, a person who is overtly "judgmental" (hypercritical, dictatorial, controlling) is probably ruled by multiple hidden addictions.

Harsh or dictatorial judgment may be looked upon as a twisted expression of the will, just as addiction may be looked upon as a twisted or conflicted expression of the feeling nature. If we wish to resolve that inner conflict, we must understand the nature of that twist. They are twisted because they are incomplete.

In outer relationships, when two parties are in conflict, each expresses knowledge that the other represses (previous chapter). The same may be said for the relationship between an addiction and the harsh judgment of the addiction.

One of the reasons we may have difficulty removing an addiction, even when it is clearly harmful to the body and mind, is that we don't recognize it as the incomplete awareness of a deep desire. The addict has partial awareness of the deep desire to feel alive, whereas the average person, with no obvious addictions, simply represses the desire and robotically plods along. The addict feels a deep emptiness and urgently tries to fill it. However, since the addict doesn't have the will to listen deeply and respectfully to the desire, there is no fulfillment, only a facsimile of fulfillment at a heavy price.

Likewise, one of the reasons we have difficulty in our earnest attempts to remove excessive or harsh judgment, is that we don't recognize that the judgment is simply incomplete knowledge. We do not remove incompleteness. We just complete it! The harsh judgment or condemnation of addictive behavior is the incomplete knowing that the "fix" isn't really what we want. The desire for the fix is a signal that says, "Pay attention to this desire, this is important!" At the core of the craving is the desire to simply feel fully alive.

Again, harsh judgment of the addiction is partial knowing. The rest of the knowing is contained in the addiction itself. When both are understood, they merge into wholeness.

Understanding the Inner Addict

In everyday life, we feel aliveness by eating, touching, laughing, crying, expressing ourselves creatively, telling the truth, emotional contact and giving of ourselves freely and sincerely. If we close the door on one form of aliveness, we tend to use the others more frequently. For example, if we suppress creative expression or deny the need for intimacy, we might compensate by overusing food or sex. The judgment we then place on the food or sex is the incomplete knowing that we are using them as replacements for what we really want. In the recognition of this, we can do one of two things: We can freely engage in the addictive behavior, or we can abstain from it. Either one can work. It depends on the individual and the circumstance. If it works, both the addiction and the harsh judgment diminish.

In one sense, they don't really "diminish", they merge. This might be the hidden wisdom within the (sometimes) controversial teaching of twelve step programs; they assert that you never really "get rid" of the addiction. This is taken to mean that you will always have the problem. What it really means is that the problem becomes a blessing; through the problem, you are given the greatest of gifts – yourself.

Whether or not the addict is aware of it, the process of undoing the addiction involves a gradual cultivation of will. The common practice (in twelve-step programs) of admitting one's powerlessness might seem contrary to that goal, but is, in fact, based on another bit of hidden wisdom. Admitting ones powerlessness is intended to remove pretence, denial, defensiveness and other patterns of a weakened or rigidified will. Such honesty allows feelings to flow more freely. Thus, the will is gradually purified, sharpened and deepened. When this is done consistently enough, passion emerges, followed by grace.

Passion sets us free from the addictive pattern – through focused intention and persistence. When passion reaches the end of endurance, grace appears serendipitously as an encouraging phone call, a letter from a friend, a spontaneous wave of inspiration, an insightful dream, a job opportunity, or money that appears just in time to pay the rent or repair the automobile.

Understanding the Inner Dictator

Just as the addict appears to have no will, the dictator appears to have no feelings. It is goal-oriented with little regard for the path. The will, cut off from the feeling nature, gets the work done, but has no regard for the workers. To the tyrant, the end justifies the means. It has no conscience, because conscience is born of the feeling nature. The tyrant only has a code of honor that may or may not include respect for truth and justice.

Whereas the addict is afraid of addressing inner conflict, the dictator is afraid of peace. In one sense, the dictator is addicted to conflict. He breeds conflict and uses it as a control tool or as a means of acquiring power. On the personal level, this "addiction" often shows up as the tendency to criticize and find fault in others.

For sure, there is value in expressing criticism toward others if we feel violated by them, or if we genuinely feel that their behavior is unethical or destructive. In fact, keeping silent in the presence of such behavior tends to increase our feelings of weakness and impotence. If, however, criticism and fault-finding become habitual, they act like a drug that produces a temporary high, but ultimately weakens us even more.

The Addictive Cycle

The addict is, by definition, out of control. The addict is depleted of energy because the will that is capable of gathering and focusing energy has been weakened. The addict responds to the lack of energy in such a way that depletes energy even more. This cyclic behavior tends to spin more and more out of control, eventually shattering any illusion of being in control. In other words, the individual "hits bottom" and can, therefore, start climbing up.

The Tyrannical Cycle

Whereas the addictive response is characterized by going deeper and deeper into chaos and loss of control, the tyrannical response is to go for even tighter control. Excessive control must breed rebellion – including inner rebellion. In the presence of this rebellion, the tyrant tightens the reins of control and declares martial law. The tyrant pulls tighter and tighter on the reins, which could culminate in a reign of terror, wherein the zeal to maintain order results in complete breakdown of the system. We see this pattern in society, in interpersonal relationships, and within the individual. In the case of the addict and dictator within, the pattern might look like alternating binging and purging.

Symbiosis of the Addict & Dictator

Just as pure will and fullness of feeling are a complementary pair, so are addiction and tyranny. Each maintains the other, whether it is within the context of society as a whole, interpersonal relationships or entirely within oneself.

Within the individual, the dictatorial will exploits the addicted feeling nature, but has no respect for it. Likewise, the addicted feeling nature depends on the will but is secretly afraid of it. We see this mirrored in the outer relationship between the pusher and the drug addict. On a larger scale, the real life dictator draws power from the frenzied and fearful mob. The dictator feeds on the fears, cravings and addictions of the masses, while holding them in contempt.

In other words, rigidified will, having no life of its own, seeks out the addict. The ruling will of one individual harnesses the chaotic feeling energy of another. The controller uses the fears and desires of the addict to control the addict, just like an unfeeling animal trainer might use food and a whip. Likewise, the addict seeks rigidified will for structure and containment; it is water seeking a channel.

The two parties form a relationship in which the controller has distain for the addict, while the addict is afraid of the controller. They tolerate each other because they feed off each other. Both are content, but neither is free. Freedom comes when each side goes within and discovers the element that is mirrored by the other.

Freedom From Addiction

Freedom from a potentially harmful desire occurs when we no longer judge it harshly. Not judging it harshly means that we can judge it correctly. The desire is seen for what it is. It is desire for aliveness. The absence of harshness allows us to experience and learn what we need to experience and learn from the addictive behavior, so that we can be complete with it.

Such completion may not be evident at first to the casual observer. Nonetheless, a deep invisible change occurs. It is the deeper union of the will and feeling nature. That union shows up as a greater capacity for calmness on the emotional level and stillness on the mental level. More tangibly, there is a reduced tendency to exhibit behavior that is harmful to the body and mind. The absence of such harmful behavior is an unmistakable sign that the will is strong and the feelings are free.

For Your Own Good

The will can develop only when feelings are free. There is no will without freedom, and no freedom without will. If we try to externally impose freedom, it is not freedom. If we try to force or con others into developing will, they will not be able to sustain it, for it is not theirs.

A strong and free will includes a boundary that does not violate the free will of others, even "for their own good". For sure, there is such a thing as respectful intervention, but that path must be walked with exceeding care and thoughtfulness, or our efforts backfire. Each of us carries a deep instinct that values free will as much as the survival of the body. An individual may destroy the body if that is the only remaining avenue for freedom.

In the colonial days of the United States, Patrick Henry issued a political decree: "Give me liberty or give me death." His statement had an emotional impact that reverberated throughout the world and is still ringing in our ears. It is a powerful political statement because it isn't just political. It emanates from the depths of our humanity and is therefore deeply meaningful for us.

Patrick Henry was giving voice to the soul's desire for freedom. That desire emanates from a place that does not distinguish liberty from life itself. Patrick Henry and the rest of the colonial rebels were challenging the commonly accepted belief that liberty is a license granted by government or any external authority. Patrick Henry recognized that freedom, though it is a laudable political goal, is not given to us by a political system; it is the product of a will that yields only to the truth emanating from within.

The Will of Iron

We cultivate a will of iron through keen awareness and respect for the truth carried by the feeling nature. This is the will doing what it does best – listening. Such a will cannot be broken by fear or discomfort. It cannot be distracted, deceived, sidetracked or seduced by promises of riches, power, special privileges, creature comforts or sensual pleasures. In the presence of truth, however, it yields completely. The will that recognizes the source of its strength is a will that has cultivated wisdom.

Three Wise Men

The inner truth that melts and reworks the will of iron is recognized in many cultures and has been depicted in a number of ways. In the Christian world, that truth has been depicted as a newborn infant resting in a stable. Purified will has been depicted as three wise and wealthy men, accomplished and successful in worldly endeavors, and adept in mystical and esoteric knowledge. These three men enter the stable and stand among the farm animals and peasants, bringing to the infant the fruits of their worldly endeavors. In essence, they say, "All that we have accomplished and all that we have built is for you. We stand before you, knowing that, in your eyes, we are not greater than these shepherds. We bow before this truth that you carry." These three wise men personify the will elevated to nobility by bowing down and respectfully listening to the truth carried by the feeling nature.

CHAPTER 21

Thoughts & Emotions

One of the major functions of the will is to think. One of the major functions of the feeling nature is to generate our everyday emotions.

Emotions are those feelings we can identify as fear, anger, sadness and happiness. There are, of course, many variations or tones of these four basic emotions, but their basic identity is clearly evident and is usually experienced tangibly in the body.

We are also capable of experiencing feelings that we would not call emotions. Instinct, intuition, empathy and inspiration are more ethereal and difficult to define than emotions. These other feelings typically blend with our emotions. For example, the feeling of empathy may be associated with the emotions of fear, sadness, anger or happiness, depending on the situation.

Furthermore, suppression of one feeling results in suppression of all feelings. Therefore, if we wish to sharpen our intuition, receive more inspiration and deepen our capacity to empathize with others, we must cultivate the ability to honestly address our everyday emotions.

IQ and EQ

Though we can argue about the best way to measure intelligence, it is, none-the-less, measurable. Therefore, we can speak of a person's *intelligence quotient* or IQ. However, to apply a similar measurement to emotions is ridiculous. In "testing" our emotions, we are attempting to judge things that function best when they are not judged.

If we try to test our emotions, they will "fail" the test. If we try to beautify them, they become ugly. If we try to make them more functional, they become more dysfunctional. If we push them away, they come back with a vengeance.

A person who seems to "pass" an emotional test has simply suc-
ceeded in censoring emotions. In that regard, we are not really testing
the emotions, we are testing the will's capacity to control emotions.

We may ask many questions and devise many tests to evaluate the
thinking capacity and the will in general. The will is tempered and
strengthened when it is tested and challenged. With regard to our
emotions, however, there is just one fundamental question – perhaps
the only one worth asking: *Are the emotions genuine?*

In the Beginning

The story of the Garden of Eden, like many myths and legends,
may be viewed as an outer dramatization of an internal or psychological event. In one interpretation, the relationship between Adam and
Eve represents the relationship between our thoughts and emotions.

The order of creation of Adam and Eve might represent the order
of creation of our thoughts and emotions. God created Adam and then
created Eve out of Adam. This can be taken to mean that our spirit or
essence gives rise to thoughts, and then our thoughts (our perceptions
and beliefs) give rise to our emotions.

The idea that emotions spring from our thoughts is not new. Emotions do seem to flow in accordance to our perceptions and beliefs.
This is why it is extremely difficult to try to change emotions directly.
However, if we change the associated perceptions and beliefs, the
emotions tend to change spontaneously.

It is also true that a particular emotional pattern, once established,
exerts a powerful effect on our every day thoughts. If we look deeper,
however, we see these established emotional patterns are maintained
by perceptions and beliefs that have become so deeply entrenched over
the years that we might not even know we have them.

The Relationship of Thoughts & Emotions

We can get a deeper understanding of the relationship of thoughts
and emotions by, once again, examining the story of Adam and Eve.
As the story goes, God created Eve out of Adam so that Adam
wouldn't be lonely. We might ask, why would Adam be lonely with

all the animals and God to keep him company? We might say that Adam needed someone more like himself. Well then, why didn't God create another man? Besides the fact that two men cannot make a baby, there are emotional reasons. If there was another man, the most that they could do is work together, share their loneliness or go to war (unless they happened to be gay). Thoughts are, by their very nature, analytical; they tend to break things apart into ever smaller pieces, losing sight of the big picture. It is the feeling nature that maintains contact with the wordless essence that unites all of life. It is with our emotions that we reach out and create relationship. Without such contact, thoughts become reclusive, alienated and self-destructive.

Emotions & Spirit

The importance of emotions in contacting our spiritual nature or essence is indicated by the attention that many religions place on emotions. The drawing power of most religions is not intellect or the power of reason. The typical religion is a set of rituals and techniques designed to access the emotions and cause them to flow in a particular direction. If the religion is ethical, the techniques are used in conjunction with reason to guide the practitioner toward the creation of a harmonious relation with God and the rest of life. This occurs through the natural evolution of emotional energy into spiritual awareness.

If the religion is not ethical, the same principles and techniques are used to emotionally imprint the followers to the religion, keeping them in a state of dependency. The same techniques that can facilitate the evolution of emotional energy into spiritual awareness can also be used to exploit emotional energy and arrest its evolution. Just as an unethical health care provider might not want the patients to get healthy too fast, short-sighted religious leaders may not want their followers to achieve spiritual freedom.

In other words, the followers might be maneuvered in such a way as to maintain emotional dependency on the religion. This is relatively easy if the individual becomes a member of a religion at a very early age. Adults too can be imprinted through a slight-of-hand magic trick in which the followers are given an emotionally impactful experience, a sense of wholeness, or a taste of freedom. Since the freedom was apparently provided by the religion, it really doesn't belong to the seeker, it belongs to the religion and its leaders. To the seeker, the experience of freedom and wholeness is emotionally tied to the religion in question. The experience can only exist within the context of the religious belief that housed the experience. This is one source of the common belief or attitude that says, "My religion is the one true religion."

The above paragraph is not an indictment of any religion, or of religion in general. A given religion and its doctrines may be benign and ethical. The religion might be an effective system of techniques and principles for facilitating the natural evolution of emotional energy into spiritual awareness. How those techniques and principles are used is entirely up to the members.

For sure, there is wisdom in being entirely focused on one's own religion as if it were the only one. Yes, it is the only one. It's the only one for *me*. This makes it easier for the individual to master the principles and techniques of that religion. This is true for any teaching, religious or otherwise. The more devoted we are to a given system, the more it will reveal its secret to us. Not only does it sharpen our thinking, but it also opens the door to intuition and inspiration.

Deep devotion to a given religion, practiced intelligently and ethically, results in the cultivation of emotional serenity and spiritual awareness. Therefore, even though the individual is not tempted to "stray," there is a tendency to quietly respect the religions of others. On the other hand, when the methodologies of the religion are used to instill emotional dependency, the individual is likely to adopt the attitude that "my religion is the only true religion".

Resolving Paradoxes

The relationship of emotions to spiritual awareness makes our emotions indispensable for resolving paradoxes. When we attempt to *think* our way beyond duality (beyond the play of opposites), we frequently encounter paradoxes and unsolvable riddles.

Most paradoxes are really not that mysterious; they are the result of thoughts dissociated from emotions. Paradoxes are the result of the cognitive nature trying to find meaning and understanding separate from the feeling nature. The more we allow our emotions to dance freely about our well-disciplined thoughts, the fewer paradoxes we encounter.

We can bring thoughts and emotions into the deep synergy by methodically applying a simple formula: *Question your thoughts and accept your emotions.*

Question Thoughts and Accept Emotions

The ability to question thoughts and accept emotions is the key for maintaining sanity in daily living. A perception or belief can be either true or false and must, therefore, be questioned for validity. An emotion is neither true or false; it simply is. When we allow our thoughts and emotions to co-exist in this manner, they tend to complement one another. The willingness to question thoughts allows emotions to flow more freely and genuinely. Likewise, acceptance of emotions gives us the serenity to question our perceptions and beliefs.

When we are at peace with ourselves, we generally do not have to make a conscious effort to question our thoughts and accept our emotions. Both happen spontaneously. When there is inner conflict or confusion, we can help ourselves by intentionally questioning our thoughts or accepting our emotions. It is not necessary to try to do both at the same time. In fact, that would probably be awkward. We need only tend to the one that seems to be calling for attention. The other follows naturally.

There are a number of specific ways of putting this principle into application. For example, if we get upset because the car won't start and we might be late for work, we can repeat over and over again, "The car won't start and I might be late for work." By focusing on the fact or physical event, our perception of it is likely to undergo a subtle change – it doesn't seem so terrible any more. As our perception changes, the associated emotions are also likely to change.

The resolution of cosmic paradoxes is one result (and, really, a minor one) of integrating thoughts and emotions. The more tangible results are mental clarity and emotional serenity. Life becomes simple, relationships become simple, spiritual and religious practices become simple.

Simplicity is not well tolerated when thoughts and emotions are disconnected. Simplicity is the natural result of thoughts and emotions in a state of balance and integration.

Such simplicity does not preclude intellectual pursuits and the evolution of intricate ideas. In fact, when such learning occurs in the presence of emotional connectedness, the intellect evolves more readily and more humanely. This is possible because intellectual activity is not used as a replacement for emotional connectedness. It is an *expression* of emotional connectedness.

How do we know we have attained such connectedness? Must we be overtly passionate about everything we do? Not necessarily. One common way to know that we have such connectedness is that, regardless of how complex our thoughts become, we still have the capacity to delight in simple things.

Thoughts and Emotions at War

When we reject our emotions, the result is a gradual erosion of self-esteem. We then try to compensate by rigidly holding on to our perceptions and beliefs. We see this most frequently and dramatically in religion, but it can also occur in other areas, such as politics, health care, and even in the domain that is supposed to be the bastion of objectivity – science. We also do this in our every day existence. Just as we put on clothes to hide and protect the body, we put on perceptions and beliefs to protect our sense of identity and cover up our insecurity.

If personal identity and self-esteem have become deeply invested in a particular belief system, we will not stand by quietly while it is criticized or questioned. We will defend our beliefs like we would defend our mother, even if the criticism has an element of truth (*especially* if the criticism has an element of truth). We become fiercely protective of our beliefs because they have replaced emotional truthfulness as a source of inner stability. The beliefs have also replaced emotional contact with others as the source of nurturing.

Mental Laziness and Emotional Numbness

The unwillingness to question thoughts and accept emotions often shows up as mental laziness and emotional numbness. These two responses are closely related. What appears as mental laziness (the unwillingness to think for oneself) might be a defense against feeling hidden emotions. The presence of these suppressed emotions disrupts clear thinking. We reflexively close our eyes to anything that might evoke feelings that we don't want to feel. We do not allow our thinking to stray into areas that would trigger the unacceptable emotions.

Mental laziness and emotional numbness, once established, tend to be self-perpetuating, and can reduce the individual to a robotic state. On the larger social level, this invites dictatorship. A population of individuals who are mentally lazy and emotionally numb call forth social and political structures that can spare them from the toil of thinking their own thoughts, and save them from the anxiety of feeling their own feelings. As long as everyone thinks and feels the same way, we have a sense of safety. This, however, becomes increasingly difficult as communication and travel encourage the mingling of different cultures and beliefs. As the world contracts, the mind must expand.

If we want to develop the ability to think for ourselves and enhance our emotional aliveness, we need only bear in mind that the two are complementary. Clear thinking supports and enhances emotional freedom. Emotional freedom supports clear thinking.

Worship of Emotions

Acceptance of emotions does not mean worshipping them. Worshipping emotions is the same as being addicted to emotions. When we truly accept our emotions, they gradually evolve into spiritual awareness – which is what they want to do. If this evolution is not allowed to occur, we are likely to become addicted to our emotions.

We can become addicted to anything that gives us a facsimile of serenity or a sense of aliveness. We can become addicted to chemicals, relationships, work and our own emotions. Addiction to emotions simply means they are not felt in fullness. The void that is created from not fully feeling our emotions causes us to silently crave them – we worship them. As with other addictions, the addiction to emotions causes us to become seductive and vulnerable to seduction.

Factoring Out Emotional Bias

When there is a need to interpret data, as in science or legal matters, the ability to question perceptions and objectively examine evidence requires that we factor out our own emotional bias. The way to factor out emotional bias is simply to be aware of it. The more we are in touch with our own emotions, the more capable we are of being objective. A conscientious scientist, who recognizes his own emotional bias or private agenda, is able to be reasonably neutral and objective, or, at least, recognizes that he is incapable of being neutral and objective.

The history of science and politics reveals that such objectivity has frequently been lacking. This is understandable. In the last several hundred years, civilization has placed little or no emphasis on the value of emotional connectedness. As a result, emotionally biased reporting has been more the rule than the exception.

Emotions: Hedonistic and Expansive

When we take the time to understand our own emotional nature, we discover that it is hedonistic and expansive. The emotional nature is driven by the desire to satisfy personal urges. When this hedonistic tendency is allowed its natural modes of expression, the emotional nature can then express its other tendency, expansiveness. The expansiveness of emotions is what drives us to reach out and create relationships, family, communities and social order based on fairness and justice.

In contrast to the emotional nature, the cognitive nature, or intellect, tends to focus in and break things down. The intellect focuses in to find out how things work. The intellect's ability to separate things allows it to dissect and analyze things down to minute details. Consequently, it can easily lose sight of the big picture – the simplicity of the whole. Then, the intellect tries to reconstruct the whole through elaborate philosophies and theologies, only to repeatedly encounter the familiar wall – loops in logic and paradoxes – until it rediscovers its beloved mate, the emotional nature.

Who's In Charge?

We are powerfully driven by our emotions, even if we think we aren't (*especially* if we think we aren't). The destructive behavior of the intellect in the realm of politics and technology is simply the result of repressed but still powerful emotions, secretly controlling the overtly dominant intellect. The repressed hedonistic nature of the emotions manifests as intellect striving to achieve self-centered political and economic goals at the expense of others. The expansiveness of the emotional nature, when repressed, manifests as intellect on an explosive path of imperialism and megalomania.

In summary, we often try to purge ourselves of our emotions, casting them out because we see them as dysfunctional, treacherous, hysterical and unpredictable. Yet, when we look deeply enough, we see that emotions get that way precisely because they *have* been cast out. The same emotional nature, when integrated with a strong and dependable cognitive nature, becomes quite predictable – it wants to create family.

CHAPTER 22

Intellect & Intuition

(Two Sources of Information)

Intellect and intuition are two ways of understanding things. Intellect is a function of the will. Intellect is our capacity to understand things through logical thinking. Intuition is an expression of the feeling nature. Its understanding of the world is visceral and silent.

The intellect asks questions and then formulates answers that fit into the framework of three-dimensional space, linear time, cause and effect. It can discern how past events influence future events. Intuition does not ask questions. It is non-linear. Its comprehension is not limited by words, time or space.

Integration

One of the important functions of the will is to listen and provide safe boundaries for the expression of feelings – all feelings. In so doing, the rational mind receives the intuition included within those feelings.

We might get a gut feeling to take a different route to work on a particular day and, later, discover that the usual route is blocked by a fallen tree. We cannot explain the gut feeling in terms of observable events; there is no tangible evidence to explain how and why we know what we know. We just know; the same way we know when it's time to empty the bladder; the same way we know we are happy or sad. Furthermore, this feeling might be so elusive that it cannot be traced to any specific emotion or body sensation.

Intuition rises from the primordial knowing that life is singular. This same knowing also manifests as curiosity, which drives the intellect to gather information. Little children, endowed with keen intuition, also demonstrate curiosity. They ask questions. The baby is intensely fascinated by mother's eyes because of a wordless feeling that seems to say, "I am looking at myself from the outside in. This huge mysterious beast is myself, and it is different from myself." The baby's intuitive knowing and intellect are merged as curiosity. This curiosity diminishes with age, but persists throughout life; it is what drives the pure scientist.

In other words, pure intellect, the capacity to question and to gather and organize data, is not far removed from intuition. Our drive to understand the world by questioning and looking for proof, emanates from the place within us that already feels its relationship to the rest of the universe, and wants to give birth to that knowing as a body of tangible, provable, recordable data.

When we take the time to understand the relationship between intellect and intuition within us, the two can complement each other. It is not uncommon for scientists to admit that their methodical searching and eventual breakthrough began as an intuitive hunch. Dr. Einstein reported that he *felt* relativity long before he hashed out the mathematical proof.

Likewise, by using the intellect to question our own perceptions, we cultivate objectivity. Such intellectual honesty feeds back to the intuitive process. Thus, we can distinguish between genuine intuitive insight from the many forms of fake or fuzzy intuition, such as:

- *Wishful thinking*: "My intuition tells me that she really likes me," which really means, "God, she's pretty, I hope she likes me." In other words, excessive or unrecognized desires frequently obscure intuition.
- *Self-fulfilling prophecy*: "I just knew the bank wouldn't give me the loan."
- *Justifying laziness*: "I don't have to study; all knowledge is within me."
- *Relinquishing responsibility for one's choices*: "I feel we should spend some time together because we have a deep soul connection," as a cover for, "You have nice legs."

Typically, intuition is influenced by excessive or unrecognized fears and desires. This is not surprising. Since intuition rises out of the feeling nature, any sort of emotional bias or unresolved emotional issues can obscure intuition.

Emotions interfere with intuition when they are censored, denied, exploited, or justified. We might censor or deny emotions because they are regarded as threatening. We might exploit them by using them to manipulate or overpower others. We might try to justify them by saying, "I don't trust you because you stole my horse in a past life." For sure, such an extraordinary accusation could very well have a basis in reality, however, the instant that we use it to justify our emotions, the emotions become twisted, and, therefore, intuition is obscured. Intuition is strong and accurate when emotions are reported simply and honestly without condemning or justifying them.

Ethics and Empathy

The complementary relationship between intellect and intuition is based on the fact that they are expressions of the will and feeling nature, respectively. The same applies for ethics and empathy. Ethical behavior is a choice; an act of will. Empathy is a feeling that emerges spontaneously from within.

Every mental function is inseparable from its emotional counterpart. Clarity on the mental level translates into serenity on the emotional level. Confusion on the mental level translates into anxiety on the emotional level. Clear thinking on the mental level translates into peace on the emotional level. Likewise, ethical behavior is the mental equivalent of empathy.

The overt expression of ethics is rooted in the unspoken feeling of empathy. Likewise, the intentional adherence to ethics and principles can trigger our genuine feelings of caring and empathy. Each side can provide the foundation for the emergence of the other.

Knowledge and Wisdom

As mentioned earlier, both our intellect and intuition give us understandings. The knowledge conferred by our intellect is learned through time and organized in a linear fashion. The knowledge conferred by our intuition is instinctual; it is inborn and not limited to linear time. The intellect stores and organizes knowledge that begins at birth and ends at death, while intuition allows us to gaze beyond the boundaries of birth and death. The knowledge gathered by the intellect is rational and tangible and can easily be communicated in words, while the knowledge emerging form the feeling nature may be so mysterious as to defy verbal description.

When the bits of knowledge conferred by the intellect and intuition are deeply blended, the result is wisdom. Wisdom is more subtle than knowledge. Knowledge is simply information – we can gather it fairly quickly. Wisdom tends to evolve gradually. We tend to cultivate wisdom over time, through the harmonious relationship of our intellect and intuition.

CHAPTER 23

Love

(A Feeling and Beyond)

If something has no opposite, it is virtually impossible to define. The only way we can even discuss it is to mentally create (or imply the existence of) an opposite. Even so, any definition of love is likely to be extremely fragile and crumbles in our hands if we hold it too tightly or stare at it too hard. In fact, in the very act of naming it, our knowledge of love becomes incomplete. Nonetheless, as long as we recognize the limits of our definition, it has value.

Conditional & Unconditional

In everyday life, one of the ways that we understand love is by separating it into two forms that are diametrically opposed. Thus, we can understand each side by comparing it to the other. The two basic expressions of love are called conditional and unconditional. As long as we do not try to make one superior to the other, both are easy to understand, and both find their rightful place in our lives.

Under the light of mutual illumination, we understand that unconditional love is infinitely inclusive, while conditional love has boundaries. Both have to do with recognition. There is recognition of kinship or connectedness that shows up as respect and caring.

Conditional love is a form of partial recognition or partial knowing and, therefore, carries some judgment or potential for separation. There are conditions under which the bond can be broken. To love unconditionally is synonymous with complete recognition or fullness of knowing. When we are moved by unconditional love, we are moved by a sense of knowing so deep and vast that it can encompass any possible situation that might threaten the bond.

Loving Oneself

Love of oneself has been called the greatest love and the greatest folly. It is a folly if we attempt to love ourselves without knowing ourselves. In this case, self-love translates into self-deception, self-indulgence, avoidance of responsibilities and disregard for others. On the other hand, if self-love is understood to be inseparable from self-knowledge, self-love eventually translates into an easy and respectful relationship with others. We know what we are responsible for, and what we are not responsible for. Commitments toward others are made naturally and fulfilled graciously.

If loving ourselves seems difficult, perhaps we simply do not see the connection between self-love and self-knowledge. Perhaps we do not love ourselves because we have a false image of ourselves. Likewise, if we seem to be having a hard time seeing ourselves clearly, perhaps we are blocking knowledge because we do not love ourselves sufficiently to see the various hidden facets of ourselves without freaking out. Either way, there is a need to see the unity of self-love and self-knowledge.

Echoes of Singularity

When we feel deep affection for each other, we do not merely feel "close". There is a silent feeling of being part of each other. In everyday life, compassion, thankfulness and kindness represent the emotional echoes of unity or singularity reverberating in the world of separateness. These feelings are typically forms of conditional love, in the sense that they are defined by the boundaries of our individuality.

Most of our expressions of love have some conditions. For example, if our love is not gracefully accepted, we might feel hurt or angry. Conditional love also implies *preference, boundaries* and *discernment*. Most of us would agree that it is healthy to respect one's preferences, but if we have a hidden belief that conditional love is somehow inferior to unconditional love, we will deny that having preferences is synonymous with conditional love. Most of us would also agree that it is healthy to have boundaries and show discernment in giving affection in our relationships, but we might deny that our discernment is an expression of conditional love.

In other words, although we do the healthy thing of respecting our own preferences, we conceal from ourselves the simple fact that we are practicing conditional love. By not recognizing that our personal boundaries and preference are the same as "conditions," those conditions remain and may become covert power tools. For example:

- We might justify our behavior by calling it *preference,* while condemning the same basic behavior in others, by calling it *conditional love.*
- We might think that we are being kind to someone out of unconditional love, while we are unconsciously trying to maneuver them into doing what we want them to do.
- Our show of affection toward one person might be a way of buffeting ourselves against another. For example, two or more people may unknowingly bond to one another as a way of forming an alliance against a common enemy, and call it love.

Having thus used love as a power tool, we add to our secret guilt, and therefore have additional motivation to keep hidden the conditional quality of our love. Consequently, we look into each others' eyes and say, "I love you just the way you are," even as the chest and tummy get tight, breathing gets shallow, the bowels slow down, blood vessels constrict, tissues are deprived of oxygen and become cluttered with waste products, and the body dies a little.

On the other hand, we might say, "Yes, my love is conditional, and these are my conditions..." This is when breathing becomes deep and even, the tummy and chest relax, blood vessels dilate, tissue oxygenation improves, and the body can regenerate.

In summary, when conditional love is regarded as inferior, we are, in effect, judging our own judgment, and thus drive it underground. Once it becomes unconscious, it will probably be used as a covert power tool. When the conditions of our love are recognized and allowed to be, the conditions tend to gradually widen. The *conditional love* becomes more inclusive and eventually returns to its primordial form, which is *unconditional love.*

CHAPTER 24

Truth

(Small t and capital T)

When our focus is on truth, we are not concerned about whether our love is conditional or unconditional; we simply want to express love honestly. When we are fully genuine, we need not be concerned about having love, for we are *being* love.

When truth is denied, simple acts of love are somehow overlooked and neglected, even as we verbally exalt love. The home is neglected, the body is neglected and work is neglected. The father who denies his truth neglects his family. The mother who denies her truth neglects her children. When we are truthful, we tend to give loving care and attention to the body, the home, and our loved ones.

The Carrier of Truth

Love rides in on the wings of truth. Truth rides in on the wings of feelings honestly expressed. The truth that sets us free is revealed to us when we stop trying to find it as a rational thought separate from the feelings. Self-doubt vanishes when the rational mind accepts the simple task of putting words to the feelings rising from within.

Our feelings can change from moment to moment. Therefore, our personal truth can also change from moment to moment. Our truth is not something that we hold on to. It evolves. We give voice to truth as it unfolds before the witness of the rational mind. In fact, it is the ability of the rational mind to report the gut-level truth that allows truth to change, unfold and evolve.

The expression of personal truth has a simplifying and unifying effect on life. The expression of personal truth dissolves self-condemnation and its byproducts – denial, excuses and defensiveness.

When we are free enough from self-condemnation, our personal experience of truth evolves into truth with a capital "T".

Truth With a Capital "T"

Like the God of the ancient Hebrews, Truth with a capital "T" is nameless and faceless. It has no opposite, for it is all encompassing. There is no bottle that can contain it. There is no single book that can describe it. There is no static picture that can fully reveal its beauty, nor any prayer or invocation that can capture it in fullness. The vessel in which we try to trap Truth eventually shatters. The string of words we use to describe Truth becomes contradictory. The only way we can even speak of it is to compare it to our own time-bound personal truths.

Infinite Truth becomes finite truth when it is spoken as *the word*. The formless takes on form by curling in upon itself. This is how boundless Truth has the experience of boundaries. This is how immortality has the experience of death and birth. This is how limitless Truth has the experience of limitations.

Human Limitations

Conscious awareness of our limitations in the absence of humility can be very disturbing. This is the experience of "impotence". The associated feeling is shame. Shame about our perceived impotence is then covered with the facade of omnipotence, inflated self-importance or arrogance.

Arrogance, born of impotence, looks upon itself and says, "My form is the best of all possible forms. I'm better than others." This assertion sees other truths as lesser truths. It seeks to conquer and establish its dominance over other truths. The archetypal creator of this experience is often called "Satan". The name, however, is inconsequential, for it is not limited to one form or one name. Its potential exists in any corner of creation where individuality or separateness has forgotten its origin, thus setting the stage for the experience of impotence and the arrogance that follows.

Likewise, any person using any method can, at anytime, wake up to his or her wordless, formless, timeless identity, at which point the awakened one looks at the rest of creation and perceives oneself. This can be a life-changing vision. More likely, it shows up as our own personal sense of morality, ethics and conscience.

The Boundaries of Truth

Absolute Truth (Truth with a capital "T") has no boundaries and, therefore, has no opposite. In the world of duality, truth does have boundaries. Every truth has boundaries beyond which it becomes a lie. Likewise, a lie is typically a truth that has violated its boundaries. We can exceed the boundaries of truth by blatantly falsifying information, or by telling a little white lie – exaggerating just a bit in order to make a point.

Warring Truths

To stretch the truth beyond its boundaries is to take things out of context or blow things out of proportion. When a truth violates its own boundaries, it must, of necessity, encroach upon a neighboring truth. When one truth tries to displace another truth, the invading truth becomes a lie. On the other hand, a truth that respects the integrity of a neighboring truth has reached wholeness. Neighboring truths can only be reflections of each other, each bringing to the surface what the other holds in secret. To be at war with a neighboring truth is to be at war with a hidden part of oneself.

The concept of "racial purity" (chapter eighteen) is one example of a truth that has violated its boundaries. Another is the concept of the "final battle", the hypothetical event that will eliminate the enemy and bring lasting peace. "The War to End All Wars" (World War I) and "The Final Solution" (World War II) are two recent historical examples of final battles.

The reason we keep falling for the lie of the final battle is that we do not recognize its core of truth. The lie is that we will have lasting peace when we finally defeat our enemy. The truth within the lie is that we will have peace when we no longer *require* an enemy.

We may be tempted to point an accusing finger at the fanatical groups that push the idea of the final battle, but they are simply acting out a caricature of a basic truth the rest of us have denied. There is, indeed, a "final solution". It is the calm recognition of our mutual need to have an enemy; a need that is so deeply engrained and so pervasive that it influences us in every area of our lives. It is not to be condemned or justified. It is to be recognized for what it is — the secret belief that if we don't have an enemy to push against, we have no basis for living.

In thus recognizing this belief, it eventually transmutes into the desire to simply know that *I am alive.* When we experience our primordial aliveness, we do not require an enemy to validate our existence.

Another example of a truth that has violated its boundaries is the belief that says, "I am special in the eyes of God." Many religions and mystical teachings use this belief or some variation of it. Such beliefs are not to be laughed at or scorned, for they do emanate from truth. Every individual who is touched by it has tapped into the deep memory of our true relationship with our source. We remember ourselves as a special spark of life that emanates from God. The eye of God is singular and can therefore do nothing else but look upon every spark of creation and declare, "You are my one and only, for you are all that I am." The fullness of this memory can be overpowering and disorienting if we experience it too quickly. It can also be gradually awakened through ethical living.

Why Do Criminals Leave Clues?

To the habitual liar, the thing that is feared the most is the same thing that is deeply desired – recognition. Those who engage in deception, often leave subtle but enticing clues. This may be done as an oversight or intentionally as a way of being cute or clever.

When we hide, we must suppress the need to be recognized. If we remain hidden long enough, the suppressed need for recognition becomes the silent ruler, manifesting itself in covert ways. The very thing we try to suppress seduces us. When we chronically deceive others, we gradually start doing little things to expose ourselves. The longer we remain hidden, the more obvious the clues become. The need to be recognized *as I am* cannot be denied indefinitely. The liar/criminal who absentmindedly or mischievously leaves clues, is acting out the baby's need to be recognized and appreciated by mother (Life).

Lying

Truth withheld is likely to explode into violence. If it doesn't explode into overt violence, it lingers as covert hostility, often taking the form of resentment, gossip or neglect.

We cannot lie in one aspect of ourselves and be totally truthful in other aspects. The total self may be likened to a hologram in which every "part" contains every other part. If we lie in one part, the entire hologram is affected. When we lie in a seemingly insignificant activity, we are affected in our most exalted activity. When we lie at work, it affects our home life.

Most individuals do not enjoy lying. It produces tension and eventually leads to fatigue, depression and self-hatred. If we are attentive enough, we may notice a feeling of deprivation. Truthfulness is one of the ways we emotionally nourish ourselves. We then devise methods of alleviating the pain and filling the void, such as loud music, drugs, excessive work, excessive play, etc.

To be a self-aware human is to have an instinct for truth-telling. Truth creates a sense of ease and a steadiness of the mind. Habitual lying is usually done without conscious awareness, or at least without conscious awareness of the effects of lying.

Why We Lie

There are two basic reasons for lying. First, we lie because we are afraid of the truth. Truth is withheld because we believe that our expression of truth will be rejected, attacked, or misunderstood.

The second reason for lying is typically unconscious and has to do with energy. A child dams up the flow of water in a gutter or a creek and lets it accumulate so as to experience the fun of breaking the dam and watching the water rush through with greater force. Lying (active lying or withholding truth) results in the accumulation of pent-up energy in the body and mind. The release of that energy feels good.

I have childhood memories of myself as a busy little beaver, joyfully placing rocks, mud and other debris in the path of the stream, letting the water accumulate into a good-sized pool, and then breaking the dam with one swipe of the hand or foot and watching the water flow furiously out, washing away other debris further downstream. If an adult had walked by and asked me why I was doing that, I would have shrugged my little shoulders. It was just a neat thing to do!

In a similar manner, as adults, we might unconsciously hold back the emotional waters (by actively lying or passively withholding truth) to let the energy build up so that we can have the thrill of watching them burst forth. This can be very therapeutic (chapter fourteen). If we do this repeatedly, however, it can become a subtle, but powerful addiction to drama and conflict.

Addiction and Lying

Habitual lying *is* an addiction. If the nervous system is allowed to develop naturally, the individual finds pleasure in telling the truth. On the other hand, if the individual has learned to equate truth with punishment, the only way of experiencing safety and normalcy is through deception. The approach of truth produces panic and disorientation not unlike an addict withdrawing from drugs.

As mentioned earlier, when a drug is taken as an escape from a painful situation, the experience of euphoria (the "rush") is partially due to the experience of *no pain*. If a person is in a constant state of physical and emotional pain, the deadening of that pain (by any means) is experienced as "pleasure". Deception creates the same rush of "pleasure". It is simply a momentary relief, a sense of safety produced by the absence of threatening exposure to truth. This is why addiction of any kind must be accompanied by an addiction to deception – especially self-deception.

Lying Consciously

Lying consciously is one way of undoing unconscious lying. In a situation where we are unwilling or unable to be truthful, we simply play it out without condemning it, justifying it, or denying it. In essence, we say, "Right now, I'm lying; I'm withholding my true thoughts and emotions." By lying consciously and without condemnation, we begin to resurrect the natural inclination to tell the truth.

Fake It 'Til You Make It

Fake it 'til you make it is a way of lying consciously. We know we are faking it; we know we are wearing a mask, and we give ourselves permission to do so.

Fake it 'til you make it means we are acting. When we act polite, we are acting out the form of love without necessarily feeling genuine love. However, if this is done with no condemnation or justification, we are performing a powerful shamanic practice; we soon begin to feel genuine love.

CHAPTER 25

Evil Spirits & Troubled Mind

Telling the truth in a threatening situation is a bit like taking a cold shower. We may dread the thing at first, but after we jump in, it is invigorating, exhilarating, energizing and seems to drive away many demons. If the latter is true, we might also say that the act of lying *attracts demons;* which brings us to the subject of the current chapter: the distinction between evil spirits and troubled mind.

Admittedly, evil spirits and troubled mind do not constitute a pair of true polar opposites. However, we often *do* place these two concepts at odds with each other, and that is why they are worth examining.

Are Demons Real?

Are we troubled by evil spirits and externally imposed dark clouds of "negative energy", or do our troubles come from our own troubled thoughts? If we attribute distress to negative energies or evil spirits, we might light a candle, burn some incense, offer a prayer, do a ritual, or invoke the presence of a master or saint to kick out the offending spirit or transmute the objectionable energies. And, by golly, we feel better! Or, we might examine our own mind. We tell the truth with regard to what we did to create the situation. And, by golly, we feel better!

In truth, we can come up with convincing arguments for both sides of this issue. If, however, we cling to one and reject the other, we are likely to face a situation that can't be adequately explained by the side that we favor. Either point of view can make us crazy if we adhere to it dogmatically. For example, if we try to explain troubling or bizarre experiences in terms of psychology, while rejecting astral influences, we will have to conjure up increasingly convoluted psychological mechanisms to explain the unexplainable. On the other hand, the tendency to blame evil spirits and externally imposed curses and bad vibes can result in a state of paranoia. The fear simply increases, because such eerie experiences tend to re-enforce the belief in astral influences. If we get too preoccupied with trying to keep astral nastiness at bay, we become increasingly entrenched in astral wars. The result of successfully fighting off demons, is that we get to fight off bigger demons next time.

The way out of this loop is to consider both sides of the coin – evil spirits and troubled mind. This is possible when the rational mind is in harmony with the feeling nature. We are then free to navigate from one polarity to the other without being inhibited by the fear of appearing inconsistent or fickle. We simply relax and embrace what feels true in the moment, unrestrained by what we think we *should* believe.

Haunted by Guilt

Those who claim to see or feel non-physical entities report that demons and unfriendly spirits seem to have easy access to a troubled mind. Our struggle with nasty spirits seems to reflect a deeper struggle with our own unresolved emotional issues, especially guilt. This is understandable because when guilt is severe enough, we are likely to obsess about anything – including evil spirits. Any sort of troublesome obsession suggests the presence of hidden guilt. The deeper the guilt, the deeper the obsession. When guilt is resolved, obsessions tend to dissolve.

Once the troubling spirits gain entry, however (which simply means that they become real to us), it is counterproductive to pretend they are not real to us. Such denial simply deepens the struggle. A more workable solution is to acknowledge they are real to us, and then address the psychological issue that allows them to enter.

The nature of haunting spirits is such that we can't seem to get away from them. This is understandable because guilt doesn't reside in any particular corner of the mind. Guilt isn't simply a space-occupying object that can be removed. Its influence is distributed throughout the mind, and it affects every aspect of life. We can't feel guilty in one area without having it affect other areas.

This situation might seem hopeless because, like a haunting spirit that has latched on to us, guilt seems to follow us around and we can't escape from it, no matter where we go. If we try to expel it, it seems to come back, perhaps stronger or more subtle than before. The deeper we bury it, the more we deepen its affect. The more we struggle against demons, the bigger the demons become. On the other hand, when we recognize our guilt without trying to make it go away, it's not so bad anymore.

As we learn to relate to our own troubling thoughts and emotions in a healthy manner, we become more effective at handling the nasty spirits and bad energy that seem to haunt us. We discover that the most potent way to free ourselves of evil spirits is to quietly acknowledge they are real to us, and then address the guilt or other emotional issues that seem to attract them.

Dreams and Nightmares

The most common time to be troubled by unsavory spirits is while we are asleep and dreaming. There are two ways of addressing our dreams: from a Western or psychological perspective, or from an Eastern or multi-dimensional perspective.

From the psychological perspective, dreaming occurs during a phase of sleep characterized by rapid eye movements and the production of certain brain waves, known as beta waves. Some schools of thought, such as Jungian psychology, regard dreams as an attempt to integrate the emotional issues of waking life. Not surprisingly, the more effectively we handle our emotional issues while we are awake, the less troubled our dreams become.

As our dreams settle down, we tend to spend more time in the deeper dreamless phase of sleep. This deeper phase is characterized by the production of brain waves known as delta waves. During delta sleep, we experience a deeper rest. It is during this phase of sleep that the body can more effectively regenerate itself. For most of us, healthy sleep includes a balance of delta sleep for physical regeneration and beta sleep for emotional integration.

If we consider the Eastern or multi-dimensional perspective, our existence can be roughly divided into three planes: physical, astral and causal. The physical plane corresponds to normal waking life. The astral plane corresponds to the beta or dream phase of sleep. The causal plane corresponds to the delta or dreamless phase of sleep. The causal plane may also be called the spiritual or transpersonal plane because we are not identified with physical form or the thoughts and emotions that define our personality.

Using the two models of sleep described above, here are two ways of addressing the spirits and entities that trouble our sleep:

- During the day, we tend to business. We take care of the body, conduct ourselves honestly in our relationships, and do our work ethically and effectively. If we do these three things during the day, we will be more likely to have pleasant dreams during the night.
- Before going to sleep at night, we can give ourselves the suggestion that our dream-time will be used for healing of unresolved emotional issues and healing of relationships. We can also give ourselves the suggestion to spend a goodly amount of time in the delta phase of sleep – the transpersonal realm – beyond the reach of the astral drama. This can be done through prayer, meditation, or by saying *deep delta sleep* over and over.

In other words, we can keep the real or imagined demons away by being very physical during the day and very spiritual at night. We let ourselves be very down to Earth during waking time, and soar to the restful and dreamless transpersonal realms during sleep time. The two are quite compatible and mutually supportive. The "higher" we go into the spiritual or causal plane, the more smoothly we flow through our physical existence. The more effectively we handle our waking life, the more easily we flow into the transpersonal realm of deep delta sleep. The more diligent we are about tending to the physical plane and spiritual plane, the more the astral plane tends to settle down.

CHAPTER 26

Sanity

One of my patients once gave me an interesting perspective on sanity. She said, "Sane people think they're crazy, and crazy people think they're sane."

Though she said it jokingly, the comical value of her statement is at least partially derived from its element of truth. To jokingly say that sane people think they're crazy, calls attention to the fact that a heightened awareness of oneself can be troublesome. It is troublesome if it is not accompanied by an equally heightened ability to sort things out.

Likewise, to jokingly say that crazy people think they're sane, calls attention to the fact that the inability to sort things out, can result in a generalized state of protective numbness and denial. We create a facade of sanity, to conceal the chaos within. We blind ourselves to our own inner inconsistencies that might be glaringly obvious to those around us.

Most of us have such inner inconsistencies. They become troublesome only when we habitually try to cover them up with a facade of normalcy, chronic defensiveness, and the illusion of certainty. The result of such denial is a gradual erosion of sanity.

Inner and Outer Sanity

Since the terms *sane* and *insane* carry so much emotional charge, we might, in the interest of open-mindedness and liberalism, be tempted to avoid this pair of opposites altogether. However, whether we like it or not, the duality of sane/insane exists in our collective consciousness.

We can get some perspective on the sensitive issue of sane/insane by remembering that it has both an inner and outer component. Inner sanity has to do with how we feel. Outer sanity has to do with how we behave.

Inner sanity is simply a state of mental clarity and emotional seren-ity. Outer sanity refers to behavior that allows the individual to be free and autonomous, while doing no harm to oneself or others.

The two are obviously related. Inner sanity translates into outer sanity. How we think and feel determines how we behave. When thoughts and emotions are sufficiently dissociated or conflicted, per-ceptions no longer reflect reality and emotions become proportionately unbalanced. This can eventually translate into the inability to function and, perhaps, the tendency to harm oneself and others.

In everyday life, we tend to equate sanity with outer behavior, while ignoring the inner condition. This is understandable, since outer behavior is more visible. However, in placing the emphasis entirely on outer behavior, our criteria for sanity usually drift away from autonomy and functionality to conformity. A person who controls their outer behavior sufficiently enough to fit into society is regarded as sane.

The Key to Inner and Outer Sanity

The key to sanity is our willingness to question our perceptions and accept our emotions (chapter 21). These two complementary ac-tivities help us to maintain conscious contact with a certain indefinable feeling. It is the feeling embodied by the laughter of a child, the touch of a loved one, a home filled with laughter and trust, and acts of kind-ness with no ulterior motives. This wordless feeling is the keeper of inner sanity.

The feeling is kept alive through the cultivation of honesty. Most of the stressors that challenge our sanity are effectively handled by just practicing truthfulness. When we are honest, we tend to question our thoughts and accept our emotions, resulting in mental clarity and emo-tional serenity.

The Causes of Insanity

As long as we are inwardly sane, we do not have to give much attention to outer sanity. However, as we neglect to question our perceptions and accept our emotions, inner sanity erodes – we lose touch with that indefinable feeling of serenity. Our perception of the world around us becomes increasingly warped – reflecting our own inner chaos. We then have to consciously control our outer behavior to keep it in the realm of what is considered sane by the rest of society.

Paradoxically, if we try too hard to appear sane, it can make us insane. As we try harder and harder to maintain the outer appearance of sanity and normalcy, our inner sanity erodes faster and faster. This is likely to happen as long as we give greater importance to the outer appearance of sanity, while neglecting how we feel.

In other words, we give up our inner sanity because we value something else more. As one insightful songwriter once pointed out, "…You're giving up your sanity for your pride and your vanity…"

To indulge in excessive pride and vanity, we must conceal or contort our truth, and live in a perpetual state of pretense. This is inherently stressful, contributing to emotional unrest and mental fogginess.

And, yet, excessive pride and vanity are not to be cast out, for they are simply frozen self-respect waiting to be set free by truth.

Harsh judgment of insanity is probably the single greatest obstacle to sanity. What we do not realize is that our seemingly irrational perceptions and immoral urges have within them the very energy we need to maintain sanity. Even those fleeting morbid thoughts that embarrass or frighten us have the potential to save our sanity and even uplift us to greater happiness and deeper serenity. Each of those dark specks of inner insanity contain energy and vitality waiting to be set free. If we curse them with rejection, they become a curse to us. If we bless them with acceptance and truth, they become a blessing to us.

Remembering Who I Am

The same songwriter mentioned above, implies that sanity is simply, "the serenity to just remember who I am." The process of *discovering who I am* or *remembering who I am* is difficult to evaluate from the outside, especially when we remove the usual outer criteria regarding what is sane and insane. We might be somewhat unpredictable and obey rules and customs only when we want to do so. Onlookers may experience this as a threat because it is difficult to say what the person who is *really* engaged in self-discovery will do next.

Such a person, however, is less likely to steal, kill, rape, cheat, injure or lie. Persons who are really engaged in self-discovery, do so by looking deeply within. It is impossible to harm others while we are looking within.

CHAPTER 27

Austerity & Wild Abandonment

(Two Ways of Seeking Freedom)

Austerity is an act of will. Wild abandonment is surrender to the feeling nature. When we practice austerity, we seek purity. When we dive into wild abandonment, we seek fulfillment.

There is no cause for conflict between austerity and wild abandonment, provided that each is an expression of truth instead of a suppression of truth. When we use them to suppress truth, we cling to one and fearfully reject the other.

If either one is practiced as an expression of truth, we eventually discover the other. There is a tendency to recognize the value of what appears to be the opposite. The individual who practices austerity purely, recognizes the deep desire to feel the fullness of *I am alive.* The individual who is actively engaged in wild abandonment and does it in fullness will eventually hear the deep yearning to just be, pure and simple.

If we do not discover the other, the one we favor gradually degenerates. One side becomes a state of struggle, the other a state of yearning. One withers away from lack of use, and the other becomes exhausted from overuse.

The two sides of this duality achieve harmony when the individual realizes that the preference for one over the other is just that – a preference. It is important to respect one's own preference, for it emanates from an inner wisdom that probably is not apparent to others, and sometimes not even apparent to the individual. That same wisdom quietly recognizes the value of the opposite. That same wisdom carries the quiet realization that our choice to do one or the other does not make us better than others.

Binging and Purging

When one side becomes excessive or dogmatic, it can easily lead to the excessive or dogmatic expression of the other side. The orgies of ancient Rome were followed by exaggerated purity of medieval Europe, where Christians supplemented austerity with deliberate acts of self-inflicted pain. The medieval Christians believed that self-love is evil, and pleasure is dangerous, while poverty, suffering and sacrifice bring us closer to God.

Today, we might laugh or shake our heads at the pious barbarism of the dark ages. If, however, we look deeper, we do find a core of truth. Many individuals who endure great pain often do experience a breakthrough, followed by a sense of peace and fulfillment. Physical and emotional sufferings cause us to remove frivolities, drop all pretenses and break the armor of denial, so we can experience the purity of who we really are.

It is not the pain, however, that produces purity. It is the removal of pretense. When we lose sight of this, we arrive at the conclusion that painful penance must precede wholeness. Pain is unnecessary to the extent that we are attentive and truthful.

Neither austerity nor wild abandonment produces the desired outcome (freedom) if they are used as a means of escaping from oneself. All attempts to escape everyday physical reality through austerity or wild abandonment result in mutilation of the body. Each side is unconsciously saying, "I don't like who I am; I don't like where I am." This translates into a gradual (or, not so gradual) destruction of the body. Attempting to purify ourselves so as to escape from our self-hatred harms the body. Likewise, pleasure-seeking to escape from pain (or boredom, which precedes pain) harms the body. On the other hand, when we use either principle wisely, there is a natural tendency to respect the body and accept our humanity.

Wild Abandonment That Really Feels Good

The healthy use of the pleasure principle involves the awareness that the pleasure we experience in the body is but an echo of the primordial state of aliveness that is beyond pleasure and pain. If we harshly judge our experience of pleasure, we do not feel the fullness of it, so we indulge more and more, until we simply saturate our senses. The naturally occurring channels of pleasure quickly become insufficient, and we must resort to more invasive methods to produce the same level of pleasure.

When the will is pure, we can experience the fullness of feeling in every little moment of sensual pleasure, whether it is the delicate fragrance of a flower, the touch of a loved one, or a fascinating book. Without even trying, we ride the pleasurable feelings of daily living to their source, which is the feeling of aliveness beyond pleasure or pain. And, we do so in a way that respects the body.

Austerity that Really Works

Austerity, like wild abandonment, is about freedom. The call to do one or the other is simply a question of how we want to experience our freedom. Austerity works if we remember two important principles:

- Judging the opposite as inferior sabotages our efforts.
- If harsh judgment is present, austerity eventually precipitates a crisis point where we become uncomfortable and are tempted to go to the opposite pole.

For example, a person who attempts to become slim and trim might, at some point, start craving rich foods and go on a binge. If the person chooses not to binge, the alternative is to persist just a little bit beyond the perceived limit of endurance. This generally produces a breakthrough in which the person exposes the secret self-judgment, and makes emotional contact with the deeper desire. This is somewhat analogous to the runner who runs right through the feeling of, "I can't go another step," and suddenly experiences the runner's high, which is particularly sweet because it was generated from within. When we experience this sort of breakthrough, the thing that was tempting us is no longer all that tempting. And, if we do partake of the tempting thing, the natural inclination is to do so in a way that is thoroughly enjoyable and respectful of the body.

Union

The monk who goes deeply enough into the practice of austerity is naturally at peace with the individual who freely engages in sensuous experience. Such acceptance is not patronizing tolerance – which is even more dishonest and insulting than overt rejection.

The deep experience of austerity is the experience of purity. It is an emptiness that is deep enough and vast enough to embrace all things. It is the silence that allows all voices to be heard. Such purity has so thoroughly let go of everything and has become so free, that it can allow all others to be free. Such austerity can cherish the sensuous experience, as the lover cherishes the beloved. The lover neither envies the beloved nor fearfully tries to convert the beloved into a facsimile of self.

For sure, a monk who is being a pure monk is likely to inspire others to follow a similar path. Such a monk, however, is simply creating an atmosphere in which others can see themselves and be themselves. If we allow ourselves to be ourselves, we naturally allow others to be themselves.

CHAPTER 28

Fasting & Feasting

(Two Ways of Nourishing Ourselves)

We fast when we seek purity. We feast when we seek fulfillment. Either one works, provided we know that purity and fulfillment are inseparable. Either one works if the call to feast or fast comes from within. If the choice to feast or fast does not spring cleanly from within, we tend to be dogmatic about it. The way we know we are using our fasting or feasting dogmatically is that we invariably place harsh judgment on the other, actively rejecting it or passively regarding it as inferior, silly or useless.

The full value of each side is not realized as long as it denies, rejects or belittles the other. Each has its own expression of truth, which we can fully comprehend only when one polarity is allowed to dance about the other; each recognizing the other with a knowing that says, "We are different, yet we are the same." In other words, each side, used properly, is way of inviting the experience of freedom. Freedom recognizes freedom, regardless of outer appearance.

A Matter of Taste

The wisdom that creates the body also instills within us the gut-level knowing of what to eat, what not to eat, when to eat and when not to eat. Therefore, knowing what to eat is (theoretically) as simple as knowing what tastes good. Knowing when to eat is as simple as knowing when you are hungry.

When the nervous system is allowed to develop naturally, the presence of hunger means the body needs food. The absence of hunger means the body doesn't need food. In its natural form, food that is nutritious and life-sustaining also tastes good. Likewise, things that are not particularly nutritious do not taste good, and food that is poisonous tends to be very bitter or otherwise unpleasant.

Through the commercializing and processing of food, we create products whose taste doesn't necessarily reflect nutritional content. Yet, even after our sense of taste no longer entirely reflects nutritional content, we must still to be respectful and attentive to what we crave, for it reflects not only the nutritional needs of the body but the sensual and emotional needs as well. Taste includes a desire that says, "I want to have a certain experience." The experience that is desired might be the food itself, or it may be something else represented by the food. Either way, the choice to eat or not to eat must be made by the individual. Either way, the experience remains incomplete as long as we place harsh judgment on the food in question.

Eating whatever we want whenever we want is one way of completing that experience. Likewise, fasting may be used to restore the body and mind to the pristine condition in which we hunger only for those foods that truly nourish and strengthen the body, freeing us to pursue what we desire on other levels.

Feeding the Whole Person

It is important to emphasize that giving the body the necessary nutrients is just one way that we sustain ourselves. The purely sensual experience of eating is also important. Furthermore, these two levels of nourishment are very closely related. How the food tastes to us greatly influences how it is handled in the body.

We also nourish ourselves through loving touch, speaking the truth, emotional contact, giving and receiving. If any of these are denied, we try to compensate by overusing the existing ones. For example, we might overeat. Likewise, if all the portals of "nourishment" are fully accessible, we might find that our desire for food changes in both quality and quantity. In fact, we may not have to eat at all – according to some schools of thought.

Do We Really Have to Eat?

There is a belief that we have the potential to sustain the body without having to eat. This is an extreme form of fasting, to say the least. The idea of not eating at all might seem far-fetched for those who have no direct experience of it. It certainly goes against our assumptions about the limitations of matter. It also goes against the evidence of our own senses. As far we can tell, if people do not eat, they lose weight. They can even become emaciated and starve to death. Yet, spiritual disciplines in both the East and West claim (and offer evidence) that we have the potential to sustain the body without eating. Reports of such individuals are numerous enough to make the skeptic take notice. For example, Theresa Neumann is a Catholic saint who lived in France in the 1940s and '50s. For over twenty years, she reportedly consumed nothing except the daily communion wafer. Meanwhile, in India, another woman, Giri Bala, was doing pretty much the same thing, minus the communion wafer. They were separately asked if others could learn to do the same. Both offered the same answer. They said, yes, it is possible, but it is not for everyone. They both felt that God was allowing them to live without eating so they could show others that such things are possible.

The Source of Sustenance

The belief that we do not have to eat to live might seem more believable if we take a broader view of how life sustains and expands itself. That broader view simply says, *Life contacts life, thus creating new life.* In the purely physical sense, this translates into eating. When we eat, we draw on the energy stored in the molecules of life. The other forms of nourishment, such as emotional contact and spiritual awareness, also involve life touching life, but in more subtle ways.

The evidence of Theresa Neumann, Giri Bala and others suggests that it is also possible to sustain the body by communing with the "source" of life directly. We might call this process *life touching Life.* Such extraordinary individuals seem to receive life-giving energy in its "raw"and pristine form, while the rest of us must consume it after it has been "predigested" by other life forms. In other words, we can sustain ourselves (physically and emotionally) by communing with the life around us or by communing with the source of life within us.

The secret of tapping into the deeper spiritual source of life seems to be *consciousness*. The individuals who reportedly don't need to eat seem to have one thing common: they recognize the presence of a life-giving force that they access by focusing the mind. They emphasize the importance of being at peace with oneself and the rest of life.

And the Rest of Us?

It is not unreasonable to suggest that the same current of life that sustained Theresa Neumann, Giri Bala and other non-eaters, also flows through every one of us. The difference might simply be a matter of degree. Perhaps when we physically or emotionally contact the life around us, we unconsciously tap into the very source of life. In other words, we stimulate the silent awareness of our spiritual origins, like two tuning forks resonating with each other. For sure, when we eat food, we do draw energy from it. Similarly, when we interact with one another, we do "exchange energy" in various ways, but there is also energy being *generated* from within – from nothing, apparently. For There is physiological evidence suggesting that our body cells get some of their energy directly from the "avoid."

Perhaps our health and well-being requires that we give and re-ceive energy with the life around us, while also bringing in "new" en-ergy from "nothing." Fasting (done with the proper focus) might be one way of increasing our capacity to receive life-giving energy di-rectly from the source.

CHAPTER 29

Vegetarian & Carnivore

(What You Eat and What's Eating You)

The controversy between vegetarian and carnivore is frequently a split between the quest for purity and the desire for fullness of experience. Denial of this inner split causes it to be projected out into our personal relationships, religion, politics and food. Each becomes a battlefield where we unconsciously play out the inner split.

Many years ago, I became aware of how I was using food to buffer myself from the reality of my own emotions. This (plus my other health issues and the reports of abuses in the production of flesh foods) compelled me to "purify my diet". I made a few attempts to remove all meat from my diet, but I found myself constantly hungry and edgy. The more I avoided meat, the more I craved breads, cakes and cookies. I struggled with this issue off and on for a while. Then, one evening, I was blessed with a solution. At that time, I was ending a close relationship with a woman. As I sat in my apartment, moping, I felt like eating something rich and heavy, yet I did not feel like I was really hungry. Finally, I slammed my fist on the table and asked myself, "Damn it, what do you want? To hell with the distinction between physiological and psychological needs! What do you want right now?" The first answer that came to me was, "I want to go out and get a dozen chicken nuggets." Without hesitation, I proceeded to Colonel Sanders. Once I got there, I experienced the split once again. I was looking forward to eating the chicken nuggets, even as I silently judged it harshly.

I then looked around and proceeded to judge the other people in the restaurant in the same manner that I was judging myself. The judgment was barely noticeable. I would have forgotten it immediately if it weren't for a gentle wake-up call that I received while I was there in the restaurant. I sat at a table, half of me getting ready to enjoy the chicken nuggets, the other half silently judging it. Directly in front of me, perhaps twenty feet away, a man and woman had just sat down. They were having a quiet conversation. As I glanced at them, they stopped talking, bowed their heads and gave prayerful thanks for their food.

My mind stopped in its tracks, and I experienced several seconds of blessed stillness. The first thought that emerged from the inner silence was, "Thank you."

After that day, I still wanted to experience a meatless diet, but I also knew that I would much rather eat a greasy pork chop prepared with love than a "healthy" vegetarian meal prepared with holier-than-thou arrogance.

I also knew that when it was time to stop eating meat, I would just know. Years later, on the day of my 35th birthday, I was sitting in a seafood restaurant, eating chicken and feeling rather blissful about things. By the time I finished eating, a quiet feeling went through me, which translated into, "No more meat, until I really feel like eating it again." Following that guideline, I abstained from eating meat for about the next seven years (except for one time at a Fourth of July picnic, when I accidentally ate a turkey hot dog, thinking that it was a soy wiener).

Vegiterrorism

When I first made the choice to abstain from meat, I coincidentally met a number of people who were vegetarians for spiritual, moral or humane reasons. Some of them did it light-heartedly, while others obviously had an ax to grind, insisting or implying that eating meat was only for those who were spiritually unevolved and socially uninformed. Without realizing it, I was gradually adopting this attitude.

Since my self-esteem needed some bolstering, I was easily seduced by the idea that my dietary choice made me "better" than those who ate meat. I was inwardly responding like the people of Germany who, after the devastation and humiliation of World War I, were seduced into believing that they were the master race. In my case, the seduction was much more subtle, but the principle was basically the same.

Fortunately, the silent voice of reason, once again, ended my silent strutting about. While I was preparing a tasty vegetarian dinner, a sentence formed in my mind. The words were clear and distinct, as if a voice was speaking them into my ear. In fact, I imagined that the voice was rather jovial and lighthearted. "No one," said the voice, "is further from heaven than an arrogant vegetarian." I paused for a moment, and then burst out laughing.

I Yam What I Yam

During those seven years, I did not crave meat. The most uncomfortable part of my diet was having people call me a "vegetarian". I didn't like that, though I wasn't sure why. I convinced myself that I was irritated because they were simply not being accurate. "No, I'm not a vegetarian," I would say. "Once in a while, I might have eggs and cheese, and, on rare occasions, even a bit of fish. These are not vegetables." I explained, "Therefore, I'm not a vegetarian! I simply do not consume the flesh of land-dwelling vertebrates."

I repeated this explanation many times. It wasn't until the end of the seven years – when I started feeling inclined to eat an occasional chicken leg – that I discovered the real cause of my irritation. I did not wish to be called a vegetarian, because I was unconsciously rebelling against the idea of having my identity based on my dietary choice. I was irritated because I was being defined by what I was eating. When I became aware of this, it was with a sigh of relief that I finally declared, "Vegetarian or carnivore is not who I am. I am who I am. Eating is simply something I do."

CHAPTER 30

Male & Female

(Gender and Beyond)

If we address the male/female duality from a biological standpoint, it's pretty simple. The vast majority of humans are clearly either male or female. If, however, we include the softer and less tangible aspects of the person, gender becomes less clearly defined.

Some would argue that it is pointless to dwell on what is psychologically and behaviorally male and what is female, because the distinction is heavily influenced by the culture in which we happen to live.

As with other dualities, however, the act of denying or rejecting the male/female distinction is just another way of becoming more tangled up in it. If we wish to recognize the "lie" in the male/female duality, we may do so by first recognizing the truth in it, and then we may discern where the truth derails into a lie.

Maleness as an Expression of Duality

Maleness is about comparing, competing, setting boundaries and establishing hierarchies. Maleness may also be said to be analytical, linear and goal-oriented. Male consciousness is on a journey, a mission. It is willing to sacrifice itself for something greater than itself. In this respect, maleness is an expression of duality. In contrast, femaleness tends to be more merging, embracing, non-linear, inclusive, unifying, and, as such, transcends duality.

Femaleness as an Expression of Duality

If we look within the embracing, inclusive nature of female, we see cycles, seasons, birth and death. In other words, we see expressions of duality. In contrast, maleness, with its single-minded persistence and power of penetration, is able to break the cycle, stop the repetition, transcend the existing order of birth and death, thus ushering in non-dualistic awareness.

In other words, both male and female have qualities that simultaneously express duality and transcend duality. The dualistic nature of one is drawn to that which is beyond duality in the other. Maleness disrupts the dualistic (seasonal) nature of female. Likewise, the all inclusive "Isness" of female absorbs and dissolves the logical hierarchical structure of maleness.

Creation

When opposites interact, creation happens. Duality establishes a potential difference, an energy gradient – a charge. The interaction of male and female is just one way of establishing that polarity, so we have energy with which to create. In each other's presence, men and women release their stored emotional energy as romance, deep affection, sexual intercourse, procreation and the establishment of a home. This discharge of emotional energy is also re-directed and channeled to bring forth spiritual awakening, poetry, dance, music, architecture and other such creations that form our culture.

"Sperm Consciousness"

The very essence of male may be called "sperm consciousness". Sperm consciousness is dumb guts that does not stop or hesitate; it plunges headlong through the obstacle course of life, until it reaches the center of life itself – the great sphere, and then it surrenders totally, for it has reached the ultimate goal.

Sperm consciousness is the desire that says, "I want to give all that I have and all that I am to something greater than my finite self." As finite beings, we want to be nestled within something greater than our finite selves. Occasionally, the isolated self wants to merge deeply into the greater presence. This instinct also expresses itself in every-day life as the desire of the individual to belong to a family; of the family to belong to a community; and the community to belong to the greater community (culture, religion, etc.).

Sperm consciousness is a fundamental drive. If it is not allowed to express itself freely in relationships and creative work, it can be exploited and twisted into kamikaze pilots, suicide squads and crazed crusaders who unquestioningly sacrifice themselves for the glory of the empire or some other perceived "greater presence".

Sperm consciousness typically expresses itself more dramatically in men, but it is also present (though more subtle) in women. Sperm consciousness in women is typically hidden within the much more obvious *egg consciousness.*

"Egg Consciousness"

"Egg consciousness" is the very essence of female. Egg consciousness has no place to go and nothing to do. It does not have to sacrifice itself for life, for it *is* life. It does not identify itself with the ephemeral seed that is born and then dies; it identifies itself with the essence that goes on and on. It does not perceive that it devours and annihilates the sperm. It carries a vision of life that is beyond the duality of egg and sperm, beyond winning and losing, beyond conquest. It is, thus, able to appreciate sperm consciousness in the only way that sperm consciousness can feel appreciated. Egg consciousness embraces sperm consciousness and says, "Welcome home, Beloved."

Egg consciousness is present in men. Typically, however, it is not very obvious. It may be likened to a translucent halo, a cool and pastel aura that envelops and quietly stabilizes the fiery passion of sperm consciousness.

Men, Women and Trust

A number of factors determine how much trust two individuals share. The personal history of the individuals is certainly one factor. Another important (but usually overlooked) factor is the degree of harmony between the will and the feeling nature of the individuals. Inner harmony leads to outer harmony. Inner conflict leads to outer conflict. Conflict between the will and the feeling nature contributes greatly to conflict in relationships.

A man's hidden (or not so hidden) belief that he cannot trust women is based on the even more hidden belief that he can't trust his own feeling nature. He is justified in this belief. Once the feeling nature has been subjugated, repressed and exploited, it becomes chaotic and unpredictable. Hell hath no fury like feelings scorned! As in other forms of internal warfare, this one is projected out. It typically turns into hostility and distrust of women. The mirror image of this internal warfare exists in the woman who trusts men just about as much as she trusts her own will.

What About Spontaneity?

For most of us, gender is an important part of our identity. If we regard gender simply as a role that we play, we must also recognize the strong emotional charge associated with this role.

If we take the gender role *too* seriously, spontaneity is lost and genuine expression is censored. We suppress genuine expression so as to fit the established model of how a man or woman is supposed to behave. For example, it has been stated that women under stress feel better by talking freely, whereas men feel better by prioritizing their problems and then developing a plan of action or solution. The woman is said to handle troublesome feelings by just talking about them and not necessarily expecting the listener to provide an answer; while the man handles troublesome emotions by being alone, thinking it over and then taking the appropriate action.

These insights can be most helpful in creating understanding between men and women. The man can understand that he does not have to solve the problem for the woman. He can just relax and listen, which is probably what the woman really wants him to do.

Likewise, when the man feels overburdened and withdraws into himself, the woman can understand that his actions may not have anything to do with her or the relationship. So, rather than frantically trying to draw him back (which causes him to withdraw even more) she can relax while he finds himself in solitude.

141

Thus, we can drop the destructive comparisons and realize that each, in their own way, is instinctively carrying out the very useful practice of just letting themselves be. When a woman talks in a seemingly random manner about her problem, she is letting herself be. When a man withdraws into himself, he is letting himself be.

A word of caution: The guidelines describing male and female behavior, though useful, can become a hindrance when used rigidly. Our spontaneous expression doesn't necessarily follow the established gender guidelines. The desire to talk and to be heard is a natural human desire, which tends to show up more obviously in women but is also present in men. The desire to withdraw and go deeply into oneself is alive and well in both genders, though it tends to be more obvious in men. This simply means that the woman need not think herself abnormal or unwomanly if she wants to withdraw and then take action in a definitive manner, and the man need not think himself less of a man if he feels compelled to just talk about a troublesome issue without having a specific plan of action. This level of spontaneity, combined with an awareness of the how men and women tend to behave, allows the fullness of masculinity and femininity to express, and opens the door to the deeper sense of our personal identity, which includes both, and goes beyond both.

Feminine Men and Masculine Women

On a purely biological level, any given individual is clearly masculine or clearly feminine, usually. If, however, we look at behavior and psychological disposition, some men show more feminine mannerisms than others, and likewise for women.

We might be afraid of displaying behavior associated with the other gender because it could threaten our safe place in the existing social order. This is particularly significant when such behavior is erroneously associated with homosexuality. Sexual preference and degree of masculinity/femininity in one's mannerism are best addressed as two separate topics. This is true whether we approach it from a physiological or psychological level.

For example, high levels of testosterone are likely to make a man or woman more sexual and aggressive, but does not influence sexual preference. Likewise, the outward appearance of masculinity or femininity is not a reliable indicator of sexual preference. A gay man can be very masculine or very feminine in external mannerism. A heterosexual man can seem very masculine or feminine. This also holds true for women.

If, however, an openly gay man is inclined toward feminine mannerisms, he is more likely to express them freely through his gestures and speech. Whereas the heterosexual man who has the same feminine mannerisms is more likely to keep them hidden because he has been programmed from childhood to act "manly". Heterosexual women show a similar tendency to censor and conform, though it seems to be less pronounced than that of men.

Synergy of Male and Female

The embracing nature of female (egg consciousness) gives equal value to male and female qualities. For the male (sperm consciousness), egg consciousness is the goal. He has to climb for it. When thinking is linear, life is a journey and the path is always upward. The goal, the highest point on the climb, is the wholeness and vision of equality carried by egg consciousness.

In other words, male consciousness, at its purest, regards female consciousness as, somehow, superior. This translates in everyday life as the man who instinctively protects his mate with his very life.

The women, thus feels honored and loved, and embraces the man with deep appreciation, which she can do in a balanced and wholesome manner because of her natural inclination toward equality.

Such harmonious interaction between male and female consciousness does not happen by forcing it or pretending that it is present when it isn't. Such harmony evolves naturally when we are honest with our fears and desires, irrespective of how we think we're supposed to act. In the presence of such honesty, the wholesomeness of our innate male or female qualities tend to assert themselves. In this manner, the synergy between the two genders unfolds and comes to life in a way that is unique and natural for any woman and man in a relationship.

CHAPTER 31

Mother & Father

(The Two Sides of Parenthood)

While I was attending a support group, I was listening to one of the participants, whom I will call "Jill". She said that she felt guilty about asking us to help her find clarity on a certain major issue in her life, because if she found that clarity she would probably leave the group and move away. She felt that in receiving support from us, she was obligated to stay with us and "pay us back." On the surface, this little confession does not seem extraordinary. It's the sort of thing that people routinely reveal when they are attempting to sort out their personal issues. When she said it, however, something clicked inside me. *"Mother!"* I declared. I then shut my mouth and, somehow managed to restrain myself while she continued talking. When she finished talking, I responded by saying, "Jill, to me, there is something very important about us giving to you even though you will no longer be here to pay us back."

On the surface, my words did not seem extraordinary. When I spoke them, however, something clicked in Jill. She started crying, feeling overwhelmed, unable to comprehend why she was so emotional about such a simple exchange of words. When she finally did speak, she said – in so many words: "I feel recognized... I feel like I have a right to exist just as I am." She realized that for many years, the care she received from her mother had a hidden price tag on it, which had been weighing on her quite heavily. Until that moment, she had been unaware of that price tag.

Her healing involved allowing herself to receive from us even though it meant she would leave "the nest". For those few minutes, we were, in a small way, carrying out the function of the ideal mother.

Mother

Mother gives to the child the experience of receiving unconditionally and thereby imprints into the brain the nonverbal message that silently says, *This is your home, you are welcomed here... You deserve to have your needs met, simply because you exist.* This message is accepted by the baby, and establishes a pattern for life. Without it, we walk the Earth, feeling like strangers. We feel we have no right to claim anything for ourselves. We feel we must negotiate for everything, or depend on the good graces of others who are more privileged than we are.

Mother has the nonverbal vision that *allows* the baby to be a baby. She asks nothing of the baby, relating to it in a way that cannot be understood with masculine business mentality. Mother consciousness needs no practical reason to nurture the new life; she doesn't weigh the baby's life in terms of profit and loss. She knows what the life in her body wants to do, and she allows the life around her to support her. She carries the nonverbal knowing that the life within her and the life around her are simply expressions of the same life, dancing the dance of life. Mother consciousness does not see her function as an investment. If it were an investment, she would not think twice about putting the child up for adoption if she found a more profitable investment. When a woman does give up her child for adoption, she typically does so because she feels incapable of properly caring for the child. It would be meaningless to say that she being "selfish", because, as long as she is responsible for the child's well-being, her needs are inseparable from the needs of the child; if she is deprived, the child will also be deprived.

Mother is the nest where the child can simply *be*, without having to prove or accomplish anything. The child's needs are instantly met. In the safety of mother's arms, the child's very existence is validated, allowing for the development of self-worth in the years that follow.

Now the question is: How does the above flowery description of motherhood relate to the flesh and blood reality of the exasperated young mama who can't believe that screaming monster came out of her? She might be tempted to condemn herself as a "failure", or she might get cynical and declare that the above description of mothering is idealistic but not realistic. Another alternative is for her to remember that "mother" is more of a *function* than a fixed identity. The mother is a person before and after she is a mother.

Nurturing can be extended to another person only if it is simultaneously given to oneself. The young mama discovers that her sanity (and her baby) are saved by allowing herself the same kindness and tenderness that she would extend to her baby. In essence, she is being *mother to herself.*

Father

Maleness is a focused, linear, driving force. *Father* is an aspect of maleness, expressing itself outwardly to give support and acting in unison with mother as she brings forth and nurtures the new life. Male becomes father by stopping the established monthly cycle; breaking the earth, planting the seed, thus initiating something new; transforming undifferentiated female energy into mother energy.

As an expression of the will, the father function establishes firm boundaries to protect and tend to the physical needs of the mother so that she can have the safety to nurture the child. The father function, however, doesn't stop there.

Son

Father is the child's introduction to the world outside the nest. Father is the source of worldly knowledge. Unlike mother, father is not satisfied to just let the child be a child. Father encourages, pushes and sometimes demands that the son be more than he thinks he is. Father is the role model. He might also be the brick wall the child must climb over or break through. Through father, the child cultivates resourcefulness, courage, stamina, self-reliance and will.

Daughter

For the female child, the mother/father functions are similar to those described for the male child, but are less clear cut, because many of her worldly lessons ("fathering") come from the same parent who does most of the mothering. The mother tends to be more exacting with the details of the daughter's life and tends to be more lenient with the son. In contrast, the father tends to be relatively lenient toward the daughter, but demanding with the son. (Note: We are speaking here of general *tendencies,* not hard and fast rules.)

The Continuum

In truth, for both the daughter and son, the biological mother can fulfill some of the roles that fall under the category of fathering, just like a man can fulfill some of the roles associated with mothering. In fact, in the average home, this is precisely what happens. The loving mama knows where to draw a hard line with her kids. Likewise, a stern father who teaches the child the ways of the world, instinctively knows how to temper his lessons with a quiet acceptance that allows for imperfection.

The interaction of the mother and father functions moves along a continuum throughout the life of the child. At birth, there is a dominance of "mother" energy in both parents. At this point, the biological mother provides most of the mothering; she gives birth to the child's body from her body, holds it against her skin and feeds it with her milk. In those early years, the biological father also does a good bit of mothering. He relates to the baby with undemanding and unquestioning acceptance – hopefully.

As the baby grows, both parents shift steadily in the direction of fathering. They instinctively become more exacting with the child. Their parenting takes the form of instruction and guidance.

At the other end of the continuum, the child is no longer a child and the parents are no longer parents. Together they have traveled to the realm that is beyond parent/child; they have become equals, joined by a love that is made tender and sweet by the memory of a childhood and parenthood experienced completely.

Both Must be Present

It is tempting to give mothering greater value than fathering, or vice versa, depending on our upbringing and social conditioning.

Even when we make a concerted effort to be unbiased and diplomatic, most of us have an emotional leaning toward one or the other.

For the developing child, however, the mother and father functions must both be present, even if provided by the same parent. Mothering, in the absence of fathering, will eventually consume the child, and the nest becomes a tomb. Fathering, in the absence of mothering, looks at the child pragmatically in terms of assets and losses, and will therefore exploit the child.

Mother, in the absence of father, looks upon the newborn baby and says, "Oh, you are precious, so divine, so delicious! I want to eat you up!" Father, in the absence of mother, looks upon the newborn baby, at first, with total bewilderment, and then says, "Oh, I see. It's a tube...you put food into one end and shit comes out the other end."

The quality of love that creates a free and independent life is the gift of mothering and fathering acting in unison. Mother is the nest; father teaches the child to fly free from the nest.

Over-Identification

Over-identification with the mother or father role exacts a toll on the child as well as the parent. When the child leaves home, there is a void in the parent's life. This is temporary and not problematical, unless he or she has no well-defined identity beyond the mother or father function.

When the parents have reached advanced age, it is normal and natural for grown sons and daughters to care for them. However, when the aged parents are helpless to the point that they become a drain to their children, the grown children may swallow their guilt and place their parents in a home for the aged. In contrast, individuals who fulfill their parental functions, and then take the opportunity to discover who they are beyond the parent role, tend to stay physically, mentally and emotionally healthy and therefore less dependent on their grown children. The bond is still present, but rather than being a reversal of dependency, it is a non-verbal bond of mutual affection in which giving and receiving are done freely.

CHAPTER 32

Child & Adult

To be an adult is to work and be responsible. To be a child is to play and be free. Both exist within every individual.

We relate to children out there as we relate to the child within. Likewise, we relate to authority figures around us in accordance with the condition of the adult within.

The child within us is an expression of the feeling nature. It is innocent curiosity flying freely on the wings of unquestioning trust. It is large round eyes that see the world as an amazing mystery, and a heart that knows it is always at home. The adult is an expression of the will. The adult weighs the options, analyzes the past, ponders the future, makes choices, and exercises discipline.

The child within says, *I want to be seen.* The adult within says, *I want to see.* The child within needs to be heard and understood; a need that can only be provided by the inner adult that is capable of listening and understanding.

The question as to who is in charge is effectively answered when we notice which one we repress. Whichever we repress unconsciously runs us. As with other dualities, child and adult define one another. The truth felt by the child within shapes and sharpens the will of the adult. Our innocent curiosity and capacity to feel give meaning to the tasks we assign to ourselves as adults. Likewise, when the adult is present, the child feels safe to be a child. The adult sets the boundaries that allows the child to safely express, explore and take joy in life.

As in other dualities, imbalance between the adult and child within oneself results from judging one as more important than the other. As a result, the one that is rejected is driven into the unconscious and silently runs the show, controlling the one that is on the surface. For instance, if the inner child is seen as greater than the adult, the repressed adult (the capacity for logical planning) is not lost. On the contrary, it takes over and distorts the visible expression of feelings. Thus, the outer child-like behavior becomes a tool of the repressed adult to control and manipulate his/her environment. Likewise, if the child is repressed in favor of a rational adult persona, our so-called rational decisions become the tools of the hidden desires, fears and fantasies of the repressed child. I am reminded here of my oldest brother. Since he had so many younger siblings, he had to grow up very fast. Essentially, he had to become an adult before he was through being a child. He became self-sufficient at an early age and learned his way around the world of commerce. By his early twenties, he had generated enough capital to start his own business: *The Kitty-Kat Toy Company*.

Parent & Offspring

In real parent/offspring relationships, the tyrannical parent stifles the child and, therefore, stifles the capacity to enjoy life. On the other hand, the absence of the parent creates panic in the child, who will then create chaos in order to elicit a response from the parent. In essence, the child says, "Please give me some boundaries so I can feel safe." Both of these scenarios precisely parallel the dynamics of the adult and the child within oneself.

Suffering occurs when the parents force themselves to give out of a sense of lack or guilt. Parents who force themselves to give are likely to force the child to receive. The parents' suppressed needs silently suffocate the child, as the parents try to shape the child into something that will bring some semblance of parental fulfillment.

This tendency is undone when the parents sort out their own needs. Thus, the parent can yield to the deeper instinct that is capable of simultaneously protecting and guiding the child, while setting them free to be more than the parent could have imagined.

Young & Old

Early one morning, I woke up from a dream in which I was watching an old man and a boy. The old man might have been in his eighties, and the boy looked like he was around fifteen years of age.

The old man was clearly very wise and learned. He was Oriental, which, to me, symbolized wisdom and harmony. The boy was obviously impatient, bubbling with enthusiasm, eager to show the world what he could do. Unlike the old man, the youth was a Westerner, reinforcing the symbolism of drive and ambition.

There wasn't much explicit action in the dream. The two characters simply sat facing each other, as they conversed quietly. The aspect of the dream that made the biggest impression on me, was that the two characters had great respect for one another.

The dream dramatized the relationship between youthful enthusiasm and the wisdom of advanced age, as they relate within the same person. The dream was a picture of harmony between the passion of youth and the serenity of old age.

Youth is desire. It wants to reach out, explore, play, build, experience more, do more, be more. Youth wants to discover itself as it unfolds moment by moment.

Old age is tranquility. It is surrender and serenity. It is the inner stillness that can allow life to be as it is. Such tranquility begins as youthful enthusiasm that is allowed to unfold freely. It is the youthful mind, free to be and do, that eventually evolves into the serene wisdom of the learned sage. Likewise, it is the wisdom of advanced age that allows youthful enthusiasm to be born again.

Any attempt to devalue or subjugate one in favor of the other results in premature degeneration and death. Youthful enthusiasm, stifled or exploited, never matures. It withers into bitter and decrepit old age, unfulfilled and, therefore, unable to nurture the young. Fear of growing old and fear of death result from youthful enthusiasm that was not allowed to bring itself into fulfillment.

The stillness and wisdom of the sage within provides a stable base from which the youthful passion within may launch itself. When youthful enthusiasm is allowed to find fulfillment in worldly activities, it evolves into wisdom and serenity, which in turn gives birth to new buds of youthful enthusiasm. And so, life goes on, always fresh, always new.

CHAPTER 33

Time

(The canvas on which we create)

The experience of youth and old age occur in linear *time*. To experience young and old simultaneously within oneself is one way of inviting the experience of *timelessness*.

Aging

The body responds faithfully to whatever emotions and beliefs that are consistently held in the mind. Apparently, thoughts move molecules. If we follow this line of reasoning, we might come to the startling and perhaps frightening conclusion that if we consistently maintain the peaceful awareness of timelessness, the body simply does not age! Even more surprising, respectable healthcare practitioners are putting this knowledge into practical application!

If we are not in touch with the quiet awareness of timelessness, the rallying to immortality or longevity becomes a fearful rejection of the death experience, which, in turn, causes the body and mind to age more rapidly. For example, a useful practice for reducing the fear of aging is to refrain from celebrating birthdays. The use of this strategy does away with the fear that says, "Oh, God, I'm one year older." If, however, we obsessively avoid the celebration of birthdays, we are denying the human experience that says, "Gee, one more year has passed." Such denial perpetuates fear. On the other hand, when we allow ourselves to quietly reflect upon our experience of the passage of time, we invite serenity. If we are attentive and quiet enough, we might become aware that such serenity stems from the silent knowing that seems to say, "I am, I always have been, and I always will be." Such awareness encourages rejuvenation of the body.

Release the Past/There is No Past

How can we release the past if there is no past? This seeming contradiction can lead to fascinating debates or heated arguments between those who advocate remembering and releasing memories of the past and those who insists that these "memories" are not memories at all, but stories we make up here and now.

One side advocates looking at one's behavior and correlating it to childhood experiences. Though this is valuable, the rigid adherence to this model could very well be a way of avoiding full responsibility for present behavior. The other side states, "There is no painful past to explain current behavior. There is only now and the choices we make now. We create all experiences here-and-now, even the experience of 'memories' are created here-and-now." This perspective also has value, but it can easily be used to justify the denial of memories that are too uncomfortable to contemplate.

In other words, one side uses linear time to validate and justify feelings of hurt, anger, guilt and the belief that there are victims and villains. The other holds on to the concept that there is only *now,* so as to hide the same basic feelings that the other is dramatically playing out.

Merger of these two concepts does not happen with compromise. When each is experienced in fullness, we see the pure essence of the other. Remembering and healing hurts from the past opens the door to the perception of the eternal now. Likewise, to actively seek the transcendental experience of timelessness can very well open the door to the unresolved issues from the past. In fact, to force the experience of timelessness when we are not ready to release the past, can produce psychological disorientation and insanity.

Time & Space

The experience of timelessness is potentially disorienting because time and space are inseparable. This has been demonstrated mathematically and experimentally. It has also been reported by sages, saints and countless individuals in and out of mental hospitals.

153

Since time and space are inseparable, a change in one affects the other. Therefore, if the mind dives into a strong experience of timelessness, the normal experience of "space" also goes out the window. We lose the friendly and familiar frames of reference, such as up, down, left, right, front, back, large, small, self and other.

Carl Jung, one of the early pioneers in the field of psychology, coined a phrase to identify the timeless/spaceless realm of the mind. He called it the *collective unconscious*. He once told the story of a client, a level-headed military man, who was exploring the collective unconscious. This client had a daughter in a mental hospital. The client learned that both he and his daughter were tapping into the same collective unconscious. He, therefore, wanted to know how his experience was different from that of his daughter. Dr. Jung replied, "You dove in; she fell in."

Just a Moment Ago

The experience of timelessness does not necessarily have to be dramatic or disorienting. A mind that is happily operating in linear time, routinely gets little hints of timelessness. These hints are subtle feelings. They may present themselves as a quiet sense of wonder; the world takes on a newness, a brightness; everyday events seem quietly miraculous. If we are attentive to these little feelings, they grow. We look at the same oak tree every day, appreciating its majesty, and one day, we may feel something. If that feeling could speak, it might say, "That oak tree...wasn't it an acorn just a moment ago? Behold the mountain; it was a valley just a moment ago. Behold the grass-covered plain; it was an ocean floor just a moment ago; and in yet another moment, it will become a deep canyon. Behold the star; just a moment ago, it was a nebula; in another moment hence, it will be transformed into a flower."

The scientist who looks at the ordinary landscape and marvels at what is, what was and what will be has merged the rational perception of linear *time* with a subtle feeling of *timelessness*. By the calendar, eons have passed since life first appeared on Earth. Yet, when our feeling nature is open, the event is stunning and miraculous, as if we had witnessed it just a moment ago.

CHAPTER 34

Birth & Death

Linear time makes possible the experience of birth and death. To be aware of timelessness is to be aware of life beyond birth and death.

Birth is a beginning. Death is a completion. When we embark on something new, we must, at some point, reach completion. Likewise, as long as linear time marches on, every completion ushers in something new.

On the consciousness level, we are complete with a given experience when we no longer cling to it or push it away. It simply falls away like a dry leaf. When a journey begins, we feel excitement and expectancy. When a journey is ended we are at peace with the outcome. We cherish it as a complete experience. Therefore, we are ready to rest, renew ourselves and move on.

Grief

The inability to experience the "completeness" of a given event can show up as lingering *grief*. The grief that follows the death of a loved one may be looked upon as the emotions trying to catch up to external reality. The more unexpected the death, the longer the period of grief.

As with birth, grieving over a death has it own timing and rhythm, unique in every individual. It is not wise to rush the grieving process, just as it is not wise to try to speed up or slow down the birth process so as to conform to the doctor's schedule.

If we try to expedite or censer the grieving process so we can "get on with life", the neglected feelings are likely to remain, preventing us from *really* moving on with life.

Grieving is complete when the life of the loved one is seen as a complete experience. At that point, the grieving individual experiences a "birth" or renewal.

The Ever-Present Cycle

Every day of our lives, we dance the dance of starting and finishing. It is relatively rare that we experience grief over it. We experience starting and finishing in many small ways and a few grand ways. How gracefully who move through this cycle depends on how gracefully we embrace the unknown.

Fear of birth is fear of the new and unknown. Fear of death is pretty much the same thing. As with other opposites, we are ruled by the side that we reject or resist. To experience both as partners in the dance of creation is to invite the timeless quality of life beyond birth and death. Which reminds me of a story…

The Old Tree

I awoke at about 3:30 am, I found myself curled up on a couch in the waiting room next to the intensive care unit of a hospital in northeast Pennsylvania. My father was in critical condition. My oldest brother was sleeping on another couch in the same room. His snoring was thunderous, and I was feeling restless anyway, so I went for a stroll.

I walked slowly through the dimmed corridors, my footsteps echoing softly on the linoleum. To my surprise, I remembered a cartoon I had seen at the age of ten. It was called, *Kimba the White Lion*. The cartoon was a TV series that had aired every day after school. The show was about a community of animals ruled by a young lion named "Kimba".

I had long forgotten the actual contents of the show, but as I walked through the corridors of the hospital, I clearly remembered one particular episode. It had to do with a large, ancient tree standing in a clearing in the midst of the jungle. For the animals in the community, the tree was a common gathering point. For many of them, it was a source of food or shelter. It was far older than the oldest animal in the community. From season to season, through countless storms and droughts, it stood steady and firm. The tree was their home base, the center of their universe. It defined them as a community.

When the animals realized the old tree was dying, they frantically did everything possible to keep it alive. Eventually, they resorted to tying strong vines around its trunk and branches to prevent it from breaking apart. In the end, however, the old tree broke the restraints and began to crack in various places.

The animals stood in a circle around the tree. They watched as it crumbled to the ground. In a matter of seconds, their lifelong companion was reduced to a heap of splintered logs and broken branches.

For a while, the animals stared in silence at the remains of the tree. Kimba stepped forward, fell on the debris and sobbed.

In the depth of his grief, Kimba looked up and fell silent. He walked slowly to the center of the fallen rubble. There, he saw a single tiny seedling. That was when Kimba understood. The old tree wanted to die. It wanted to make room for new life. Their old friend had become a new friend.

Beyond Birth and Death

I stood in the darkened corridor of the hospital, looking out the window. Thirty years had passed since I had seen that cartoon. As I gazed down at the snow-covered rooftops and the two rows of glowing streetlights, the images continued flashing through my mind. I recalled the cartoon vividly…as if I had seen it just a moment ago.

The next day, as my father took his last breath, my brothers and sisters and I stood around his bed. All seven of us wept, some of us loudly, some of us quietly. Yet, as I let myself feel the loss, I was also became aware of something new and innocent in our presence. The feeling was subtle, yet quietly overpowering. I was experiencing both *death* and *birth,* and something beyond both – Life, ever-changing and always the same.

CHAPTER 35

Power

(It's About Contrast)

Whenever we use the word *powerful* we are (perhaps unconsciously) making a comparison. Our assessment of who is powerful is based on contrasting one person with another. Superman is powerful by earthly standards, but, on his home planet of Krypton, he would be considered just one of the grunts.

I am not implying that such comparison is to be discarded. If we reject or deny the tendency to compare, it persists covertly and assumes a greater role in our perception of ourselves and others. If we allow ourselves to consciously make comparisons, our perception of powerful and powerless tends to fall into proper perceptive.

The Power of Truth & Silence

Knowledge is power. How we express what we know will greatly determine how powerful we are. Two ways that we use knowledge to generate power are through secrecy and truthfulness. When the two are balanced, we cultivate power effectively. If one is exalted at the expense of the other, power is diminished. If both are present as pure silence and the fullness of truthful expression, power is maximized.

Secrecy, as a power tool, is effective when its use is motivated by respect for oneself and others. It derails when it is motivated by fear or the desire to harm or otherwise control anyone. The same applies for speaking the truth. Expression of truth increases our sense of power when it is motivated by respect for oneself and others. Truthfulness derails when it is used to control others. Such expression of truth is not much different from a lie, for it is being used to conceal other truths.

Overt & Covert Power

Since powerful and powerless are experienced through comparison, they must be in close proximity to each other in order for either one to have any meaning. The powerful individual and powerless individual seek each other out for mutual validation.

In truth, each has its own way of exerting power over the other, while yielding power to the other. One displays its power and conceals its weakness, while the other displays its weakness and conceals its power. The individual who is considered powerful may be said to have *overt power*, while the individual who is considered powerless or simply less powerful may be said to have *covert power*.

Overt Power

A person who is outwardly powerful exerts power by utilizing tangible assets, such as greater physical strength, sharp intellect, verbal skills, money, property and politics. Such an individual is able to dominate others through a visible frontal attack, using intimidation or logic. In this form of power play, the attack is obvious; what you see is what you get. The primary weakness that exists within the overt power play is also obvious. The individual provides a large and visible target. Furthermore, regardless how much overt power an individual appears to have over others, victory ultimately depends on the other person's perception of greater power. Taken to extreme, if the other person does not even perceive the power play, there is no comparison. With no opponent to push against, we have no basis for claiming greater power.

Covert Power

The purpose of concealing power is to increase it. Covert power is generally developed by the individual who appears to be weaker or more dependent. Covert power is about pretending. It relies on secrecy, deception or seduction. It makes itself invisible or innocent looking. It hides in small, low and dark places, beyond the reach of those who are overtly powerful. Covert power is the employee who steals from the company when the boss isn't looking. It's the wife who buys an expensive item and hides it from her husband. It's the person who intervenes in an argument between two other individuals, pretending to side with one and then the other, so as to profit from both. A variation on this is the child who plays the two parents against each other, and then gains favors by becoming a secret ally to both.

Covert power is the follower who tries to play upon the leader's vanity, in essence saying, "I will give you power over me, now you are obliged to take care me. You are now responsible for my well-being; treat me nice and make sure to fulfill all my expectations or I will be hurt and disillusioned and I will no longer worship you."

Gender & Power

One of the misconceptions regarding the nature of men and women is that men are inherently domineering, while women are inherently sly and deceptive. These two stereotypes – whether or not we admit that we believe them – contribute greatly to the subtle hostility that sometimes exists between men and women. In truth, a man who acts weak and wimpish utilizes the same covert power tools as the passive woman with a domineering husband. Likewise, the woman who has cultivated the more visible forms of power may engage in overt power plays as readily as any man.

As long as the primary motivation is the desire to have power over others, any individual, regardless of gender, may use overt or covert power tools. In fact, most of us can shift back and forth from overt to covert power plays, depending on which one we deem as more effective in any given situation.

And the Winner is...

Overt power seems to win the battle, while covert power, being more patient, seems to win the war. In the long run, however, both lose. Overt power experiences the satisfaction of immediate and obvious victory, visible for all to see. Such victory, however, is quietly undone by covert power. Likewise, covert power seems to have the last laugh, but at a great price. Its victory is subtle, and the price for that victory is also subtle. In the very act of being covert, the person must hide the genuine self and suppress the fundamental desire to be as *I am*. This results in self-hatred. It is subtle self-hatred that quietly and slowly destroys the individual from the inside out.

Pure Power

Recognition of our overt and covert power plays allows us to move beyond them and into the realm of inner serenity. We may also call this the realm of pure power. Here, we experience a sense of self worth that is not strained or inflated. Pure power does not need to establish its self-worth by diminishing anyone; therefore it cannot be diminished by anyone. It is sustained by truth, which is freely available from within and cannot be stolen from without. It is simply shared.

The sharing of our truth increases our sense of pure power. The sharing of truth translates tangibly into the act of giving what we really want to give and receiving what we really want to receive. Since no one feels cheated or exploited, no energy is wasted through attack or defense.

Potential

We can get a deeper understanding of pure power by looking at the concept of *potential*. Potential is the ability to get things done. Potential is established through the juxtaposition of opposites. Potential is established when fullness encounters emptiness. Potential energy is released when fullness rushes in to fill emptiness.

Superficially, untapped potential looks like no potential all. An unfired stick of dynamite looks exactly like a dud. Either way, there is no movement, and no work is done. The difference between the two is that untapped potential, on the human level, can be quite painful to bear if it is not eventually released.

Unexpressed potential is tense to the point of immobility, while no potential is just relaxed and content – it has no need to move. The balance point is a condition called *flow,* wherein potential or tension is present, but is allowed to continuously release energy in the direction that the energy wants to move.

One of the ways we express our potential is through comparison. We frequently express our "power" and abilities by being in the presence of those who have less of that particular power or abilities. We feel our "fullness" by comparing ourselves to those who are "empty". Again, this tendency is benign when it is expressed honestly. When we do this, we eventually discover that the tendency to compare ourselves to others is an outer projection of a process that occurs entirely within.

There is an emptiness within, and there is a fullness within. The overt power play stems from the inner fullness that has lost touch with the inner emptiness. The overt power play is the inner fullness exploding outward because it has lost access to the inner emptiness. The covert power play is a caricature of the pure, inner emptiness that has lost touch with the inner fullness, so it tries to quietly siphon power from others.

Through simple recognition, the projection is withdrawn and the flow is established between the inner fullness and the inner emptiness, resulting in a surge of pure power, a realization of potential, a surge of creative expression, which is then shared freely.

The more deeply we contact the emptiness, the more profound the flow of fullness. At its peak, the surge might be experienced as the fullness of orgasmic merging, a moment of sublime communion between the emptiness and fullness within, a profound rapture in which we know who we are and what we are doing.

Yet, this experience does not have to be overwhelming or otherworldly. It occurs in everyday life. It happens every time we give voice to any secret place that feels "empty", whether it is experienced as a quiet acceptance of our humanity, or a painful sense of inadequacy. Regardless of how we experience our inner emptiness, when it is cleanly recognized, fullness rushes in to fill it, resulting in a feeling of aliveness, a surge of pure power that is beyond the perception of having more or less power than anyone else.

CHAPTER 36

Responsibility & Freedom

(Two Necessities for Harmonious Relationship)

Power, addressed in the previous chapter, is abundant when freedom and responsibility are synergistically united. Quite often, however, they are at war with one another. Most of us believe we must sacrifice freedom to fulfill our responsibilities, and vice versa.

On the surface, the relationship between responsibility and freedom does appear to involve the need to cut back on one in order make room for the other.

We might agree in theory that freedom and responsibility are complementary, but as long as we believe we must sacrifice one to accommodate the other, they are not complementing. They are competing or compromising. If we assume that we must give up an important freedom so as to be responsible, we are not really being responsible, we are submitting to something akin to slavery.

Likewise, if we feel we must get rid of our responsibilities in order to have freedom, we really don't understand responsibility. We cannot relinquish anything for which we're truly responsible. When we realize that we are truly responsible for a thing, we embrace it freely.

In other words, if we take on a burden for which we feel genuinely not responsible, we are trapped. If we attempt to disown something for which we are truly responsible, we are trapped. We are free when we know we are fulfilling *our* responsibilities, not someone else's.

It's About Relationship

We can get a deeper understanding of freedom and responsibility by considering relationship. We each have an innate desire for freedom. We have an equally strong desire to be in relationship with the world around us. Relationship with the world around us translates into responsibility.

Responsibility that reflects our own genuine desire for relationship is easy and natural. It is not a burden imposed from without, but a yearning that rises from within. When we really want to be in relationship with someone, we gladly accept the responsibilities that come with it. Therefore, we feel free.

When our relationship with life is to our liking, freedom and responsibility tend to be supportive of one another. It does not matter which side is more visible at any given time. We might be actively engaged in fulfilling our responsibilities or just playing and feeling free. Either way, freedom and responsibility are complementary.

Drawing the Line

In everyday life, freedom translates into determining what is our responsibility and what is not. However, when guilt is present, responsibility becomes twisted into self-blame, or becomes obliterated under a smokescreen of excuses.

When responsibility translates into self-blame, the tendency is toward abuse or neglect of oneself, while assuming excessive responsibility for others. We act under-responsible for ourselves and over-responsible for others. Truly responsible action tends to promote freedom for all concerned.

Responsibility for Others

The desire to care for and nurture others is normal and natural. When it is done freely, it does not imprison the loved ones but sets them free to blossom into themselves. Such responsibility is not a loss of freedom or self-sacrifice. On the contrary, the very act of giving in this manner *is* fulfillment.

However, caring for others can be twisted into *giving to get*. This is a way of living our dreams through our loved ones, pushing them to be the person we secretly want to be. In essence, we are unconsciously saying, "I am going to take care of you so that you will take care of me." This might be as subtle as helping others so we can receive their gratitude and take credit for their success.

Fullness of Freedom

As mentioned earlier, freedom increases with our willingness to be responsible for the details of our lives. Quite often, we do not appreciate our freedom until someone threatens to take it away. We might even unconsciously draw the enslaver or marauder to us, so we can rebel against them and thereby experience freedom. However, as long as we require the presence of an enemy to make us appreciate our freedom, we cannot be totally free. Fullness of freedom is freedom that cannot be taken away. Nor do we need to have our freedom repeatedly challenged so that we can know that we have it.

Pure Responsibility

Total or absolute responsibility means we are personally responsible for every detail of our existence – the body, mind, relationships, professional success and everything else that happens to us. This sounds rather cosmic, but is it real? And, do we really want it? Let us examine this idea more closely.

Accepting total personal responsibility for one's life means two things: no excuses and no self-blaming.

"No excuses" means we are free from the need to defend or justify ourselves when we stray from the path we have set for ourselves. Absolute personal responsibility means we no longer see ourselves as victims of circumstance. We no longer need to excuse ourselves by blaming the weather, the government, the devil, the drug pushers, the school system, society, the greedy boss, the dishonest salesmen, the sins of our parents, the foibles of humanity, the hypercritical clergymen, the power-hungry capitalist, blind chance, or the limitations of time and space.

In other words, every detail of our world is a reflection of what we have consciously or unconsciously called forth. Such removal of *all* excuses can only happen if we also remove all self-blame.

165

Underneath the cover of excuses or self-justification, is a pool of self-blame. Beyond self-blame is the possibility of absolute personal responsibility. Freedom from all self-blame is absolute freedom, which allows for total responsibility.

In Everyday Life

So, how do we move toward that ideal state of synergy between responsibility and freedom? Just by being honest. Truthfulness gradually dissolves self-blame and self-justification. We don't have to force the issue by attempting to surgically remove self-blame or self-justification. Our hidden feelings of self-blame and the need to make excuses tend to quietly dissolve when we simply express them honestly. When we do so, we quietly deepen our capacity for responsibility and expand our personal freedom.

CHAPTER 37

Be Your Brother's Keeper & Mind Your own Business

(Setting the Boundaries of Responsibility)

Shall I be my brother's keeper, or should I mind my own business? If we are clever enough, we can come up with convincing arguments that glorify either one over the other. As with other dualities, elevating one at the expense of the other leads to inner struggle. The side to which we cling becomes shallow or without meaning, while the one that is rejected becomes the silent ruler.

Ultimately, the ability to care for oneself is inseparable from the ability to give respectful support to others. The honest expression of one is inseparable from the honest expression of the other.

The unity of *Be Your Brother's Keeper/Mind Your Own Business* rests on the idea that we are a lot more connected to one another than we think we are. It matters not that the other is perceived as friend, enemy, good, bad, wise, foolish, worthy, or worthless. When we look deeply enough into others, we see ourselves. If we like what we see, the feeling is one of *wholeness*. If we don't like what we see, we are likely to deny that we are looking in a mirror.

In other words, we might feel fear, anger or pain in seeing someone's self-destructive behavior if the other person reminds us of us. This does not mean that we censor our thoughts and feelings. On the contrary, we express them fully. In so doing, we awaken within us the courage and clarity to recognize the source of our inner disturbance.

Likewise, by recognizing oneself in the other, we are better able to express genuine caring toward the other – caring that is not based on a perception of superiority, but rather, is rooted in a gut-level feeling of equality.

Walter's Girl Friend

My friend "Walter" was having a problem with his girlfriend "Janet". On a number of occasions, Walter and I would sit and talk, as he described his latest encounter with "Janet". We discovered two repeating patterns:

- Walter saw that the relationship went well when he was just being honest about his needs and wants, rather than bending over backward to accommodate Janet.

- He got into trouble and lost his perspective when he denied his needs in order to take care of her. In fact, he had the courage to admit that part of his attraction to her was his desire to "heal her" of her emotionally traumatized past. Such behavior is probably a lot more common than we like to think. Our genuine attraction is often intermeshed with the desire to somehow heal or reform the other into our image of "wholeness". It is rare, however, that we encounter an individual like Walter, who is conscious enough to see what he is doing – and courageous enough to be honest about it.

As Walter played out his drama over a period of several months, we were both under the assumption that taking care of himself was "good" and playing the role of Janet's caretaker was "bad" and therefore had to be purged. Several times, he tried to end the relationship on the grounds that it was draining him. However, he kept going back to her, and each time, he found himself tempted to drift into the role of Janet's caretaker.

One day, as Walter and I reviewed his dramatic encounters with Janet, we, once again, discovered that he had the greatest impact on her when he was just minding his own business. His ability to be a caring friend to her was a natural outgrowth of his willingness to just be himself and tend to his own needs honestly. Of course! We both knew that already! Why had he repeatedly forgotten this principle in his relationship with Janet?

The answer is that Walter was unconsciously drawn back to Janet precisely *because* he (and I) had silently judged his desire to help Janet. We had judged it as dysfunctional. Therefore, every attempt to discard his "caretaker" role drove it into the unconscious, where it joined the other hidden forces that drew him back to Janet – over and over again.

So, we came up with a solution. The idea was to stop treating his desire to help Janet as a sickness that had to be purged. Instead, we looked at it as a basically healthy desire that deserved to be recognized and respected. That was when he *really* understood that his ability to take care of himself and his ability to be truly supportive of Janet were one and the same. Shortly after that, his relationship with Janet ended for good.

Compromise

Walter's experience underscores an important concept regarding compromise. Compromise is a form of sacrifice. It is based on the belief that we must give up something of value to get something else of value. In this case, sacrificing oneself to take care of some else or vice versa.

Sacrifice has its rightful place in our lives. However, when we begin to feel the unity beyond opposites, we become aware that it is impossible to lose something that is truly important to us as a means of gaining something else that is truly important. In reality, we give up what we don't need and want, so that we can make room for what we really need and want. The more we contact this deeper reality, the less inclined we are to see life as a compromise.

Caring for oneself is an instinct. Caring for others is also an instinct. These two instincts are, ultimately, the same instinct. If one is sacrificed, both suffer. If I am really minding my own business and doing it properly, I am, simultaneously being my brother's keeper.

CHAPTER 38

Sex

Sex is one step in life's elaborate dance of opposites. Even if there is no sexual intercourse, the inner flow of sexual energy is a dance of opposites. It is a dance between energy that is hot and impulsive and energy that is cool and stable. The two yearn for one another. The hot impulsive energy searches for a home where it can be nested, while the cool stable energy is looking for the spark of life. Like any dance of opposites within a living system, the flow of sexual energy has to create something.

A number of authors have indicated that fear and shame prevent us from knowing the truth of our sexuality. These same authors agree that sexual repression greatly contributes to prostitution, pornography and child molestation, as well as subtler forms of sexual exploitation.

Sexual energy can be the focal point of silent terror and psychosis largely due to our repression of it. Montak Chia, a teacher of Taoist healing techniques, writes, "In my travels, I have noticed that prostitution seems to flourish side-by-side with the most fanatic religious communities..." As an example, he noted that Switzerland had fairly tolerant attitudes toward sexual expression, as compared to the bordering country, Italy, which traditionally controls and censors sexual expression. The incidence of sex crimes, pornography and prostitution is far more prevalent in Italy than in Switzerland. We can also add that, of this writing, Sweden, which has a tradition of sexual openness, has the lowest rate of teen pregnancy of any western nation.

Montak Chia and other authors agree that if we explore sex on its deeper levels – beyond the shame, power games and exploitation – we discover a source of power that goes well beyond biological procreation and "feeling good". Through the ages, many religions and spiritual disciplines have recognized this power, and have tried to control or cultivate it through celibacy or through the intelligent and ethical

170

expression of sexual energy. They all agree on one thing: we cannot fully comprehend sex, nor can we use it wisely without including the spiritual element. Of equal importance is the need to address any emotional issues. If we do not recognize and resolve the murky corners of the mind, they silently rule our expression of sexuality.

The transcendental quality of sex is realized when it is used as a way of knowing oneself, rather than as a weapon for gaining power over others. It can take us to a place that is beyond sexuality and beyond duality. There is a sense of wholeness or "oneness" that can be experienced as a physical sensation, as a thought, as an emotion, and even as a pure awareness that is beyond physical, mental, and emotional. This is the fullness of orgasm.

Fullness of Orgasm

Montak Chia and others state that men can realize the transcendental quality of sex by cultivating their sexual response so that it begins to resemble the female's response. The male response is typically brief and self-limiting, characterized by a rapid excitation, orgasm and ejaculation. The female response is characterized by a slow building of energy, multiple orgasms that increase in intensity, and a retention of fluids – for the most part.

In some systems of sexual cultivation, the man learns to retain the semen and slow himself down to harmonize with the woman's rhythm. There are two obstacles to this. The first is the belief that orgasm is synonymous with ejaculation of semen. In reality, ejaculation is what *terminates* the orgasm. The second obstacle is more subtle. When the man is faced with the task of changing his sexual response to resemble that of the woman, he (perhaps unconsciously) feels like he is losing his masculinity. In truth, he must cultivate and sharpen his masculine will, so as to move beyond his typical self-deflating sexual response.

Fullness of orgasm is possible only when fear, hatred and the desire to control the other person have been honestly addressed. Such an orgasm is easier to achieve within the context of a long term relationship that is rooted in mutual love and respect; a relationship that has gone beyond exploitation, beyond the thrill of pursuit and being pursued, beyond conquest, beyond the barrier of shame.

Within the context of such a sexual relationship, we can experience deeper and deeper levels of connectedness, that eventually lead to the awareness that life is singular. As described by Montak Chia, "The man who cultivates his subtle (sexual) energy, eventually experiences in his body the fact that all living beings are the same life."

One who has experienced the fullness of orgasm recognizes that the same result may be achieved through a lifestyle that is celibate. However, neither sex nor celibacy works in the above-mentioned manner if either one is practiced in a way that denies or rejects the other. Each one, done in fullness, respects and recognizes the value of the other, and then recognizes itself in the other.

If the mind is already at ease, sexual contact can be used to gradually and gracefully discover the bliss that transcends sexuality. The individuals simply do what comes natural. Even when the man is practicing seminal retention, he is doing what comes natural to him; he is developing his masculine will.

If, however, the mind harbors unspoken anger, fear, guilt or shame, the process becomes more complicated. If there is less than perfect peace in the mind, the intentional cultivation of sexual energy requires mindfulness, attention to ethics and personal integrity, and the determination to be true to oneself. In this respect, the sexual path is the same as that of the celibate monk.

Censorship

Those who advocate control and censorship of sexuality seem to be at odds with those who advocate free expression of sexuality. The two sides do appear to be mutually exclusive. Their commonality becomes visible only when we address the human emotions that underlie the two polarities.

The desire to give full and free expression to sexuality comes from the knowing that it is a potent creative force as well as a source of pleasure. The fear that compels us to censor sex is based on the same unconscious knowing. It is a sealed memory that knows the potency of sex. The fear expresses itself as a moral judgment against sexual expression.

We, thus, have two opinions, both of which come from the same knowing. One says, "Sex is a source of great power, let us set it free." While the other says, "It is a source of great power that can destroy us, let us tightly control it!"

Each polarity carries important information. Each remains incomplete as long as it denies the wisdom contained in the other. Those who endeavor to establish laws to censor sexual expression are forever the slaves of sex, simply because we are slaves to anything we fear or suppress. Such individuals are forever battling pornography, prostitution and other forms of sexual exploitation, as well as their own secret desires to experience those very same things. Likewise, individuals who advocate the free and full expression of sexuality cannot do so (and survive) if they minimize or reject the fear that compels us to censor or control it; for this same fear is the echo of a deep memory of the potentially explosive emotional and psychic force of sexual energy.

In other words, one side is advocating freedom and the other is advocating responsibility. Neither option is possible without the other. Therefore, one who earnestly wishes to realize the full potency and of sexual energy will respectfully listen to both the advocates and the critics of sexual expression, recognizing the knowledge contained in both.

Sexual Preference

One of my patients, whom I will call "Chuck", once attended a weekend seminar. Upon his return, he reported that he had sat in a large room with about 250 other men, listening to a slightly overweight man who looked like a truck driver. He was forceful, authoritative and spoke boldly and bluntly about delicate issues concerning men, women and sexuality.

During one segment of the presentation, one of the participants asked about homosexuality. The seminar leader immediately responded with, *"All gay men in the room, stand up, please! "*

About a dozen men stood up. "There is a disease in our society," the seminar leader continued in a loud voice. "It is called homophobia. These men now standing are going to help the rest of you conquer this disease."

Chuck was among the few men standing. That was the first time in his life that he had allowed himself to be publicly recognized. He stood looking at the crowd of heterosexual men staring at him, and he wept.

Chuck's story would have been profound enough even if it had ended right there. Months later, however, to his surprise, he began to get the notion that maybe he liked women after all!

For many individuals, heterosexual and homosexual do not represent a benign distinction between two choices. One side is flatly regarded as good and normal, while the other is regarded as bad and abnormal.

As a young child, I remember engaging in sexual play with other children of my age, irrespective of gender. At that age, it seemed perfectly natural, either way. As I grew older, the child-like sexual play faded away, and girls became increasingly more attractive (and mysterious) to me. This too seemed perfectly natural. However, this normal developmental process was accompanied by indoctrination. We were deeply programmed with the idea that sexual play among same-gendered individuals is perverse and shameful. Not surprisingly, we basically pretended that it never happened. This is, apparently, common among children. The experimenting fades away and is perhaps forgotten. If it isn't forgotten, it is probably not discussed. It remains as a low-grade fear that subtly disturbs the peace of the adolescent mind.

Admittedly, I was perfectly content to pretend the whole thing never happened. However, as a young adult, I found myself interacting in professional and social circles with a significant number of gay men and women. I saw how inwardly tortured some of them were. This, plus my own unintegrated childhood experiences, led me to ask two questions: *Why have they been emotionally alienated from the rest of society? Why is there such a strong taboo against same-gender sexual contact?* I was curious enough to engage in some same-gender sexual experimentation to determine for myself what all the fuss was about. I already had some understanding of how prejudice clouds our ability to reason. I recognized the human tendency to make others conform to our ways. I also recognized the desire to maintain social order and family structure. These factors can certainly create a cultural bias against the gay lifestyle. However, the exaggerated fear and loathing of homosexuality was beyond reason. I was puzzled by it. Eventually, it occurred to me that the function of any taboo is to conceal knowledge.

What Do They Know?

Gay men and women know something. For the most part, however, they don't know that they know it. It is just a vague feeling. With no social sanctioning to explore their gut-level knowing, they usually bury it, and act it out unconsciously through clandestine encounters or romantic relationships that parallel heterosexual relationships.

They may take on the role of rebels fighting against an unjust society, or martyrs suffering at the hands of the ignorant masses. Since they are too busy fighting off the shame projected on them, they do not reveal to themselves what they secretly know: *I am simultaneously both man and woman and beyond man and woman.* This idea is not new. It has been expressed by saints and mystics of many cultures. Gay men and women know it as a visceral feeling that they act out, but rarely understand. They are in a unique position to show us that our deeper identity goes beyond gender roles and sexual preference.

This is not to say that taboos against homosexuality should be rejected as total nonsense. To do so guarantees that the nonsense remains. One of the major objections regarding homosexuality is that it undermines the family. Whether we agree with this or not, there is no question that the integrity of the family is essential for the health and well-being of the individual and of society. Another objection is that the gay lifestyle is just a developmental disturbance, perhaps due to the presence of a weak father or a domineering mother. This might be true for some individuals. If so, the freedom to be as they choose is the ideal way for them to discover (like my patient, "Chuck") that they might prefer the other gender after all. If heterosexuality is normal and natural, it does not have to be enforced by the law.

One thing is fairly clear. The right to do as we choose with our own body is not granted by any government or regulated by any institution. It is simply one of truths that we hold as self-evident.

Adult Sexuality & Child Sexuality

Children are sexual. In fact, they are sexual from birth. It is equally important to point out that child sexuality is different from adult sexuality. Sexuality in the infant is innocent and trusting, whereas adult sexuality carries a lifetime of memories and conflicting feelings. Sexual intrusion by the adult can be devastating to the emotional health of the child. The child experiences confusion and chaos, for an area that was formally pleasurable and safe is now alien and scary due to the presence of adult sexuality, with all of its intensity and contradictions.

There are two ways that adults intrude on the sexual development of the child. Child molesting is the more obvious way. Pedophiles unconsciously act out the strong longing to re-experience the innocence and freedom of childhood, wherein there are no boundaries placed on the senses, and there is no distinction between sexual and non-sexual experiences; there is just life communing freely with life. The other, less obvious, form of intrusion takes the form of overzealous parents who project their own issues on the children.

The parents who are at peace with their own sexuality can allow the child's sexuality to unfold naturally. They are unlikely to consciously or unconsciously use the child to act out their own sexual needs. Nor do they panic if the child innocently expresses sexual curiosity toward the parent.

Repression leads to violation. Violation leads to repression. Unexamined, each side sets the stage for the other, played out from one generation to the next. When recognized, the cycle is ended.

Breaking the cycle translates into taking personal responsibility for one's sexuality. We neither blame our past nor pass on the wounds to the future. For sure, part of that personal responsibility might involve examining our sexual past. If we get still and quiet enough, we might reconnect with the lost sexual innocence of early childhood. We might even remember the beginning of repression or the intrusion of adult sexuality.

Healing

Healing happens when we remember those childhood wounds with the understanding of the adult. When the memories first start to emerge, there might be some anger. It is natural to get angry when we feel violated. When the violation occurs on a very intimate level, the anger is likely to take the form of rage.

A parent might become enraged if his or her child is violated. We might feel the same sort of rage if our own tender and vulnerable places are violated. If that rage is repressed, it is likely to show up as shame. Healing the sexual wounds of the past might involve remembering the forgotten grief, shame and rage that quietly control our everyday behavior.

Techniques for the cultivation of one's sexual energy, taught by Montak Chia and others, are valuable because they offer a way of relating to our own sexuality in a way that is practical, sensible and free of the fear-based programming of our own past. Such techniques recognize sexual energy as a source of power that can be used to heal the body and mind. One tangible benefit of cultivating our sexual energy is that we can use it to help restore sexuality itself to a state of innocence.

CHAPTER 39

Self-Defense

There is certainly nothing wrong with defending oneself. When we speak of being "defensive", however, we are usually referring to the chronic tendency to assume a defensive posture with little provocation. Here are some ways that overt acts of self-defense can be counterproductive:

- Defensiveness often provokes a stronger attack.
- Emotional defensiveness can re-enforce feelings of guilt.
- When we are chronically defensive, we tend to become somewhat blind to ourselves. It is difficult to look deeply within while fighting an enemy. The same shield we use to defend against external attack is likely to shield us from our own deeper truth.

On the other hand, though defensiveness can be harmful to the person doing the defending, *not* defending oneself can be just as harmful, as illustrated by the following story.

I Didn't Do It

One of my patients, whom I will call "Jane", had been advised by a counselor to practice "defenselessness". The rationale was that her need to defend herself against verbal challenge or accusation was giving others power over her. The advice seemed practical and seemed. However, shortly after Jane received that bit of guidance, she had an opportunity to apply it. That's when she discovered there is more than one way of being defensive. She was shopping in her favorite grocery store when she overheard one of the clerks tell the manager that she (Jane) had stolen a piece of halvah and placed it in her purse. It was a mistake. Jane had no idea why the clerk made that assumption. However, since the clerk did not confront her directly, Jane decided not to explain herself – as part of her intention of practicing defenselessness. Consequently, every time she entered the store, she felt as if she was being watched. Furthermore, she felt hostile toward the clerk who had wrongly accused her.

Several months later, when she finally told someone (me) about it, she realized that her attempt to be defenseless translated into withholding her truth, which generated greater defensiveness. She did not eliminate her defensiveness by refraining from speaking out, she simply drove it underground and thereby caused it to intensify.

To Fight or Not to Fight

Jane was caught up between two choices – to confront or not to confront. To be defensive is to be in a confronting or fighting mode. To be defenseless is to be in the surrender mode. As in other dualities, if we cling too tightly to one, we are mysteriously driven to act out the other.

The value of surrender is clear if we understand that it means giving up our pretense that alienates us from others. Such surrender is surrender to the truth as we experience it in the moment.

However, when we generalize the virtue of surrender – we consider it to be inherently superior to confrontation – we fall into a trap. We do not surrender to our truth, we deny it. This plays itself out as the child who withholds expression due to fear of being punished by the parent. The adult version of this is the act of selling one's soul to save one's skin or to gain the acceptance of others, or hiding one's truth in order to control the behavior of others.

How Do I Know I'm Being Attacked?

The attack is obvious if it is physical. The attack is not so obvious if it is verbal or mental. In all forms of attack, however, there is one generality: If we genuinely perceive that we are being attacked, we will tend to respond accordingly.

Attack requires the presence of at least two participants. At any give time, one party is giving the attack and the other is receiving it. Either way, the attack is real to both of them, and so is the defense.

In general, the attacker and attackee interact in one of three ways:

- Neither party is aware of being in the attack mode. This form of attack can show up as mutual back-biting with a smile, or a game of subtle one-upmanship that goes on indefinitely.

- Only one side is aware of battle. This mode can be most infuriating if the one who is aware of the battle happens to be on the "losing" end. This is the situation in which we feel victimized by someone who is convinced that they are being saintly or loving. We feel flustered because we see the other individual unconsciously elevating themselves by using us a foot-stool. On the other hand, if we are on the "winning" end, while being unaware of the battle, we will probably enjoy a mild feeling of euphoria; we quietly knock the other person down in our own minds, as we bask in the perception that we are on a higher spiritual plane.

- Both are aware of being in the fighting mode. This is the preferred way of doing battle, if the goal is to complete the conflict as quickly and cleanly as possible. To be fully aware that we are in the fighting mode opens the door to resolution. We expose mistaken perceptions that were fueling the conflict. In addition, we open the door to deeper truths that underlie the hurt feelings and perception of attack. For example, we are likely to encounter the hidden personal issues that triggered the conflict. We are also likely to contact even deeper feelings that make resolution and friendship possible.

It is conceivable that, during the confrontation, one of the attackers suddenly "wakes up", no longer perceiving an attack, and therefore stops defending. In that moment, the battle is over, for the other individual suddenly feels totally understood and respected. This is rare. If one of them really *is* significantly more peaceful in disposition, the confrontation probably never would have happened to begin with. The more likely scenario is that the two parties are "symmetrical" in their consciousness. If they "evolve" from conflict to friendship, they tend to do so organically, as equals. The lingering perception of superiority and inferiorly prolongs the conflict. The perception of equality expedites the evolution into friendship.

When Should I Defend Myself?

When should we defend ourselves? If we look to others for an answer to this question, we are immediately in trouble. If we listen to someone else's call to war, we will be fighting *their* battle, not ours. If we blindly follow someone else's choice to practice defenselessness, we are leaving our own house unprotected to march in their peace parade. Either way, we deny our own truth and our own needs. If we do this habitually, the accumulated denials add up into a deep pool of hostility, resentment and other repressed emotions. Repression leads to violence, whether we repress the instinct to fight or the instinct to hold our peace.

When we make a daily practice of listening to our own instinct—to fight or not fight – we open the door to the deeper feeling place where we feel our connection with the other individual. In other words, the more we connect with self, the more we connect with others. We might experience such connection as a sense of kinship or relatedness. More commonly, the feeling quietly rises to the surface of the mind as conscience, empathy or the inclination to avoid harming the other party.

CHAPTER 40

War & Peace

According to Zen teachings, if we wish to achieve anything, we must have an understanding of its opposite. If our social and political goal is *really* peace, we must have an understanding of war. We do not have to go to war to get that understanding. If we, however, fail to cultivate such understanding, we will go to war to get it.

Understanding War

War consciousness can be understood on several levels:

- On the surface, war consciousness is about survival. It says, "You have something I *must* have, and war is the only way I can get it."
- On other levels, war consciousness says, "I want to join with you, but I'm also afraid of you, so I will conquer you."
- On a still deeper level, when two parties are at war, they are acting out the predicament of the traumatized newborn baby described by Dr. Robert Leboyer, "Don't touch me, please don't leave me."
- War allows us to bring forth qualities and abilities that we did not allow ourselves to develop during peacetime. When our survival is at stake, we tend to forget minor inconveniences and petty arguments. We become single minded, resourceful and efficient.
- On the personal level, violence results from the repression of our vitality. Our vitality typically takes form as playfulness, spontaneous self-expression, creativity and our deepest dreams and aspirations. When vitality is repressed, it accumulates like steam in a pressure cooker. When we repress vitality on a personal level, we eventually do harm to

ourselves and others. When repression of vitality occurs on a larger social level, the result is social conflict and war. In one sense, warfare is one way of collectively "letting off steam".

Understanding Peace

The desire for peace is about relationship. If the desire for peace and friendship is genuine, it stems from the place within us that says, "I know you, I want to be in relationship with you." We tap into this place through the daily practice of truthfulness. Truth leads to peace. Truth hidden under the facade of peace explodes into war.

Does peace consciousness ultimately conquer war consciousness? From the perspective of war consciousness, yes, it does (and war consciousness is deeply grateful for being thus conquered). From the perspective of peace-consciousness, there is no conquest; there is simply the desire to be in relationship with ones friend. In other words, the power to focus, forged during war, is allowed to come home. It is honored. Its wounds are healed. It is allowed to do what it deeply yearns to do – build the foundation for peace.

Allies & Enemies

The enemies are those from whom we try to steal power, or those who can steal power from us. The allies are those whom we enroll to defeat the enemy. Since the bottom line is survival, today's ally can become tomorrow's enemy, and vice versa. When war consciousness encounters a new face, it asks the question, "Is this an enemy, or is this an ally who can help me against my enemies?"

If we are at war, we are in survival mode. Therefore, real loyalty and affection are luxuries we can't afford. While the battle is in progress, life is reduced to kill or be killed, which means those around us are allies or enemies. Though war can forge the beginning of friendship, we must wait for the battle to end before allies and enemies can become real friends.

We Have It Because We Want It

The outer reality for most of us is a desire for peace and fear of war. The inner reality is often reversed. We secretly desire war and fear peace.

As long as the inner reality remains unrecognized, it continues to silently rule. This is one reason that war and social conflict in general seem to reappear regardless of how much we consciously try to stamp them out.

When we no longer condemn war, we begin to understand it. We begin to see our hidden desire for war. We understand why we desire it, and why we have been terrified of peace. We realize that we desire war because we emotionally equate it with purpose, movement and vitality. We are afraid of peace because we equate it with stagnation. Secretly, most of us regard peace as boring. Underneath the boredom is intense fear of oblivion and death.

Midway

Historically, some war movies have glorified war while others have condemned it. Then came *Midway*. On the surface, *Midway* looks like other war movies. It combines thrilling battle scenes with menacingly beautiful warplanes and battleships, interwoven with captivating human drama. However, this particular war movie had another source of appeal unique among other World War II movies.

In the movie, the Japanese military personnel are portrayed as sailors and airmen with names, faces and families. We get to know them personally. Their fears, doubts and pain were the same as their American counterparts. Their highest-ranking naval officer, Admiral Yamamoto, is first seen sitting in a peaceful garden. He has a contemplative, sage-like countenance. His words and mannerisms reveal a man of honor and conscience who sees the war beyond the perspective of winning and losing.

The human drama in the movie includes a relationship between an American pilot and his fiancée, a Japanese-American young lady living in Hawaii. We also meet her parents, an elderly couple being held in a detention camp.

One scene depicts a Japanese reconnaissance plane that is eventually shot down by two American fighters. This scene is preceded by a series of other scenes in which we look inside the cockpit of the same Japanese plane and get to know the young men flying it. As the plane is discovered by American radar, we find ourselves wanting the Japanese plane to escape. When two American planes begin shooting at the Japanese plane, it is already crippled, low on fuel and unarmed. As the plane starts descending toward the water trailing smoke, its young occupants wounded and still under heavy fire, the viewer is silently saying, "Stop shooting, for God's sake!" When the plane finally hits the water, it explodes and we see a mushroom cloud rising from the point of impact, reminding us of Hiroshima and Nagasaki.

In previous war movies, the same basic plot and the same action-packed scenes were used to create nationalism and hatred of the enemy, who were depicted as nameless, faceless bad guys.

That movie probably would not have been well received if it had come out shortly after World War II, for that time was still a season of war. The success of the move had to do, at least, partially with the fact that it came out during a season of peace.

The Season of Peace

The season of peace begins when the forces of war reach their peak and have been fully recognized and understood. The season of peace is the time that we look deeply inside ourselves. It is impossible to harm another while looking within. We cannot even harshly judge anyone while looking deeply within.

To go to war, we must first put armor around our feeling nature, shut off conscience and suspend empathy, so that we do not suffer the death of our neighbor. We might even say that the temptation to harm another is the temptation to forget oneself.

There is nothing sentimental or wishy-washy about looking within. To do so consistently takes courage, a will of iron, tenacity, resourcefulness and the willingness to be direct and honest with oneself and others. These skills are aimed against any weakness that would attempt us to live parasitically on others; the weaknesses that would cause us to turn away from the royal feast of freedom and friendship,

185

so as to feed on the crumbs stolen from the table of another. Vigilance against such weakness opens the door to the experience of pure power, generated from within.

Looking deeply within allows us to see ourselves clearly and, therefore, to see ourselves in others. This is the man of war, turning his weapons into tools of self-knowledge, thus ushering in the season of peace.

CHAPTER 41

The Serpent & the Dove

(The Secret of Harmlessness)

In Matthew 10:16 of the Bible, the disciples are advised by Jesus to *"...be wise like the serpent and harmless like the dove.* A close look at these two virtues reveals that wisdom and harmlessness are not merely compatible, they are inseparable. The wise serpent and harmless dove can exist only in the presence of one another. Wisdom that is not harmless is not really wisdom, for it ultimately self-destructs. Likewise, true harmlessness can exist only in the presence of wisdom. A wise old sage with a loaded gun is harmless. A small child with a loaded gun is not harmless.

Wisdom and harmlessness are not merely compatible, they are inseparable. The wise serpent and harmless dove can exist only in the presence of one another. Wisdom that is not harmless is not really wisdom, for it ultimately self-destructs. Likewise, true harmlessness can only exist in the presence of wisdom. A wise old sage with a loaded gun is harmless. A small child with a loaded gun is not harmless.

Harmlessness is possible only when our personal vitality is allowed to express itself. When we repress our vitality, we do harm to ourselves and others, consciously or unconsciously. When our vitality flows freely and naturally, it does not harm, it heals. It does not steal life, it enriches life. In the presence of true wisdom, vitality flows freely; expressing itself as life, liberty and the pursuit of happiness.

Don't Tread On Me

In the early years of America, some of the colonies and colonial organizations adopted a flag design that included a picture of a rattlesnake. Below the rattlesnake was a caption that read, *Don't tread on me.* The image of the rattlesnake symbolizes a deadly force that will not attack you if you just give it space and leave it alone. In essence, those spunky colonists were saying, "If you are harmless, I am harmless. If you are not harmless, neither will I be harmless."

In the presence of true harmlessness, potentially lethal power becomes wisdom. The fighter becomes the builder. However, if the dove isn't really a dove (not really harmless), the wisdom of the snake will see through the disguise, and turn its wisdom into a weapon.

In everyday life, the wise snake is always accompanied by the harmless dove. They are the power to change and the serenity to let things be. Likewise, the false dove is but the mirror image of the foolish rattlesnake that does not see the power it possesses. This is when we fancy ourselves to be peaceful and upright, blind to the harm that we do.

The Snake as the Healer

From times of antiquity the snake has been used to symbolize the healer. In the hands of the healer, the snake's wisdom takes form as techniques and tools to relieve suffering and bring balance and integration to the body and mind. In applying its wisdom to the healing arts, the snake's central guiding principle is, "Do no harm." Here again, we see the close relationship of wisdom and harmlessness. In fact, we might say that we cannot help but heal, the moment we make the choice to use our knowledge harmlessly.

Restoring wholeness to the body and mind is intrinsically important, but it doesn't stop there. There seems to be a recognition in the healings arts that the body and mind are on a journey, of sorts. The official logo of the medical profession consists of two intertwining snakes. Their vertical orientation and spiraling configuration suggest an evolutionary process.

Evolution

When wisdom and harmlessness are united in the mind, they dance together in an upward spiral of evolution. Each one is nourished by the other. The fruit of wisdom is harmlessness, and sustained harmlessness evolves into even greater wisdom, and so on. Eventually, transcendence occurs. The spunkiness that says, *Don't tread on me*, becomes the realization that says, *It is impossible for anyone to tread on me.* The personal conviction that says, *I must do no harm,* becomes the realization that says, *It is impossible for me to do harm.* From the perspective of the individual who is utterly harmless, defense of any kind is superfluous because attack has no meaning.

Free Will and Harmlessness

True harmlessness cannot be imposed. Harmlessness is a choice. It evolves from a free will that has asserted its legitimate boundaries. It unfolds naturally when the will is allowed to say, "Don't tread on me."

When the will is free to defend itself, harmlessness must follow. Wisdom, by its very nature, wants to realize its potential for harmlessness on deeper and deeper levels. The journey starts when we choose to refrain from harming those who do not harm us, and grows into an ever-increasing tendency to hold one's peace, even when provoked. It culminates with the realization that any attack has no meaning, and that harmlessness simply *is.*

For us humans, the desire to actualize harmlessness is an in-born drive. If we regard it as an expression of "goodness", we must recognize that it as an inborn goodness that exists in everyone. We can no more take credit for it than we can take credit for our capacity to experience hunger, thirst or lust. The instinct for harmlessness might be so deeply buried, that it is totally unconscious, but it cannot long be denied. If it is chronically repressed, it silently gains power in the darkness and stillness of the subconscious mind. Eventually, it becomes stronger than the instinct for physical survival. We might incapacitate ourselves so that we can know our harmlessness. We might even create the experience of death (of the body or the ego), if that is the only way that we can approximate harmlessness. For the evolving self-aware human, the will to live and harmlessness are inseparable.

CHAPTER 42

Separateness & Unity

(The First Step in the Cosmic Dance)

Creation is, among other things, a dance of separateness and oneness. We can see this dance on a number of levels. We see it in our personal relationships, in the workings of the body, in the ecological dance of life around us, and even in the cosmic dance of creation as a whole.

The Cosmic Dance

The first step in the cosmic dance of creation is the separation of primordial unity into polar opposites. The second step is that the primordial opposites rejoin to create diversity.

If the primordial opposites make love, creation bursts forth abundantly, and life flourishes. If the primordial opposites make war, they annihilate one another – like the collision of matter and antimatter – and creation stops right there. If the joining is a combination of love and war, creation happens, but there is some degree of conflict.

As we ponder this cosmic dance, we might ask, what is it that allows opposites to interact harmoniously? The answer is that opposites interact harmoniously because each carries a "memory" of the primordial unity from which they sprang. That memory translates into an affinity for each other. They fit together. To the extent that opposites "remember" unity, they make love and thus create life.

The Human Dance

On the human level, the remembrance of unity is what allows us to form harmonious relationships. However, it is important to emphasize that if our goal is to increase our remembrance of unity, progress is delayed if we try to rush it. We must bear in mind that separation is an important part of creation. This is true whether we are speaking of creation in the cosmic sense or our everyday acts of creation.

Denying our humanity (which includes separateness) in order to attain our divinity (oneness) causes us to get tangled in our humanity. If we want to really expedite the realization of oneness, we can do so by allowing it to emerge organically, here and now, in the world of separateness. Unity is experienced in everyday life as an appreciation of diversity.

Another way to invite the silent awareness unity is by recognizing the ways that separateness serves us. We express separateness in a number of ways, such as in the setting of personal boundaries, exercising discernment, making choices, expressing our individuality, stating our terms, and claiming our territory.

We should also bear in mind that the experience of unity isn't necessarily a high, exalted state of peace and compassion. In everyday life, the subconscious echo of unity can reverberate through a mind that is congested with unresolved emotional issues. It can show up as lack of respect for boundaries and property. It can show up as the irrational tendency to hurt someone (anyone) in response to one's own pain. The injured party seems to be saying, "I have been hurt by life, so now I will hurt life back." It doesn't matter who we punish because, instinctively, we know there is just one life. In such a situation, the setting of clear and rational boundaries (respecting our separateness) makes more sense than acting out our twisted experience of the unity.

My Thoughts, Your Thoughts

In everyday life, the remembrance of unity can also show up as the ominous feeling that the distinction between one's own thoughts and the thoughts of the other person are not as clear-cut as we might think. We might be sitting quietly next to someone, when suddenly we start thinking about frogs for no reason at all, or we feel resentful toward "George", even though, a moment earlier we were totally at peace with George. Are these "my" thoughts and emotions, or are they the thoughts and emotions of the person sitting quietly close by? There are two ways of approaching this question. One way is to be a true scientist: Don't assume anything! Look the other person in the eyes and honestly reveal who was thinking what and when. The other method is to communicate with no one and just go more deeply into stillness and silence. This method, admittedly, may not help us to distinguish between "my thoughts and your thoughts", but it can possibly render the question meaningless.

The Dance Within Us and Around Us

The life within the body is a dance of separateness and oneness. The heart is anatomically separate from the lungs, but the two cannot exist apart from each other. The teeth are hard and the lips are soft, because one carries a vast deposit of calcium and the other does not. During the aging process or degeneration, things appear to become more "uniform". A scientist would say that during the aging process, "entropy" is setting in. The skin becomes tougher and bones become weaker. The teeth and bones become soft and the arteries become hard as calcium leaks out of the hard places and settles into the soft places.

Youthful vigor includes the ability to keep things "separate" within the body. There is a separation of fluids and a separation of electrical charges. This is how we keep the inner battery fully charged. Our cells, tissues and organs each maintain their own internal environment. Each maintains its own separate identity, while blending and harmonizing their respective activities into a functional wholeness or oneness.

The body as a whole has the ability to separate substances that it needs from the substances it doesn't need. The useful substances are retained and the potentially toxic waste products are eliminated. The digestive system, for example, separates nutrients from waste products. The liver and kidneys do the same on a more refined level. Without the ability to properly separate things, the body quickly ages and degenerates.

This process of separating the "pure" from the "impure" occurs within the bigger dance of ecological unity. The same substances that we excrete as poisons serve to nourish other living things, which, in turn, leads to the production of food and breathable oxygen for us.

On the mental and emotional levels, we, as individuals, are exposed to many ideas and experiences. Some are useful for us, some are not, and some are more useful than others. We separate them as such. One level of separation occurs through making conscious choices. We choose the ideas and beliefs that appeal to us, and let go of the rest. A deeper level of separation occurs silently, without conscious effort. As an analogy, we might choose to eat an apple instead of an orange because we notice that apples make us feel good while oranges give us gas. Once we eat the apple, the body's own wisdom extracts what it needs and gets rid of the rest. We do not have to tell the body which parts of the apple to accept and which to excrete. On the consciousness level, the process is essentially the same. For example, we might think that we have totally rejected a given idea or experience, but the subconscious mind is quietly digesting it, absorbing and integrating what is needed, while letting go of what is not needed.

The more we exercise our own ability to separate what we need from what we don't need, the more we cultivate the serenity to allow others to do the same. This is not the pseudo-serenity of assumed superiority, wherein we bask in the perception of our own enlightenment as we graciously allow others to "grope in darkness". Our serenity is simply the understanding that what is food for us might be poison for another, and vice versa. It is the understanding that a principle that serves as a guiding light for us might be inappropriate for our neighbor or loved one. It is the understanding that each individual must digest and assimilate a given idea or experience in his or her own way. This is how separateness and oneness can dance the dance of life on the interpersonal and social levels.

The next five chapters address some everyday expressions of separateness and unity. They are *Dependent & Independent, Uniqueness & Sameness, Equality & Inequality, Rebel & Conformist, Revenge & Forgiveness.*

CHAPTER 43

Dependent & Independent

At any given moment, the average adult is independent, self-sustaining and sovereign unto himself or herself. At the same time, each person is physically and emotionally dependent on friends, family, factories, farms, the grocery store, the telephone company, the post office, garbage collectors, oil companies, etc.

The employer is dependent on the employee, the patient is dependent on the doctor, the student is dependent on the teacher, the salesperson is dependent on the customer, and vice versa for all of these. Our autonomy co-exists with our dependence on one another. I create my reality, and my reality creates me.

Beyond Compromise

The co-existence of dependence and independence is not merely a compromise. Each side is experienced in fullness only when the other is also present. When we are in the *illusion* of dependence or independence, the two appear to be at odds with each other. When we feel the *reality* of dependence and independence, we experience the two as partners in the dance of creation.

There are two ways of seeing the synergistic relationship between dependence and independence:

- My independence becomes real when I recognize my close relationship with the world around me.
- I am able to establish my close relationship with the world around me, when I become aware of my independence.

No matter which side we prefer, the other must be silently present.

Individual & Community

A community is formed when a group of individuals come together and stay together long enough for each member to bring the wholeness of their respective individuality into the community. If the individuals withhold or sacrifice any part of themselves so as not to disrupt the community, the community breaks down. We have instead a mutual tolerance of our secret fears and hostility. This is when we feel isolated or alienated even though we live in close proximity to others.

The belief that individuality must be sacrificed for the sake of community stems from a poorly developed sense of individuality. On the larger social level, the sacrifice of individuality in favor of community translates into a repressive society that can insidiously move in the direction of slavery. Each member becomes a cog whose sole purpose is to keep the machine going. Likewise, to assert one's individuality in a manner that ignores the well-being of the community, is to be a miser at best and a pirate at worst.

Either way, community breaks down. A strong and stable community (of individuals or of nations) requires free and sovereign members, for only they have the vitality and integrity to form a thriving community.

Down on the Farm

I was once given the opportunity to enter into a cooperative venture with several friends to purchase a farm. This was what I had been envisioning for myself. It looked like my heart's desire was being handed to me. After the initial excitement, however, I became progressively more fearful and doubtful. I eventually decided not to join them. At first I was not sure why. Then, I realized the fear was in response to a childhood pattern. When I was a young child, my father was a farmer in Sicily. As the youngest of seven children, I was not expected to do anything or be in charge of anything. I just went along with whatever the big people did.

When I first decided to join the collective venture, I began experiencing echoes of those early childhood years. I silently panicked. I feared that I would lose my individuality if I became part of that community. I felt I would adopt the visions and attitudes of the other members and lose myself.

Having recognized that truth, a deeper one became visible. The fear of losing my individuality was really the fear of exposing my poorly developed individuality. If I entered into a closely-knit community (or marriage for that matter) I would have to face those murky inner places where I did not have a solid sense of myself as an individual.

Common sense told me that developing healthy individuality involved recognition of those hidden places inside me where my individuality felt shaky. Fine, I did that, but it didn't stop there.

Noah's-Arc Neurosis

Not surprisingly, the recognition of my fear unearthed yet another fear. I was afraid that, if I *didn't* take advantage of the opportunity, I would be "left behind". It was as if this group was my family. I secretly feared that I would miss the boat and perish if I did not follow them. (As a child, I came to America on a ship with my family. "Missing the boat" had special significance for me). I was experiencing, as an adult, the emotions of a small child who thinks his family is about to leave without him.

As I recognized my own fragility, the fog slowly lifted and I began to see the situation more clearly: "Oh, yes, I'm an adult. I have my own business and I am self-sustaining. I don't need their approval and support to survive; these folks are not my benefactors, they are my equals. If I do not put down my roots here, I will do so elsewhere."

This declaration of independence might be self-evident to an adult, but not to a five-year-old; and that's who was silently influencing my decisions. By allowing the child to fully express his feelings of fragility and dependence, we set the stage for the emergence of independence.

CHAPTER 44

Uniqueness & Sameness

(Two Side of Personal Identity)

Separateness, on the everyday human level, includes a sense of uniqueness. Unity, on the everyday human level, includes the experience of sameness.

Uniqueness and sameness are complementary. When we feel our sameness or commonality, we tend to respect our individual differences. When we fully accept our personal uniqueness, we naturally get in touch with our sameness.

To the mind that is torn by inner conflict, the expression of uniqueness translates into fear and shame about not being good enough, while the expression of our sameness translates into the terror of oblivion. When the inner conflict is resolved, expression of uniqueness is perceived as the joy of freedom, and the realization of our sameness is experienced as the joy of relationship.

Uniqueness

To experience our uniqueness is vitally important to our well-being. The full expression of our uniqueness sets free our natural creativity. We paint a picture of the genuine self on the canvas of life. It does not matter whether the outcome is the creation of a symphony or a loaf of bread; when we express the uniqueness of the genuine self, there is no sense of superiority or inferiority, no feeling of inadequacy.

When we recognize our individual uniqueness, we seem to plug into our own personal source of power and self-esteem. Suddenly, there is no concern about being as good as someone else. We no longer fret about being overpowered or out-performed. Such fears and concerns result from failure to express our uniqueness.

When we are galvanized by the expression of our uniqueness, we establish a proper relationship with the rest of life. This is when cynicism gives way to a quiet feeling of optimism, alienation gives way to kinship, and arrogance gives way to compassion. Such compassion is not pity for the "ignorant masses". It is not patronizing tolerance of the "wayward human children". It is the echo of our primordial oneness, reaching across the sea of sameness, to touch the shores of the conscious mind as simple caring.

Sameness

The experience of our sameness is food for the soul. Without it, we slowly deteriorate mentally, emotionally and physically, as we struggle to figure out, "what's wrong, why do I feel so empty and alone."

For most of us, however, this soul food is not very palatable in its raw form. It packs too much energy and might cause emotional indigestion in the form of "edginess", anxiety or even psychosis. The remembrance of our sameness must first be cooked and mellowed for consumption. We savor this soul food as love of life and the will to live.

As more and more of our fears are resolved, we are able to tolerate larger and larger doses of our soul food in its rawness. Eventually, we can look into the eyes of another with full awareness of our sameness – without going crazy.

Concealing Our Uniqueness

In everyday life, we conceal our uniqueness by copying what others do, or conforming to the collective consciousness. This is not intrinsically good or bad. If we do it out of fear and self-hatred, we are likely to harm ourselves. However, we can also do it from the genuine desire to interact respectfully with those who appear different. If we move to a different country, we learn their language, rather than expecting them to learn our language. When in Rome, we do as the Romans do, because it is respectful and fun to do so. We put our differences aside for a while so that we can commune in sameness. This comes naturally when we have a healthy respect for our own uniqueness.

Concealing Our Sameness

As long as we live in duality, we must, to a certain extent, conceal our sameness. In the grand scheme of things, we do this to facilitate the development of our individuality or uniqueness.

On a more day-to-day level, our reasons for concealing sameness might be less sublime. For example, if we have a vested interest in remaining angry with someone, we will tend to avoid looking at our sameness. As mentioned earlier, anger and blaming are essentially the same. By concealing their sameness, however, we can justify our upset feelings as healthy expressions or legitimate anger, while labeling the similar behavior in someone else as "blaming" or "playing the victim". This is one way that we establish a separation and a sense of moral superiority.

On a more positive note, concealing our sameness allows us to break away from something that we view as corrupt, oppressive or simply not appropriate for us. For example, late one night, I was reading a passage in a book in which the author was sharing a certain philosophy for healthy living. Part of her philosophy was, "We do not love our enemies." This statement was followed by a beautiful description of how to intelligently and respectfully relate to those who are hostile toward us. In so doing, she spelled out *how to* love our enemies.

In other words, the author separated herself from the philosophies that say, "Love your enemies," and thus established her uniqueness. She gave herself permission not to follow that doctrine, and instead, allowed her own truth to well up from within. As a result, she came full circle and discovered within herself the very thing she had rejected, and turned it into a practical reality within the context of her teaching.

CHAPTER 45

Equality

(It's a Feeling Before it's Anything Else)

In everyday life, the desire to experience our sameness shows up as the desire for equality. The desire to have a basic sense of equality with the people around us is as real and as compelling as the desire to drink water when we are thirsty and eat when we are hungry. When that desire is not fulfilled, an alarm goes off. We might experience it as anger, emotional pain or a vague sense of uneasiness.

If the pain or uneasiness is not resolved, it remains as a steady irritant that does not allow us to rest, like a dripping faucet in the middle of the night. The more we try to ignore it, the louder it gets.

Ultimately, it makes no difference whether we perceive ourselves as superior or inferior. It makes no difference whether we perceive ourselves as being the wrong doers or the victims of wrongdoing. The prolonged absence of that basic sense of equality with those around us can drive us insane. Typically, however, we survive the quiet torment through various mechanisms, from rationalization to drugs; all of which have the same purpose – to numb our capacity to feel.

If we wish to cultivate a healthy sense of equality, we must have an understanding of inequality. Each finds its proper place when it is allowed to come into natural harmony with the other.

Equality and Inequality

The strong emotional charge of equality and inequality is based on the deeper desire to know both our sameness and our uniqueness (previous chapter). On still deeper levels, the charge stems from the desire to experience both our unity and our separateness

To be obsessed with equality is to be ruled by the unfulfilled desire to know our sameness or unity. To be obsessed with inequality (superior or inferior) is to be ruled by the unfulfilled desire to know our uniqueness – our identity as individuals. As with other opposites, obsession with one side results in a distorted view of the other.

The emotional charge associated with equality might be well hidden, but is still present. We see this on the interpersonal, as well as the larger social levels. If we feel a need to experience our sameness, we will have an emotional bias toward equality. Therefore, we might equate equality with justice and fairness. We would tend to deny differences and pretend that we see everyone as the same.

If we feel the need to experience our uniqueness, we will have an emotional bias toward inequality. Therefore, we might emphasize selected differences to establish a basis for overall superiority and inferiority. We certainly see this in politics. We see it on a deeper and more emotional level in religion.

Equality and Science

We can get an objective understanding of equality and inequality by using these two words in a strictly scientific manner, which is to say, free from the bias that one is good and the other is bad. To the scientist, the words *equal* and *unequal* are simply numerical expressions; they refer to specific observable features, such as height, weight, pressure, volume or density.

When using the word *equal* as a numerical expression, the scientist carefully qualifies the observation by saying something like, "These two samples have equal weight, with a possible variation of two micrograms." The scientist knows that if two objects are separate, they cannot be absolutely equal; their respective height, weight, etc. will have some degree of difference. However, the variation may be negligibly small, therefore, the scientist might say, "For our present purpose, the two samples are virtually equal."

Rudy Scarfalloto

Equality and Justice

The social usage of the word *equality* is much fuzzier compared to the scientific usage. In the social setting, equality is considered synonymous with fairness and justice. For example, in any occupation in which the male and the female have the same level of productivity, fairness dictates that they have equal pay and status. In such a situation, fairness obviously translates into equality.

Fairness and equality, however, are not necessarily the same. We would not expect a small pregnant woman to perform equally in heavy physical work as a big muscular man. Fairness, in this case, translates into special consideration we give the small pregnant woman.

Doing and Being Revisited

The perception that inequality automatically translates into better or worse stems from lack of balance with another duality, *Being* and *Doing*. Being is about feeling who we are, or experiencing our essence. Doing is about our actions.

When we deeply contact our *being*, there is a sense of sameness or equality with those around us. The more we lose touch with our being, the more we cling to the things we do. We become overly dependent on "doing" as a way of getting a sense of identity. We become preoccupied with appearance and performance. This is when inequality becomes synonymous with better or worse, superior or inferior.

The more we set free our own feeling nature, the more we make contact with our beingness or essence. The more deeply we contact our essence, the more we tend to relate to inequality as a scientist would – quantitatively instead of qualitatively.

By thus getting in touch with our beingness, equality and inequality can interact harmoniously and fulfill their function – *creation*. In this respect, equality/inequality serves the same function as any pair of opposites. The interaction of inequalities in people, groups, nations, etc. establishes the driving force to set creative energy in motion. Likewise, the silent recognition (the *feeling*) of equality allows us to look upon our creation and declare, *It is good!*

CHAPTER 46

Rebellion & Conformity

(Uniqueness and Sameness Get Serious)

Rebellion is one way of asserting our uniqueness. Conformity is one way of expressing our desire for sameness.

It is normal and healthy to rebel against oppression. It is equally normal and healthy to desire some degree of conformity so we can have community. Such conformity is not a denial of free will. It is the result of a free will that has been allowed to shape itself in accordance with the impulses rising from within. Such conformity arises organically from the collective desires and aspirations of the individuals who choose to live together.

When we are fully in touch with our uniqueness, we have no strong compulsion to rebel. Likewise, if we are fully in touch with our sameness, we do not need to enforce conformity. There is a silent sense of commonality that makes forced conformity unnecessary. Uniqueness is then free to dance with uniqueness, thus realizing the ecstasy of merging into sameness. And, sameness can spontaneously give birth to diversity.

Even when we are not fully in touch with our uniqueness and sameness, the desire for rebellion and conformity that arise can still interact somewhat peacefully and in ways that energize and enliven each other. We can write poetry because the ink and the paper are of different colors and because the two have a strong affinity for each other. Each side is free to give voice to its conviction through lively debate or passionate expression of personal truth. This is possible when the knowing of our uniqueness/sameness, though submerged, still echoes to the surface as the principle that says, "I strongly disagree with your opinion, but I respect your right to voice it. I don't like your lifestyle, but I would be even more displeased if you were persecuted for it."

When we have really lost touch with our uniqueness and sameness, rebellion and conformity start to get ugly. Nonetheless, each side still needs the other. Each can be sustained only by feeding on the other. The fanatical rebel needs a platform of enforced conformity in order to propel the rebellion. Without enforced conformity, rebellion quietly melts into the sea of sameness, which is scary if we are not in touch with our uniqueness. Therefore, if there is no evil oppressor to rebel against, the rebel is likely to create one.

Likewise, the fanatical conformist needs rebellion to stimulate reactionary fervor and thereby strengthen the walls of conformity. Without rebellion, conformity relaxes into a spontaneous stroll down the garden path of diversity, which is scary if we have lost touch with our sameness. Therefore, those who are interested in maintaining strict regimentation, will, perhaps unconsciously, create rebels and "dangerous elements" to burn in the town square.

If each side is motivated by a sincere belief in their respective cause, and not merely looking for *any* enemy to fight against, they will pay close attention to the hidden dynamics of rebel/conformist. Typically, conformists do not realize that squelching the rebellion causes the rebel to come back stronger. Likewise, the rebellion is complete and totally successful only if the rebels recognize themselves within those they fight against. If this does not happen, the rebels will eventually act out the same form of oppression they were rebelling against. This is how today's rebels become tomorrow's reactionaries. In the midst of the conflict, the qualities that the rebels fight against will surface in the rebel. The longer the fight persists, the more we become like the enemy.

Two In One

The rebel and conformist must exist together, not just in a given society but within the same person. To rebel against something, we must conform to something else. The rebel without a cause has no meaning. A rebel, by definition, must have a cause, even if the cause is not overtly stated, but merely implied. If we overtly rebel against a certain idea, we are covertly promoting conformity to a different idea. The reverse is also true. When we openly support a given form of conformity, we are, more than likely, secretly rebelling against something else. Therefore, if we consider ourselves as rebels, we must ask ourselves, "In rebelling against this thing, what am I conforming to?" If we advocate conformity, we must ask, "In actively conforming with this thing, am I rejecting something else?"

The Emotional Factor

Though it is possible to rebel or conform in a dispassionate manner, emotional involvement is typically present. The primary emotion in rebellion is anger. The primary emotion in conformity is fear. We frequently conform because we are afraid – until we finally get angry, and then we rebel.

When we want to make people rebel, we try to make them angry. To make them conform, we try to make them afraid. Rebellion is often started by provoking feelings of justifiable anger or righteous indignation. Likewise, the usual forms of mass conformity tend to play on fear.

It might be argued that both rebellion and conformity each have elements of fear and anger. This is true, especially if we remember that rebellion generally has a hidden element of conformity, and vice versa. However, in any given situation where the emotional options are rebellion or conformity, we are generally motivated to rebel through anger, and to conform through fear. Therefore, if we wish to understand why we feel rebellious in a given situation, we simply ask, "What am I angry about here?" If we feel an urge to conform for no rational reason and would prefer not to, we ask, "What am I afraid of here?"

By being aware of our own emotions, we can make choices more effectively. We can question our motives. Are we rebelling against a lie or are we rebelling against the truth? Are we conforming to justice, or are we conforming to exploitation?

We like to believe that we are rebelling against a lie and conforming to the truth. To hold this belief gives us purpose and sense of righteousness.

The Making of a Rebel

I once had a dream that illustrated my own hidden motives for rebellion. The dream had two parts to it. In the first part, I was attempting to have sexual contact with my mother. Upon awakening, I was not shocked or embarrassed by this because I knew that young children and babies have their own version of sexuality that is often directed at mother. Though I had no conscious memories of such feelings, I knew that dreams could bring to the surface the forgotten experiences and feelings of early childhood and infancy. Furthermore, I was, at the time, living with several housemates who encouraged the free discussion of such things. We were at liberty to stagger into the kitchen at seven a.m. and say, "I woke up from a dream in which I had sex with my dog", and the listeners would just sit quietly, sipping their coffee and buttering their toast, making casual comments as if we were discussing which laundry detergent to buy.

In the second part of the dream, I was rebelling against social injustice. There was no obvious connection between the two parts. Their close proximity seemed to be sheer coincidence. However, many volumes written about the workings of the mind agree that the subconscious mind is irritatingly precise in everything that it does, including the weaving of dreams.

The actual details of the dream were as follows: I was in bed with my mother and was sliding my hand up her thigh. I stopped, however, when she gave me a disapproving look. I immediately removed my hand. I felt ashamed, but proceeded to make small-talk, pretending that nothing had happened. In that very instant, the scene shifted and I found myself in the second part of the dream. I was walking on a sidewalk of a city, when I became aware that the "capitalists" were exploiting the workers by paying them wages and then effectively stealing the money back by inflating the currency. Therefore, the workers could never advance themselves financially. I was outraged. I yelled and screamed up and down the street. I was also horrified when I realized that I was helping to support this system by being part of it. So, I gave away all my possessions, my house, my car and my clothes, and got rid of my credit card. I was naked, walking along the street, totally disheartened and disillusioned. I tried to leave the city but all roads were blocked. Eventually, I became concerned about the fact that I was naked and penniless. I went back home, except it wasn't my home anymore. I looked inside the bedroom where my mother had been. I noticed how cozy it was, but realized that it was no longer mine. I began to regret leaving the comforts of "the system". As I was having that thought, I passed by a television set, which was showing a beauty contest being hosted individuals who, in my waking life, I recognized as two formally outspoken social rebels. Yet, in the dream, they were hosting a beauty contest, which, to me, meant that they had conformed to receive the creature comforts of society. As I watched the television show, I became even more despondent. I became teary eyed. As I cried, however, I became aware that I was using the situation to get attention. I wanted people to notice my moral outrage and noble tears. I wanted the onlookers to praise me for my empathy and depth of character.

In other words, I was exploiting the situation. Just as the "capitalists" were exploiting the workers, I was exploiting both of them. I was using my display of caring toward the workers and my anger at the "system" to show the world that I was worthy of love.

The capstone of this dream was the close proximity between the first part (my mother's rejection of my sexual expression) and the second part (my social rebellion).

The shame of feeling rejected by the only person who really matters sets up a lifelong pattern. Since mother's rejection proved to me that I'm unworthy of love as I am, I must do something to become worthy. I must perform an act of heroism, a great work of some kind, so that I may prove my worth to my mother (the world).

Our existence is intolerable if we do not feel our worth. Fighting injustice is a common way that we try to "redeem" ourselves. In attacking the outer evil, we are unconsciously attacking the inner place where we feel evil or somehow unworthy.

It is also interesting to note that, in my dream, after I was "shamed", I quickly denied it. At that point, I became a social rebel. In other words, it the *denial* of the shame, not necessarily the shame itself, that sets up the pattern of behavior.

Rudy Scarfalloto

Does this mean that all rebellion is a form of neurosis? Not necessarily. We must simply look inside and recognize the motivating factors for our rebellion. Is the rebellion just an act of conscience and
common sense. Or, is the rebellion a way of doing some great work so
that we can feel our worth? Is it a way of filling the void and easing
the pain of a lost childhood? If the void is not recognized, it is not
filled. We create one enemy after another to rebel against, and a great
work to conform with. We continue to do this until we see that at the
heart of the crusading conformist or angry rebel is a child who never
got to feel his or her worth. When we make peace with that child, we
will, more than likely, make peace with the world.

CHAPTER 47

Forgiveness

(The Remembrance of Equality)

Revenge may be sweet in the mouth, but it is exceedingly bitter in the stomach, toxic to the blood and corrosive to the brain. Equally destructive is the tendency to reject, repress or ignore the desire for revenge by covering it up with the facade of forgiveness. To do so is to bury a bomb in the garden of our relationships. This is not as paradoxical as it might seem. As with other opposites, the key is relationship. If we want to cultivate forgiveness, we must understanding its relationship to its opposite.

I'm Sorry

Late one night, my wife and I found ourselves in an argument. We had been married almost a year, which, according to seasoned veterans, is the time frame in which many marriages break up.

Eventually, the defenses came down (partially), and we both told the truth (sort of). On the surface, we appeared to have resolved our conflict. I became suspicious, however, when she repeatedly said, "I'm sorry, will you forgive me?" Why was she apologizing more than me? I was equally to blame!

I knew she was sincere in her apology, but I had a feeling of foreboding. I ignored it, however, because I felt too tired to continue. And so, we went to sleep, thinking we had completed our argument.

In the predawn hours, we awakened simultaneously and silently faced each other. If I had been more attentive, I would have heard the hushed roar of distant thunder. It started as a whimper emanating from my wife. Before I knew it, she came forth with a blistering blitzkrieg of blame, in essence, undoing her apology. I became furious.

In a flash we were nose to nose, firing accusations at each other, as we had never done before. The feelings we had put aside before going to sleep came back with a vengeance. My own rage was so great I felt compelled to remind myself to avoid all physical contact while we were in that state.

In retrospect, the issues we were arguing about seemed to be amplified by a storehouse of unhealed wounds and influences in our lives. These other influences seemed so prominent that the two of us seemed like pawns fighting someone else's battle.

Eventually, I started to get dressed, at which point she left the room – apparently to hide both sets of car keys. Undaunted, I got my emergency car key and stormed out of the house. However, her car was blocking mine, and I knew that she would not yield to my request to move it. So, I stormed back into the house, and we argued some more, until she was ready to move her car.

I went to my office, where I thought I would finally get some restful sleep. Instead, I periodically found myself in a half-dreaming, half-awake state, during which I seemed to be arguing on and off with my wife. As the night turned to dawn, the exchange became more peaceful. By the time I got up, the rage had lifted from me, and I had a quiet knowing that it had lifted from her as well.

When we met in person a few hours later, there were no tantrums or accusations, and we had no desire to "hash things out". We spoke quietly and freely, feeling closer to each other than we had since we were first married.

Our discussion that morning included one amazing insight. We discovered that her apologies the night before, though genuine, were a way of sidestepping the fullness of her anger. The "I'm sorry" was a way of preventing herself from going too deeply into her feelings.

A heartfelt apology emanating from genuine feelings of remorse is healing for both parties. More often than not, however, we do not reach fullness of remorse, because we do not express the fullness of our feelings. This is not necessarily a bad thing. When we hold back in this manner, there is probably a deeper wisdom at work, protecting us from expressing more than we can effectively handle at the time.

I Forgive You

Just as a premature apology can be a way of avoiding our feelings, so can insincere forgiveness. When we go through the motion of forgiving someone, we are quite often saying to ourselves, "That person has done me wrong, but I will be big about it and overlook this misdeed." This strategy runs contrary to the healing formula described in chapter 24: *The key to sanity is to question your perceptions and accept your emotions.* This formula reflects the simple harmonious relationship between the thinking and feeling parts of the mind. Our thoughts are clear and our emotions peaceful and joyful when we simply question our perceptions and accept our emotions. In attempting to "forgive" someone whom we genuinely believe has "done us wrong", we are, in essence, clinging to our perceptions of wrongdoing, while trying to force our emotions to change. The resultant inner conflict silently erodes our sanity and can make us physically ill.

Such an attempt at forgiveness, translates into a covert power play. It sounds like this: "I feel that you have wronged me, so I will get even by refraining from any overt act of hostility and thereby show you and the world that I am better than you. I will sit back and let life (God) punish you. And, as I watch you suffer I will secretly enjoy it, and I will be vindicated." This form of forgiveness is a passive form of revenge. In other words, even though we earnestly try to forgive, we (perhaps unintentionally) project vengeful thoughts, and feel vindicated when things go wrong for the other person.

A Closer Look at Forgiveness

We can get a deeper understanding of forgiveness by first getting a deeper understanding of revenge. The desire for revenge emanates from the deeper desire to experience our equality. (That's why revenge is often called "getting even".)

Genuine forgiveness is very much in resonance with that desire for equality. Forgiveness may be looked upon as the remembrance of equality.

Deep inside, we each have the desire to know our oneness or sameness. In everyday life, this shows up as the desire for equality.

When we feel like we have been wronged, the desire for equality translates into the desire for revenge. We conclude that if someone hurts us, the only way to re-establish equality is to hurt him or her equally. This is why we equate justice with revenge. We reach this conclusion on a subconscious level. Therefore, even as we sincerely endeavor to forgive, we are unconsciously plotting revenge to establish equality. When the desire for revenge is not quite conscious, it can often show up as feelings of resentment or hostility.

The desire for equality is so deep that if the attacker is not available to receive our retribution, we attempt to get even (with life) by hurting any other convenient person. This is the origin of the social pecking order in which the husband beats the wife, the wife beats the child, the child beats the younger child, and the younger child kicks the puppy. Obviously, this doesn't solve anything. Yet, if we deny or minimize the desire for revenge or feelings of resentment and hostility, they color and distort our acts of forgiveness.

If we blindly yield to the desire for revenge, we simply perpetuate and escalate the violence. Likewise, it is futile to act neutral and pretend that we have forgotten the perceived injustice. We are ruled by the feeling until we allow it to speak. When we do so, we can trace it to its origin. We see that the desire for revenge is a painful and twisted cry emanating from the place within us that yearns to join with the other person in a spirit of equality and fairness.

The straight and narrow path to forgiveness is one that recognizes the desire for revenge; neither repressing it nor acting it out. Through recognition, the emotional energy contained within the desire for revenge can transmute into its primordial form – the desire to know our equality. When we feel the primordial desire for equality, we call forth the remembrance of equality –forgiveness.

No Atheists In Fox Holes

While I was a young bachelor, a friend of mine had a fling with a woman I was attempting to court. I made no attempt to minimize or sugarcoat my feelings of anger and hurt. This was most unusual for me. My typical response was to deny or minimize my emotions and act nice, after which I would isolate myself from others and mentally rehash the drama over and over again, focusing on any detail that would make me look right and the other person wrong. If I couldn't effectively do this within the framework of the actual facts, my mind would drift into fantasy of how I would have liked it to be.

In this particular situation, however, the events had occurred too quickly for me to pull back and erect my defenses. My emotions were too strong to be hidden behind a mask of neutrality and false forgiveness.

The following morning, as I drove my car, I still felt angry and hurt. The emotional discomfort compelled me to drop the last bit of pretense about who I thought I was. Like a child, I asked God to go to the source of the pain and make everything right. In that instant, a remarkable thing happened. I "located" the source of the pain. I experienced it as a "place" within me – an infantile place – that made no distinction between what is rational and irrational, reasonable and unreasonable, sane and insane, civilized and uncivilized. Furthermore, I perceived that in this deep place, there were no clear boundaries between myself and others.

In asking for the healing of that wound, I was, in essence, asking to enter the state of consciousness in which I and my hated foe were *one*. In everyday language, I simply had the awareness of equality; his blindness was my blindness, his pain was my pain. In asking for healing, I was (unwittingly) asking for equality. My request for equality called forth the remembrance of equality.

CHAPTER 48

Hero & Villain

(Two Ways of Seeking Self-Worth)

The tendency to form heroes and villains can be very obvious or very subtle, but it is present in most of us. We are emotionally drawn to the hero/villain interaction, as indicated by the popularity of movies and novels. The popular appeal of the hero/villain dance also helps to create a market for newspapers, magazines and news shows on TV and radio.

We are drawn to heroes because they play roles that we would like to play. The hero provides a model of an individual who reaches the fullness of human potential. The flip side is that we become addicted to hero worship as a substitute to finding our own greatness or uniqueness. Or, we decide that the only way we can experience "greatness" is to copy the hero – which is impossible, but we try anyway.

The villain is someone we can blame for our misfortunes. On a more subtle level, the villain is the person we can compare ourselves to, so we can feel good about ourselves. Just as the hero gives us an image of how we want to be, the villain provides us with an image of how we don't want to be.

Whether or not our perceptions of the hero or villain are valid, the common element is our need for them to be good or bad so we can use them as a background to establish our identity. We place ourselves between the hero and villain, thus establishing the boundaries of our identity. "Who am I? I am a worshipper of this hero or that god; I am the enemy of this villain or that evil system."

We insidiously relinquish responsibility for our lives, believing that our well-being depends on the heroics of those who are greater, and that our misfortunes are due to the evil deeds of those who are morally inferior to us. To the extent we deify one, we must scapegoat another. The mere presence of the hero triggers so much hidden insecurity and sense of inadequacy that we have to create a villain that makes us look good.

In other words, on the surface we are uplifted by the hero and plundered by the villain. On another level, we give our power away to the hero and try to steal it back from the villain. To create a hero is to create a villain, and vice versa. One side cannot exist with the other.

If we think ourselves to have transcended the hero/villain duality, there's a good chance that we do it covertly. A simple way to detect the hidden tendency to create heroes and villains is simply to ask, "Do I have an emotional charge on the hero/villain dance?" If the honest answer is yes, the dance, more than likely, occurs within us.

The quickest way to move through this dance is to just dance it. We praise our heroes, and accuse our villains. We do it fully and consciously. The next step is that we won't do it at all.

The Fallen Hero

The same person can serve as both hero and villain. This is the case of the fallen hero. The fallen hero experience is quite common. It is the carrier of an important lesson. It allows us to see how much of our happiness was vested in the hero. We shift dramatically from feeling content in our admiration of the hero, to feeling confused, lost or angry when the hero falls. Yet, the person didn't really change; only our perception changed. When we become aware that we were projecting both hero and villain on the same person, we tend to quietly move beyond both.

There are two obstacles that can prevent us from realizing the full wisdom of the fallen hero experience:

- We might make excuses or otherwise deny that we were playing out the hero/villain dance.
- We might condemn ourselves for having been so gullible.

Either way, we block learning, and we can be fairly certain that the scene will be repeated. On the other hand, when we simply recognize the fallen hero experience, we free ourselves from the need for heroes and villains, which means that we are ready to embrace our own uniqueness.

Beauty in the Beast

Just as the hero can fall, the villain can be redeemed. This is what happens in the story of *Beauty and the Beast.* Deep inside the vulgar beast is nobility. The nobility is allowed to emerge through the tender kiss of Beauty. Beauty is simply truth. The graceful presence of Beauty allows the hidden nobility within the Beast to come forth.

An important element of this myth is that Beauty makes the choice to kiss the Beast without the expectation that her kiss would transform the Beast into a handsome nobleman. She saw his nobility *first.* Her seeing of the deeper nobility and acceptance of the brutish persona compel the transformation.

The tale of *Beauty and the Beast* illustrates how truth and acceptance transform the villain within us. The villain is driven by self-hatred. The remedy for self-hatred is self-love – not the pseudo-love that attempts to mask the ugliness, but the core of love that regards truth as beauty.

Beauty and the Beast is one popular variation of the hero/villain dance. There are many others, for the hero/villain dance is an important part of our cultural identity. The chapter that follows focuses another variation: *The Martyr.*

CHAPTER 49

The Martyr

Person *A* carries out a certain task, and then person *B* picks up where person *A* left off, without having to repeat the work of person A. And then, person *B* passes the baton to person *C*, and so on. This is an ongoing process in which all humanity participates. When the work includes an extraordinary amount of sacrifice and suffering at the hands of others, the individual is considered a martyr.

The martyr takes it on the chin for someone else's sin. On the larger social level, the martyr suffers at the hands of unscrupulous enemies or unworthy associates. The martyr is the individual who receives personal injury at the hands of others who stomp on the fruits that the martyr had to offer. On a more personal level, the martyr is the dutiful spouse, mother, father, son, daughter, brother, sister, employer, employee, student or teacher who goes out of his or her way to be ethical, moral, helpful and caring, only to be mistreated.

Martyrdom as a Weapon

By identifying ourselves with the famous martyrs of the past, we place a crown of nobility on our suffering. For example, let's say that I as a teacher put great effort in putting together study material for my students. If some of them don't use it and subsequently do poorly on the test, they might blame me for making the test too hard. I might show outward signs of irritation, but secretly feel elated as I compare my diligence and care with my student's poor show of character. Now I can sing the blues! I can now feel justified in showing resentment (which was there all along). Better yet, I can continue to hide my resentment and embellish my mask of nobility by demonstrating that I still feel "compassion" for my attackers. I can also magnify the drama by comparing my situation to that of well-known martyrs of the past.

Does this mean that all historical martyrs were playing out their hidden need to be recognized as being morally superior? Were they playing out their secret anger at humanity and, even more secret self-hatred? Or, was there a combination of a genuine desire to bring forth truth and justice, flavored by an undercurrent of unresolved self-worth issues? These are interesting questions that could stimulate lively debate, especially since they bring to the surface our need to see the martyrs of the past as perfect or near perfect heroes or saints.

The Martyrs of the Past

Jesus Christ is perhaps the most famous martyr in history. In telling the story of Jesus' suffering at the hands of his enemies, we must make two assumptions: that he suffered and that he had enemies. It may be argued, however, that if Jesus was the fully realized Christ, death and suffering were not his reality, but the reality of his witnesses and followers. The suffering could certainly have been real to Jesus *the man*. Christ, however, cannot die and recognizes no enemies. The mind of Christ can say, "The Father and I are one," without being blasphemous, arrogant or grandiose. The mind of Christ can say, "What you do to the least of your brethren, you do to me," because the eyes of Christ look upon the face of another with the recognition of oneness. Such recognition is not a philosophical ideal, nor a pseudo-pious gesture to someone who is secretly held in contempt. It is a genuine knowing, as obvious as a flower in bloom, as real as a sunrise. This reality is denied by the lingering experience of the martyr.

To accept the *reality* of the martyr's role, the would be martyr must consciously or unconsciously declare his or her moral superiority. This perception is unshakable until we begin to get a hint of the mind of Christ, which includes a sense of equality so profound as to transcend human actions and human understanding.

A toned-down version of that awareness exists in every one of us. Without it, we would quietly go insane or kill each other. As the awareness becomes stronger, martyrdom becomes less real to us.

Addiction to Martyrdom

Regardless of what the famous martyrs of the past actually experienced, the point is that we often use their experience to justify and ennoble our own feelings of having been victimized. It is healthy to honestly admit that we feel violated. However, we cripple ourselves when we habitually of use our suffering to elevate ourselves in the eyes of others. We feed on the idea that we are being attacked by our brethren who are not ready to receive our gifts. It is especially satisfying when we can compare our suffering to that of Jesus, Joan of Arc, Galileo, etc. We do this as reflexively as a drunk reaching for the bottle. As with other addictions, the first step in freeing ourselves is to just tell the truth about it. Sometimes, that is the only step we need.

The Reason We Suffer

In all fairness to the martyrs of history, even if some of them *were* acting out the unconscious desire to prove they were good and the rest of the world was bad, many of them were, nonetheless, genuinely noble. Given their circumstances, they acted in accordance with their conscience, showing great courage and strength of character; living their lives in accordance with their deepest truth. In times past, personal integrity often translated into the willingness to allow the flesh to be mutilated for the sake of truth. "…You can burn my body, but the Earth still revolves around the sun." In that respect, the martyrs of the past are timeless role models, reminding us to value truth as we value gold. However, while *they* suffered for telling the truth, *we*, in our modern age, typically suffer when we *don't* tell the truth.

When we consistently speak the truth, we tend to treat the body with kindness. Likewise, *when the truth is withheld, the flesh is mutilated*—through accidents, disease, substance abuse, etc. If truth is withheld, our attempts to heal the body (or our relationships) tend to back-fire. The intent may be sincere and the method may be valid. However, if personal truth is kept hidden, we will most likely suffer, physically and otherwise. I am reminded here of a story:

She Tried to Out-Martyr Her Mother

One morning, a woman called my office complaining of pain in her lower back and buttock. I had seen this particular patient, whom I will call "Diane", a number of times over the years, and we had developed good rapport. Therefore, even though I had not seen her for about seven months, she spontaneously began talking about the hidden issues that seemed to be associated with her physical condition.

She said that she had been on vacation, visiting her mother. (On *vacation*, visiting her mother. Hmmm…). During her vacation, the area she visited was experiencing severe flooding. She and her friends were eager to help. They formed a caravan and drove a long way to help fill sandbags to build a wall against the rising floodwaters.

When she first walked into my office, she stated that the physical exertion was the probable cause of the pain. As we proceeded to treat the physical imbalance, she offered more details. She stated that her mother resented being left alone by her daughters, flood or no flood.

While Diane and her friends were away filling sandbags, Diane's mother developed chest pains and was taken to the hospital. Her mother's doctor got word to Diane, who dropped the sandbags and rushed to the hospital, all dirty and grungy and sweaty. When she arrived, her mother seemed to be doing fairly well for someone who had been hospitalized for heart failure. She was alert, talkative and actively displayed how distressed she felt about inconveniencing her family and friends. The attending physician showed subtle but unmistakable disapproval of Diane, treating her like a selfish brat who had given her mother heart failure.

Diane was infuriated. She felt abused by her mother and misunderstood by the doctor. The situation, however, did not lend itself very well to venting her feelings against her mother or the doctor. At that point, her back and buttock began hurting.

The pain waxed and waned for a month before she called my office. As we treated her back, she spoke freely about the emotional implications. Since I happened to be writing this particular part of the book, I mentioned the word *martyr*. Diane's eyebrows immediately shot up, as if a light had suddenly come on in her brain.

Before this latest incident with her mother, Diane had already re-signed herself to simply accept her mother as she was. That seemed like a practical solution. However, her declaration of surrender did not register on the emotional level. Mentally, she was saying, "I accept my mother just the way she is," but emotionally she was saying, "My mother is a villain who tries to manipulate me with guilt and attacks me while I was doing a good deed."

In essence, Diane's mother was telling the world, "Look how my selfish and ungrateful daughter gave me a heart attack!" And Diane countered with, "My mother is a pain in the butt!"

Diane realized that she was unconsciously trying to out-martyr her mother; which was bound to fail because her mother was a supreme master of the art. Virtually everyone who knew of the incident sympathized with Diane's mother and vilified Diane.

One of Diane's sisters had confronted her with, "Mother is old and lonely, she's using her sickness to get attention. Why can't you feel compassion for her?"

Diane's sister's real message was: "You are bad because you don't feel compassion for mother." So, I restated her sister's question as a pure question, without the implied condemnation. "What *is* holding back the compassion?"

The obvious answer is that we would find it very difficult to feel compassion toward someone who is apparently attacking us in a very vulnerable place. It is especially difficult if the attacker reminds us of something within us that we are not particularly fond of. Under those circumstances, rather than feeling compassion, we feel anger. If we suppress the anger, we are likely to feel fear, anxiety or insecurity. If we suppress the fear, we might feel indifference or apathy. If we suppress the apathy, we feel nothing at all. As the emotional waters continue to rise behind the dam, the inner conflict is likely to show up in the body.

We go beyond the martyr's role by recognizing the wounded sense of self-worth that underlies the outer behavior. In recognizing the martyr within us, we are more likely to feel compassion for those around us who are acting out something similar.

221

CHAPTER 50

Flesh & Spirit

I was so buoyant that I did not have to exert any effort to stay afloat. I was a bit concerned about sharks, but otherwise I felt very safe. In the horizon, I saw the last hint of the setting sun. I swam toward the sun so that it would appear higher in the sky. Since I was aware that I was dreaming, I mentally tried to change the setting sun into a rising sun. I was also aware that the sun symbolized a spiritual ideal of some kind – heavenly bliss, oneness; that sort of thing.

However, my mental efforts to change the scene did not seem to work. Furthermore, I started encountering huge waves that were moving me in the opposite direction – toward shore. I thought the waves would pull me under, but they didn't because I was very buoyant; I just bobbed up and down and drifted closer to shore as each wave passed by.

Since the waves were so huge, and my own efforts so feeble, the sun was soon below the horizon. And, the waves kept coming. They seemed bigger and propelled me faster. I forgot about the sun as I became frightened of being smashed against the rocky shore. I also forgot that I was dreaming – perhaps because of my fear.

The waves *did* carry me quickly to shore. However, instead of being smashed on the rocks, I found myself flying effortlessly as I gazed down upon a lush and beautiful forest. At that point, I awoke, feeling rather peaceful.

Some of the details of the dream symbolized specific events of my life during that period of time. Many of the elements, however, had to do with life in general. The dream was yet another reminder of the subtle dance between physical reality and spiritual awareness. The message was simple: rather than trying to escape to the realm of Spirit (the sun), I would do better to just relax and accept my own humanity, especially my strong desire to participate in Earthly life (the huge waves moving toward shore). I was being gently reminded to avoid using my mind to go against the natural flow of things (trying to change the sunset into a sunrise). I was reminded that my human emotions and desires emanate from the domain of Spirit (the waves coming from the horizon). I was reminded not to fret about being overpowered by my emotions and the hard realities of life on Earth (the huge waves dragging me under and smashing me on the rocks). I was reminded that life would not drag me under as long as I was light and buoyant in the presence of those huge emotional waves. Instead of smashing me against the rocky shore of life, those same emotional waves would carry me safely to the realization that Heaven is right here on Earth (the waves carried me to dry land where I saw the beautiful forest).

Understanding Flesh and Spirit

A living being that is completely physical does not ponder its existence in the universe; it simply exists. It does not contemplate its life; it simply lives. It does not ponder its separateness from other life forms; it simply interacts. To be fully physical is to give no thought to yesterday or tomorrow, for yesterday and tomorrow do not exist in the physical universe.

To be fully physical is to have little or no sense of time. Therefore, the fully physical being is incapable of perceiving sin, guilt or shame for all of these require an awareness of history.

To be fully physical is to be free of censorship. When a bear craps in the woods, it is not inhibited by social etiquette; it is fully engaged in the act of crapping in the woods. To be fully physical is to be involved with the activities of the body as it interacts with the environment. To be fully physical means we are not thinking; we are not contemplating the rightness or wrongness of our acts. We simply follow our instincts.

As we ponder *physical*, we see that it bears a striking resemblance to *spiritual*. To be physical is to experience body sensations with no judgment. To be spiritual is to have awareness with no judgment.

Physical and spiritual are reflections of each other. Animal instinct is a reflection of spiritual awareness. The two are involved in a perpetual dance of transformation. When one side ripens in fullness, it bears the pure seed of the other. The quality of that seed depends on the quality of the parent that bears it. The corruption of one corrupts the other. Clinging to one suffocates the other. Each side, expressed in fullness, has an innate recognition and affinity for the other.

When flesh and spirit are in harmony, the spirit is free and the flesh is treated with loving care and respect. If, however, we pursue spiritual goals through rejection or mortification of the flesh, we are ruled by the flesh.

Then Came The Mind

As with other opposites, the dance of the flesh and spirit bring forth a third principle – the mind. The mind has the ability to perceive the physical body as separate and distinct from the rest of the universe. The mind records the adventures of the physical body as it moves through time and space. The mind draws conclusions and then plans future adventures. In one sense, the mind *creates* time by recording history. When the mind records and stores data, a "past" is established. In that same instant, the "future" is also created in the mind.

The ability of the mind to see the flesh as distinct and separate from spirit, is truly an *ability* that is to be respected and valued. When it is regarded as a metaphysical disability that we must overcome and transcend, it does become a disability. Such a mind perceives separation and only separation. It does not comprehend the idea that the simplicity of the kitten and the majesty of spirit are the same. However, when the mind becomes still and quiet, it can contemplate a kitten and spirit; perceiving their difference and sensing their sameness. When the mind is still and quiet enough, it is free from the programming that places flesh and spirit in conflict. When the mind is still and quiet enough, we see that the needs of the flesh and the needs of the spirit are basically the same.

Rebellion of the Animal Nature

The apparent conflict between flesh and spirit has received much attention throughout history. And, rightly so, because the harmony of flesh and spirit is very important to our well-being as individuals and a society.

What appears to be a battle between the flesh and spirit is actually the mind projecting its own inner conflict on the flesh and spirit. The apparent struggle between flesh and spirit is really our own thoughts and emotions in conflict. Likewise, as we methodically resolve the hidden conflict in the mind, we begin to sense the natural and easy relationship between flesh and spirit.

In order to understand the inner conflict of thoughts and emotions, we must recognize that such conflict is an expression of a deeper conflict that places *all* opposites at war with one another. In other words, flesh and spirit appear to be in conflict because that is what we believe about opposites in general. We secretly (or not so secretly) believe that when opposites meet, one side must annihilate or subjugate the other.

This inner warfare sometimes appears as a rebellion of the animal nature against the spiritual nature. However, the animal nature becomes "rebellious" only when the judging mind masquerades as spirit. In fact, we might even say that the "rebellion" is actually the animal nature continuing to faithfully express spirit – by overriding the repressive mind.

In the presence of pure spirit, the animal nature does not rebel for it knows that it is home. The animal nature is at home with spirit because spirit does not judge the flowerbed as being greater than the dung-heap, but simply recognizes the tendency of one to change into the other.

This is not to say that the mental realm of judgments and beliefs is less important than spiritual awareness and animal instinct. The value of intellect is unquestioned by spiritual awareness or animal instinct. The value of the intellect becomes apparent to the intellect when it cultivates the ability to be still and listen.

In summary

As with other opposites, the dance of flesh and spirit is one of transformation. Flesh becomes spirit, and spirit becomes flesh. As with other opposites, each side defines and gives meaning to the other.

Spirit animates flesh, and flesh provides a vehicle for spirit. In one sense, the life within us *is* a dance of flesh and spirit. The more balanced and integrated they are, the more readily life renews itself.

The dance of flesh and spirit is unique in every individual. It is an intimate dance that is not to be intruded upon. It is deeply personal and private. When the sacredness of that dance is respected, it bears fruit that is shared freely and abundantly with the rest of life. The dance itself is mysterious and beyond words, while the fruit show up tangibly. The fruit of that inner dance shows up as vibrant health, honest and happy relationships, and work that is fulfilling and prosperous.

CHAPTER 51

Gilgamesh & Enkidu

The balancing and integration of flesh and spirit (previous chapter) is of prime importance, as suggested by the fact that it has been dramatized for us in the form of numerous myths and legends. One such myth is *The Epic of Gilgamesh.*

The Epic of Gilgamesh, a story from ancient Sumeria, dramatizes the duality of god and animal, and how the two play in the middle ground called human. Gilgamesh was a great king, a demigod with a rich heritage. He knew many things and had performed mighty deeds. He did not know defeat, failure or death.

However, Gilgamesh had no humility and no compassion for his people. "...Gilgamesh was a godlike man alone with his thoughts in idleness. (He) left his people dreaming of the past ... longing for change. They had grown tired of his contradictions, and his callous ways..."

In response to the people's cry of distress, the gods created Enkidu. Enkidu was born in the wilderness. He suckled on the milk of wild animals and grew up in their midst. His body was covered with hair. He knew nothing of civilization, history or heritage.

Enkidu lived with the animals, ate and drank with them and set them free from the hunters' traps. "...He ran with the freed gazelle, like a brother; and they drank together at a pool, like two friends; sharing some common journey; not needing to speak..."

Gilgamesh was part god and part human. Enkidu was part animal and part human. When they meet, each becomes fully human.

Enkidu's first encounter with humanity is with a temple prostitute who is sent to tame him. The woman seduces him, after which the animals have nothing to do with him. Then, the woman takes him to the house of a local shepherd. She shaves the hair off his body and teaches him to eat people food.

While Enkidu is learning table manners at the shepherd's house, Gilgamesh has two disturbing dreams that foretell of an encounter with one who is as mighty as he, which is unthinkable to him. After the dreams, Gilgamesh feels weak and melancholy and doesn't know why.

Meanwhile, Enkidu learns of Gilgamesh, and immediately dislikes him. Enkidu finds out that the mighty king, in his arrogance and disregard for his people, forces every bride-to-be to have sex with him prior to marriage.

Finally, the newly civilized Enkidu journeys to the city. The people are excited to see him, for he looks like Gilgamesh. Enkidu is shorter and stockier, but the two have equal strength.

When Gilgamesh goes to the house where he is to deflower a bride-to-be, he is met by Enkidu who blocks the door. Gilgamesh is enraged, for the people are cheering Enkidu as loudly as they would their king. The two of them fight a furious battle, raising a big dust cloud and knocking over and breaking things until they are both exhausted. When the battle is over, Gilgamesh is the technical winner, but they both laugh and embrace like brothers.

The story goes on from there, rich in drama and symbolism, as Gilgamesh experiences the human qualities of brotherly love and humility through his friendship with Enkidu. However, things take a turn for the worse when Gilgamesh wants to do battle with the Bull of Heaven. Enkidu does not want to do this. He has a bad feeling about it. On Gilgamesh's insistence, they do battle with the Bull of heaven and Enkidu is killed.

Thus, the god-like Gilgamesh experiences another human limitation. Even with his god-like powers, he is unable to restore life to his friend.

Enkidu dies, for he is of the flesh. Gilgamesh continues to live, for he is a demi-god. However, he is stricken with a grief that also will not die.

As a mythological character, Gilgamesh represents our god-like qualities. He personifies the human mind with access to its spiritual heritage, and power over the elements. Enkidu represents our animal nature. He personifies the human mind with free access to animal instincts.

The Epic of Gilgamesh teaches us that our god-like nature, separate from our animal nature, is incomplete, dissatisfied, harsh and not quite sane. Gilgamesh finds peace only after he makes contact with his animal nature in the form of Enkidu. immortal spirit is very much at home with the innocence of the animal nature. we are also warned that if the god-king does not pay heed to the instincts and simple wisdom of his animal nature, he will lose it and come to know the sorrow of being human. likewise, if we, as true spiritual beings, are able to respect our simple and innately honest animal nature, we will know the joy of being human.

CHAPTER 52

The Vampire

(Flesh and Spirit Torn Asunder)

Extreme disharmony between flesh and spirit can show up as the "vampire." The vampire is a thief that steals on a very intimate level. The vampire steals the very life force of the individual. In everyday life, the vampire feeds on the attention and emotions of others, leaving the other person emotionally "drained". The draining can occur on a superficial level so that the other person feels fatigued just a bit. Or, the vampire can reach down so deep as to seemingly take the individual's very soul.

No one wishes to be accused of being a social/emotional/energetic vampire. The very idea evokes so much revulsion that we do not even want to consider the possibility that the tendency might exist within us. However, the very presence of such revulsion suggests that we *do* harbor the tendency. Our fear and loathing of things in the outer world, point to similar issues on the inside. To the extent that we harbor the hidden potential of the vampire, we tend to see vampires in the world around us and we react emotionally to them. The more unconscious we are of any inner tendency, the more likely that we will passionately accuse others of a similar tendency.

Revulsion of the inner vampire compels us to keep it hidden. The more deeply we keep it hidden, the more it rules us. Hence, the issue typically persists and gathers energy in the darkness of the unconscious mind. Not surprisingly, vampire-consciousness is poorly understood. It is difficult to understand a thing when we fear and hate it. We can begin to understand vampire-consciousness and how it is created, by first understanding how we nourish ourselves.

How We Nourish Ourselves

Life nourishes itself by making contact with life. This is true on the physiological level, as well as on the emotional and spiritual levels. We nourish ourselves emotionally by making contact with others. We nourish ourselves spiritually by making contact with the core self, or relating to the inner presence that is perceived as the source of life. Flesh is enlivened when it is touched by spirit.

In other words, we nourish ourselves by first making contact with our personal truth, and then sharing that truth in our relationships. Contact with one's truth is energizing, whether it is the emotional truth that changes from moment to moment, or the spiritual truth that transcends time altogether. Either way, contact with truth is inherently pleasurable.

The pleasurable quality of truth is often experienced as a sense of beauty. Even if we experience pain when we make contact with personal truth, the pain has a quality of sweetness or rightness. Even if the truth, as we see it, is ugly, the very fact that our experience is genuine gives it a subtle and perhaps indefinable quality of beauty. When we are in touch with ourselves, we would rather endure the "ugliness" of truth than cover ourselves with a pretty lie.

When we experience truth as beautiful or precious, it nourishes us. When we share our truth, we share the nourishment. When we hold back our truth in relating to others, we block the flow of life; we withhold nourishment from ourselves and others. This is how we unconsciously starve ourselves emotionally and spiritually. We then try to feed ourselves in other ways. For example, we might form many superficial relationships to compensate for the absence of deep intimacy, replacing quality with quantity. We might become addicted to attention and admiration. We might crave approval. We might find pleasure through watching others suffer. We might exalt ourselves by condemning or belittling others.

When we become seriously addicted to these forms of emotional feeding, we have created the inner vampire. We have created a consciousness that takes without giving. Like other addictions, this one tends to emerge gradually and unconsciously, and is perpetuated by a wall of denial, fear and loathing.

Not surprisingly, our fear and loathing of the vampire is accompanied by a cultural fascination with vampires. Vampirism has received much attention in the arts, suggesting that it has a significant place in our collective consciousness. Most notably, our unresolved vampire issues are projected outward as the character called "Count Dracula". By examining the legend of Dracula, we can gain further insight into the inner vampire.

Count Dracula

Blood is often used to symbolize emotional energy. In that sense, Dracula may be regarded as an extreme metaphor for how we emotionally feed on each other. Dracula craves the blood of others, just as we might crave the emotional energy and attention of others. We might be addicted to the admiration, adoration, fear or envy that others project on us. There might also be a hidden part of us that feeds on the misery, pain and perceived failure and wrongdoings of others.

For sure, it is normal and healthy to want attention and affection. It is also normal and healthy to be concerned or just curious about the problems and personal drama of others. However, when we seriously crave attention, when we are addicted to seeing others suffer or stumble, when we *have to* put others down so we can feel lifted up, we have created the inner vampire.

Vampire-consciousness is a hunger, an emptiness that tries to fill itself with the life stolen from another. Since the life is stolen life, it does not produce fulfillment and growth – it only sustains the vampire's condition so it can feed yet again.

Predator and Parasite

The vampire can function as a predator or a parasite. Predators simply overpower the victim as quickly as possible. The parasite is more subtle. It wiggles its way into the host and silently siphons off energy. If the parasite is truly efficient, it does not kill its host, or even inflict pain. In Dracula's case, when he siphons energy, the victim might actually feel pleasure. It is exceedingly difficult to fight an enemy that makes you feel good.

When Dracula is being really efficient and elegant, he does not have to overpower the body; he simply overpowers the mind. When the mind is operating according to its own inner blue print, we feel pleasure when we do things that support health and well-being, and we feel pain when we are harmed. When the vampire takes over, it overrides nature's design. The host has no life of its own, but simply exists to sustain the parasite. To do this, the host must also become parasitic on others. One of the abilities associated with Dracula is that he can turn his victim into a vampire.

Carl Jung was the first to point out that the vampire is the ultimate addict. It feeds on others, but is never filled. It cannot be filled, because it does not recognize the nature of its emptiness. This tragic condition of the vampire is a glaring reminder that we are not really nourished when we take without giving.

The Emptiness

In essence, Count Dracula symbolizes an unrecognized inner emptiness. If the emptiness were recognized, it would be filled from within; filled with the gratitude of simply knowing the truth of oneself. That truth might cry out as the simple declaration, *I am!*"

The radiance of that truth fills the inner emptiness and overflows to nourish others. The vampire is secretly terrified of this, fearing that it cannot contain the full knowing called, *"I am,"* and survive. Vampire-consciousness is correct in this perception. The shell that once sealed off the emptiness must give way, because *"I am"* is alive and ever expanding. The shell perceives that it is being shattered.

In other words, vampire-consciousness cannot tolerate the truth of its own emptiness. This is symbolized by Dracula's avoidance of daylight. The vampire, manifesting as the everyday addict, avoids the light of truth, preferring to feed secretly in the darkness of night.

The Beast Without Beauty

Dracula is often depicted as being very seductive and deceptive, and even as having hypnotic powers. To the extent that we harbor an inner vampire, we tend to be seductive and deceptive, perhaps without even realizing it. We see this in the hard-core addict. For example, the addict might pretend to be the "beast" in *Beauty and the Beast.* It says, "If you will only love me, I know I can mend my ways...if you marry me, I will stop drinking/gambling/taking drugs." The victim (the "enabler") is repeatedly seduced into thinking that a soft, tender kiss will do the job.

In the legend of *Beauty and the Beast,* Beauty provides the kiss that transforms the beast into a noble gentleman. The vampire, however, is incapable of receiving the healing *kiss* of Beauty. Beauty is truth. The vampire – by definition – has rejected the gentle kiss of truth. Therefore, it must be slain with the *sword* of truth.

In real life, the sword of truth is often called "tough love", which is sharp enough to cut through the lies, strong enough to stand firm in the face of seduction, and steady enough to refrain from self-serving interference. Tough love is tough enough to refuse to feed the vampire. When the vampire is thus slain, the noble beast is set free and is able to receive the tender kiss of Beauty.

The sword of truth – tough love – is how we address the inner or outer vampire. The vampire is likely to return, however, until we understand how it is created in the first place.

How We Create the Vampire

We create the vampire by denying our need for relationship. We create the vampire by denying the need to touch and to be touched, physically, emotionally and spiritually. We destroy our relationship with the life around us by tearing asunder the inner relationship between flesh and spirit.

The vampire is driven by the urge to fill an emptiness, but does not recognize that the emptiness can only be filled from within. Being filled from within doesn't mean we deny the need for relationship. On the contrary, when we deny the desire to reach out and touch the life around us, we shut off the flow of life from within us. We break the circuit that allows the inner current of life to flow.

In other words, the part of us that has the potential for becoming the vampire is the same part that wants to be in relationship with the rest of life. The place within us that has the potential to become addicted (to harmful substances, attention, admiration, suffering and fault-finding) is the same part that simply wants relationship. To the extent that our sensual and emotional need for relationship is denied, we create the inner vampire.

The End of Dracula

As the quintessential vampire, Dracula had his beginning during the Dark Ages (which seems appropriate when we consider that he is also known as the *Prince of Darkness*.) During the Dark Ages, knowledge and self-expression were severely suppressed. During that time, the Christian ideal of self-denial had reached its zenith.

For sure, the monastic practice of removing ourselves from the sensual world is a powerful tool for finding inner peace. However, we must be clear on our intent. The sincere monk removes himself from the sensual world, so as to create a more harmonious and respectful relationship with the rest of life, not to tear that relationship asunder. In the latter case, the ways of the flesh are rejected and condemned, and thus become a stumbling stone on the road to spiritual freedom. The monk who tries to find God by rejecting and condemning the sensual world creates the inner vampire.

When we have stumbled across this truth enough times and have created enough vampires, we can then learn from experience. We learn this: by quietly looking within, as the true monk does, we really do access the source of life. In so doing, We do not lose the sensual experience of relationship with the rest of life. It is re-born with a sensuality that is utterly free, for it is utterly innocent.

The vampire stops being a vampire (and is thankful for it) when we recognize the truth it is acting out – the need for relationship. The vampire returns no more when we reclaim our ability to make contact with each other, to savor life, to give and receive in the various ways that we are instinctively drawn to do so.

235

CHAPTER 53

Saint Francis

(Flesh and Spirit Reunited)

Count Dracula (previous chapter) dramatizes what can happen when the relationship between flesh and spirit is severely disrupted. St Francis of Assisi dramatizes the healing of that relationship.

St. Francis' great love for animals and the natural world is legendary; and, apparently, the feeling was mutual. Timid animals that normally avoid humans were drawn to Francis. Dangerous predatory animals were harmless in his presence. His own behavior was described as *impulsive* and *instinctual*. When he felt overburdened, he often sought refuge in a beautiful valley called Rieti, home to a Pagan community with whom he shared a warm friendship. At a time when devout Catholics intentionally mutilated their bodies to purge themselves of physical desires, St. Francis referred to his own body as "Brother Body."

Francis and Dracula

St. Francis is perhaps the most well-known monk in history. Most people who have any knowledge of St. Francis also have a fondness for him, just as they have a dark fascination with Count Dracula. St. Francis and Count Dracula do have some interesting parallels. For starters, both were real historical figures whose lives have been mythologized.

If we look at the historical data, we find that the real St. Francis of Assisi had his flaws. Likewise, the real Count Dracula was not as diabolical as the character in the movies. However, the legends that have grown around St. Francis and Count Dracula are as important as the documented history. The legends represent aspects of our inner reality that we have projected on the historical figures. The purpose of any legend is to teach us about us.

We fear and loathe Dracula because he reminds us of some hidden parts of ourselves that we would prefer to keep hidden. He reminds us of our potential for living parasitically on others. Likewise, we love Francis because he reminds us of the natural harmony between flesh and spirit – the spirit is free and the flesh is treated with loving care and respect. He reminds us of our potential to connect with the natural world in a sweet and intimate way. Somewhere deep inside, we would like to relate to the life around us as a young child relates to family. We would like to feel a sense of "relatedness" with the rest of creation; a relatedness that is so pure and deep that we might regard the sun as our brother, and the moon as our sister.

Both Francis and Dracula were said to have great influence over animals. Dracula used animals to do his bidding, and Francis just loved them. Both lived during the historical period called the Dark Ages. Both took part in crusades and "holy wars", which, according to their respective legends and biographies, contributed to their transformation.

Interestingly enough, Dracula could transform himself into predatory animals, mostly notably a wolf. One of the stories associated with St. Francis involves his encounter with a wolf that was terrorizing the town's people. Francis communicated with the wolf (whom he addressed as "Brother Wolf"), and was thus able to make peace between the wolf and the town people.

Another interesting point about Count Dracula was that he was a faithful Catholic prior to his transformation into a vampire. He believed that he was going to war in the service of Jesus Christ. He was a nobleman with political ambitions and visions of greatness. However, the events of the war compelled him to feel betrayed and abandoned by Christ, so he turned himself into the ultimate vampire.

On the other hand, Francis was not of noble birth. Prior to his becoming a monk, he was a fun loving, carefree, party animal. He had no hidden agenda of winning God's favor. He had no political ambitions or religious aspirations. His reason for going to war was simple: like other boys his age, he thought that wearing a suit of armor was cool and would surely win the adoration of women. When the spirit first fell upon Francis, it fell upon a naive and starry-eyed merchant's son from a town that was far removed from the religious and political centers of the day.

He Failed as a Martyr

St. Francis was one of the few religious reformers of the past who was not persecuted or martyred. He did try! In his day, if you were a serious Christian, the preferred way to die was in the service of Christ. Much to Francis' frustration, however, he was not a likely candidate for martyrdom. The martyr requires the presence of an enemy. Francis simply was not very good at making enemies.

No one wanted to harm Francis, not even the Islamic Sheik that he tried to convert to Christianity during the Crusades. In the midst of the bloody fighting, Francis had the gall to walk into the enemy camp and respectfully ask to speak with the leader. This act was considered sheer suicide. The Christian soldiers and Francis himself expected the Muslim army to make short work of him. Such was not the case, however. The Sheik was thoroughly charmed by the simplicity and unassuming humility of the little monk. They parted as friends.

The True Monk

Unlike Dracula, St. Francis knows that the emptiness within him cannot be filled from without. He does not fear his own emptiness; he embraces it. That is the distinction between the true monk and the vampire. The monk who makes contact with his inner emptiness is filled from within and shares freely with the rest of life. He becomes a *brother* to the rest of life.

When we recognize our own emptiness, we feel the fullness already in the emptiness waiting to burst forth. Francis is filled from within, nourished by the pure knowing called *I Am*. As long as he remains in pure contact with the dark and silent emptiness, he is ever filled with light. In the words of one biographer, "Francis felt the joy of the convert who sees the world vanish before his eyes...Had he been able to talk, he would have found no words to say – human language no longer made any sense... All notions of time and space faded away. He was simply lost, swallowed up in indescribable happiness. Ambition, money, power – all empty...Only one thing existed. The memory of it, which could not be communicated to anyone, made his heart flutter..."

That same biographer goes on to say, "St. Francis recognized this Presence ...disguised in the rags of poverty..." To Francis, full recognition of his own poverty (emptiness) was freedom. He claimed nothing for himself and, therefore, received everything. On the other hand, Dracula does not recognize his emptiness and is, therefore, ruled by it.

The humility personified by St. Francis recognizes that the emptiness within the vampire is also within himself. He, therefore, can only feel compassion for vampire-consciousness; not the pseudo-compassion which assumes itself to be superior – that is just arrogance wearing a mask. But rather, it is compassion born out of the knowing that says, "Deep inside we are both the same; we are both empty."

CHAPTER 54

Change It & Let It Be

(Listening to the Inner Signal)

One afternoon, I was speaking with my friend. "Richard", who shared with me the following dream. In the dream, he was earnestly searching for truth and purpose. However, he was being followed by a ridiculous-looking creature that was distracting him. It had a greenish complexion and a goofy face that resembled a cow. Its behavior was nonsensical, irrelevant, undignified, clown-like, unpurposeful and un-focused. Richard tried to ignore the creature, but it kept following him. He then tried, though various means, to drive it away, but the creature kept tagging along, unoffended and undaunted by Richard's disapproval, continuing to act silly and whimsical, apparently out of touch with reality, and too dumb to feel rejected by Richard's disapproval. Finally, Richard shot him three times with a gun.

The creature bled. However, it didn't even have the dignity to bleed properly. It just stood there, still smiling stupidly, with three streams of green fluid comically squirting out of its body. Then, as the creature was dying – in a most goofy manner, Richard recognized it as a wise and benevolent deity from ancient Egypt. Richard was horri-fied. He realized that he had shot and killed the very thing for which he was searching and striving.

The meaning of the dream was clear enough to Richard. The crea-ture represented aspects of his personality that he did not like. It rep-resented all the inferior or irrelevant parts of himself that he was trying to eliminate so he could be the man he wanted to be. In his dream, he had failed to recognize that the things he sought were contained within the same qualities he was struggling to get rid of.

When we are honest with ourselves, truth shows itself with ease and grace. To the extent that we are not honest with ourselves, truth is likely to appear in the guise of something that we might reject. To one who loves, truth appears in the form of the beloved. To one who hates, truth appears as the hated one. To one who is afraid, truth appears in a form that evokes fear.

Richard's dream dramatizes an ancient principle for changing oneself. The Bible states, "Your biggest weakness shall become your greatest strength." This principle is the basis for all inner change. It is the key for undoing any weakness, phobia or addiction.

It's About Listening

When we listen deeply within, we instinctively know when to initiate change and when to let things be. The side that is actively expressed, is supported by the side that stays in the background. Furthermore, the individual who hears the inner call to *Change* feels very much at home with someone who hears the inner call to *Let It Be.* They will recognize each other and smile.

When we do not listen, the two concepts appear to be contradictory, no matter how much we try to rationalize them into oneness. In the absence of deep listening, "making a change" takes the form of rejection, harsh judgment, forcing ourselves to do things that we don't want to do. Likewise, "letting it be" may take the form of laziness, apathy and stagnation.

The ability to listen is the same as the ability to observe. The ability to observe or listen is a function of the will. The will becomes the observer when it has been purified and deepened by the rushing waters of our genuine feelings. This observer is a *magical* observer because, in the very act of objectively observing the truth and letting it be, it changes.

Initiating Change

The science and art of focusing the will to produce outer change is very much a science and an art. It is a science in the sense that it involves a methodology and a set of principles and techniques that are available to anyone who cares to learn them. Initiating change is also an art, in the sense that we get better at it by applying the principles through diligent practice, the same way we learn how to ride a bicycle or hit a baseball.

However, there is a potential trap in using the mind to initiate change. If we consciously affirm, "I choose to double my income," it is quite possible that we are unconsciously affirming, "I choose to double my income because that's what I need in order to feel good about myself." In other words, we are unknowingly re-enforcing the idea that our self-worth is dependent on having certain material possessions or the ability to acquire those possessions. The implication is that if we don't acquire them, we have failed.

In other words, in our attempt to become the god-like creators of our physical reality, we set the stage for the surfacing of our human feelings of inadequacy or impotence. Then, we might conceal these feelings behind a cloak of excuses. We frantically try to hide the shame of not having created the things that any self-respecting god ought be able to create.

Such an experience gives us a golden opportunity to fine-tune our creative efforts. Our intention changes from, "I choose to create an apple (so I can be worthy of love)," to, "I choose to create an apple, *and* I am worthy of love." Rather than affirming, "I choose to create an apple (so that I can be happy)," we affirm, "I choose to create an apple, *and* I choose to be happy." The message is clear. Happiness is not based on having an apple, or our implied power over the environment, symbolized by our ability to manifest an apple.

We allow ourselves to remember that our worldly activities are, ultimately motivated by the deeper desire to just know ourselves and to know that we are loved. This brings a measure of sanity and humanity to our worldly doings. Our acts of creation are no longer a brutal self-trial, but a journey of self-discovery.

As we cultivate the understanding that self-worth is not based entirely on achieving our goals, we become more adept at achieving our goals. To the extent that our self-worth is shaky, we tend to use outer achievements and abilities to cover our insecurity. We use our abilities and achievements as a shield to hide our self-hatred.

When we are keenly aware that we are basing our happiness on the possession of an apple, we may discover that we no longer wish to acquire the apple. The desire for outer achievements has reverted to it primordial form: the desire to simply know ourselves and be true to ourselves. Not surprisingly, in that place of honesty and self-acceptance, *the elements yield to our will.*

Creating Out of Thin Air

When I was a young child (a *very* young child), I used to try to create objects out of thin air and move things using only the power of thought. Somehow, I felt that I should be able to do these things.

The above fantasy seems rather funny now, but perhaps the desire to levitate and manifest out of thin air is neither demented nor childish, but comes from a deep memory or an ability held in dormancy. Those who have an active interest in such things are perhaps responding to that deep memory.

If the ability to materialize things out of nothingness exists within us, there is probably a good reason why the average person can't do it. Perhaps the ability is kept dormant in the subconscious mind because we want to experience something else right now.

Nonetheless, we can still be fascinated by the idea of precipitating an apple out of thin air, and we would be deeply impressed if we witnessed such an event. Even when we know that the sudden appearance of the apple is an illusion – as in a magic show – we are still fascinated. However, there is also the enjoyment of planting an apple tree, caring for it, watching it change from season to season, and seeing the apples expand as spring changes to summer and summer changes to autumn. The mind that is at peace will regard the apple growing on the tree as no less miraculous than an apple manifested out of thin air.

How To Practice Voodoo

Actually, each of us practices voodoo throughout the day, consciously or unconsciously. Every time we have a thought toward a fellow human, we are, in effect, creating a voodoo doll of that person within our own minds. We can do all sorts of things to that doll: we fight with it, play with it, bow down to it, have a conversation with it, have sex with it, steal money from it, deceive it, praise it. In essence, we treat the doll with kindness and respect, or we stick it with pins. We have within our minds voodoo dolls of every person that we are in relationship with.

Most of us would prefer to exercise our voodoo responsibly. Black magic (which is actually a misnomer) refers to the intentional use of mind-power to harm or otherwise control another person. Such an act ultimately backfires, for it flies in the face of a basic principle that governs all forms of giving and receiving: *Whatever you do onto others shall be done onto you.* In Pagan traditions, the act of precipitating outer change begins with "making a circle". The circle symbolizes the oneness of life. The universe is "spherical," therefore, whatever you project out will return to you in some shape or form.

The only commodity that is gained by the use of "black magic" is time. Black magic is a way of borrowing time. The skillful black magician gains more time and is, therefore, able to postpone consequences longer than the less skillful magician. And, since more time has been borrowed, more interest has to be paid.

One way that we stop the tendency to unintentionally perform voodoo on others is to have no thought of them whatsoever, unless we are in their physical presence. When we are in their presence, we can minimize the unintentional voodoo by communicating directly and honestly with them.

The alternative is to practice our voodoo consciously and precisely by neither pushing the thought away nor clinging to it. We can imagine that we are placing that mental voodoo doll upon the current of the ever-present creative flow of the universe, often called the God of our understanding. When we do so, the mind becomes peaceful and we might feel a surge of power. If that peace or power could speak, we might imagine that it is saying, "Be not afraid of your own thoughts. Bring your thoughts and emotions of your brother/sister/friend/enemy unto me, so that I can love them through you." This is voodoo par excellence. This is essentially the wisdom practiced by the master alchemist/Christian saint/Buddhist sage who has learned the fine art of simultaneously *making the change and letting it be.*

CHAPTER 55

Positive & Negative

(The Dance of Yes and No)

For most of us, positive means good and negative means bad. *Positive thinking* is considered healthy, whereas *negative thinking* is regarded as unhealthy. On an interpersonal level, we generally want to receive "positive feedback". Most people would feel insulted if they were classified as "negative" and they would feel pleased if they were regarded as "positive". Positive thinking often takes the form of affirmations: intentional words and statements that describe the actualization of beneficial conditions in our lives.

Positive thinking sometimes seems to break down. More specifically, affirmations can, paradoxically, culminate in an outcome that is contrary to what we affirmed. This tendency is minimized when we understand the relationship of positive and negative thinking.

The Relationship of Positive and Negative

One of the principles regarding the interaction of opposite states that, if we wish to master anything, we must have an understanding of it opposite. Understanding its opposites means that we understand its *relationship* to its opposite. By understanding that relationship, the two sides can interact harmoniously within the mind. When the two interact harmoniously within us, the one that we actively express is silently supported by the other. The side that is visible is supported the side that is invisible.

Such understanding is consistent with another principle regarding the interaction of opposites: *If two things are opposites, each side bears the seed of the other.* Each side contains the essence of the other. Each side expressed in fullness brings forth the essence of the other. This seemingly lofty metaphysical idea has immense practical value for someone who wishes to practice positive thinking and affirmations. When we choose to be positive to the *core*, we see that negative has its rightful place too. This simply means that our choice to be joyful is in harmony with the part of us that says, "I hurt."

In other words, rather than struggling against the hurting, sad or angry place, or neglecting it like an unloved child, we respectfully recognize it. When that part of us is loved and respected, it gives new life and new meaning to our positive thinking and affirmations.

Yes and No

When we begin to understand the deeper relationship of positive and negative thinking, we see that positive translates into *yes,* which generally has an "expansive" emotional quality to it. Likewise, negative translates into *no,* which usually has a "contractive" feel to it. As we cultivate a deeper understanding of these qualities within us, we see that one side cannot exist without the other. We would not say that expansion is intrinsically more valuable than contraction. Likewise, we see that *yes* is not better than *no,* and positive is not better than negative. We recognize that each has its time and its place. And, we instinctively know which one we need to express at any given time. We express it freely and, therefore, allow the people around us to do the same.

Positive and Negative Feedback

When positive and negative expression are in a state of harmony, we tend to gravitate to the one that feels right to us, without judging one as good and the other as bad. One way to cultivate this attitude is to look at positive/negative from the perspective of the scientist.

To the scientist, positive and negative are simply convenient terms used to express opposing functions. To a physicist, positive and negative are two inseparable aspects of electricity. To a mathematician, positive and negative are directions on a number scale.

To a physiologist, *negative feedback* refers to any biological process in which a stimulus (a change) impinges on the body, and the body responds by neutralizing or negating the stimulus.

The body has many negative feedback systems. Their purpose is to maintain a constant and healthy internal environment. For example, if we introduce a large amount of sugar into the blood, the body responds by releasing the hormone insulin, which causes a decrease in blood sugar. If the blood is cooled excessively, the muscles respond by shivering, which has the effect of generating heat. If a pathogenic virus or bacteria enters the body, the immune system responds in a variety of ways to eliminate the intruder. In other words, negative feedback systems are the body's way of saying "no" to potentially harmful change.

On a personal or social level, when we say no, we are generally saying no to change. In the presence of a change or stimulus, the mind that is exercising its option to be *negative* is saying, "no, I do not want this change; let things be as they are."

Positive feedback, to a physiologist, is simply a process in which a stimulus or change impinges on the body and elicits a response that *enhances* the stimulus. The enhanced stimulus then produces a stronger response, which, in turn, enhances the stimulus some more, and so on. In other words, in a positive feedback response, the body is saying, "yes" to change, and the nature of the "yes" is such that it triggers more change – and the rate of change increases.

Obviously, a positive feedback system can easily spiral out of control and bring illness to the body. In fact, most disease processes are positive feedback responses. For example, if a stressor, such as pathogenic bacteria, impinge on the body, energy must be expended to rid the body of the infective organisms. If the depletion of energy is great enough, the immune system is compromised, thus making the body vulnerable to further attack, which depletes the body even more, and so on. On a more subtle level, lack of exercise results in stiffening of the joints, withering of bones, shrinking of muscles and breakdown of circulation. This results in lethargy and reduced mobility, which further discourage exercise, which in turn accelerates degeneration. Physiological aging appears to occur faster and faster as the person gets older because, like any degenerative process, aging operates on the principle of positive feedback.

Positive feedback also operates on the psychological level. We see it in the addicts who respond to stress by going out of control, which, in turn causes more stress, which causes them to go more out of control.

Positive feedback is not necessarily pathological. For example, development of the fetus is a positive feedback process, and so is childbirth. During labor, the pressure of the baby upon the cervix (the opening of the uterus) causes the release of a hormone that stimulates contraction of the uterus. Uterine contraction pushes the baby more forcefully against the cervix, which causes a greater release of the hormone, which in turn causes a stronger contraction of the uterus, and so on. This is why the birth contractions become stronger and at closer intervals as labor progresses.

Exponential growth of any kind, whether it is the growth of a single organism, a population, or a business, is an expression of positive feedback. Most of the current systems of economy are based on positive feedback: demand triggers supply, which triggers greater demand, which triggers greater supply, etc. Exponential growth must lead to a crescendo or "crisis point" which leads to the replacement of an old system with a new system (death followed by birth). Such is the nature of positive feedback: it must culminate with death and rebirth.

The Orgasm Revisited

The male orgasm is typically brief and singular, while females have a much greater potential for multiple orgasms, wherein each orgasm paves the way for a stronger orgasm. Essentially, the male orgasm is governed by a self-limiting negative feedback process, while the female orgasm operates more on an expansive positive feedback principle.

The use of sexual energy to achieve transcendental experience is based on the cultivation of the positive feedback quality of orgasm, inherent to the female sexual experience. In other words, the experience is allowed to become increasingly strong, each orgasm paving the way for a stronger orgasm, until the energy level reaches a critical point, and then it breaks through the existing boundaries that define sexual, giving birth to an experience that is beyond sexual.

A Symphony Of Positive & Negative Feedback

The body can regenerate and maintain itself through a harmonious blend of positive and negative feedback systems. The positive feedback systems allows the body to say "yes" to beneficial changes, while the negative feedback systems allow the body to say "no" to harmful changes.

Every living system, whether it is a single cell or a civilization, sustains itself and unfolds through time by an intricate dance of positive and negative feedback. It responds to environmental changes with a symphony of yes's and no's. When the unfolding is experienced as harmonious, the yes's and no's are balanced and integrated. When the unfolding is experienced as disharmonious, it is experienced as stagnation or chaos.

Excessive negative feedback translates into no growth or lack of vitality. Things just stay the same. This is the relationship stuck in a rut or a closed and narrow-minded society. It is fearful or repetitive behavior (neurosis). It is the absence of creativity.

Excessive positive feedback in the body translates into the inability to regulate itself and manage its resources, leading to a depletion of energy and the onset of degenerative disease. On other levels, excessive positive feedback has pretty much the same effect. It is the chaotic relationship that seems to get more chaotic. It is the debtor who responds to debt by creating more debt. It is a response to violence that breeds more violence. It is the war that sets the stage for a bigger war. Any system that functions excessively on positive feedback, and not balanced by negative feedback, must necessarily spin out of control and break down.

The Power of Positive and Negative Thinking

When we say that a person is "negative", we really mean they are (in our estimation) *excessively* negative. The attitude of healthy positive thinking as promoted by Norman Vincent Peale is actually a beautiful blend of the willingness to say *yes,* and the ability to say *no.*

Our ability to say yes, depends on our ability to say no. In devaluing or rejecting negativity altogether, we are devaluing and rejecting the ability to say "no." In so doing, the negativity is driven underground and thus becomes the silent ruler. This is the case of the individual who has a sweet smile and an angry heart. This is when we speak "positive" words but think "negative" thoughts. On the other hand, a mind that is really being positive has the capacity to see the value in all things. The truly positive attitude does not reject or "negate" negativity. As mentioned earlier, the truly positive attitude recognizes that negativity (the capacity to say *no*) has it rightful place. When we are practicing positive thinking on this level, we are being positive to the *core.*

Change and Changeless

When negative and positive are balanced and integrated, change is seen within the changeless, and changelessness is seen within change. This translates into inner stability and harmonious growth. This is the steady parent who provides a stable launching pad for the ever-changing child. It is the fiery and seemingly chaotic world of atoms and molecules continuously shifting and changing in such a way as to create a stable physical body that maintains its shape and function.

In everyday life, the dance of positive and negative translates into balance between our ability to say yes and our ability to say no. It is the natural harmony between the choice to be happy and the willingness to embrace the hurt. It is desire to evolve and our capacity to recognize what is. It is the courage to change and the serenity to let things be.

CHAPTER 56

Order & Chaos

(Freedom and Responsibility Revisited)

The duality of order and chaos shows up in many forms. It can show up as regimented and spontaneous, rigid and flexible, trapped and free, harmony and disharmony, organized and disorganized, structured and unstructured, work and play, focused and scattered, directed and wandering aimlessly, responsibility and freedom, purposeful and random, committed and uncommitted, community and individuality, symphony and cacophony, intentional and accidental, sane and crazy, sameness and uniqueness, etc.

We choose the pair that conforms best with our judgment of the situation in question. If we favor order in a given situation, we use words like *harmony, organized, responsible, symphony, purposeful, focused, sane.* We say, "I want to be organized, not disorganized. I want my actions to be purposeful not random. I want to walk with intention and focus, not wander aimlessly. I want to be sane, not insane. I want my actions to be in harmony with the flow of life."

If we favor chaos, we probably will not refer to it as chaos, since the word has an unfavorable association for most of us. Instead, we use words like *spontaneous, flexible, freedom, individuality.* We say, "I want to be spontaneous, not regimented. I want to dance in accordance with my own inner calling, not march to the beat of the collective drum. I want to *play*, I want to be *free*." However, we might be reluctant to acknowledge that freedom may appear to be chaotic or even crazy. In the words of Zorba the Greek, "A man must have a touch of madness or he will never be free."

Order/chaos follows the same pattern of other dualities. To cling to one side is to fear the other. To judge one as better is to make the other the silent ruler. Likewise, understanding each side allows the two to function as partners in the dance; each side asserting itself and yielding to the other. And, as in other opposites, their interaction results in the emergence of new life.

The Secret Desire for Order

Most of us would agree that the exaggerated need for order generally stems from fear and lack of safety. Paradoxically, if a person is playing out an exaggerated preference for freedom or chaos, there is often an unrecognized desire for order (unconscious fear and need for safety). This is the child who creates chaos, sending to the adult a nonverbal message: "Please give me structure; build a fence around me; I want to know my boundaries so I can feel safe." Adults can display a similar tendency; acting sort of crazy as a way playing out the secret desire for containment.

The Secret Desire for Chaos

There are a number of reasons we might secretly desire chaos:
- Random and chaotic events, seemingly beyond our control, give us an excuse for not achieving goals. It is uncomfortable to think that we have not become wealthy because we are not good at business or some hidden flaw in our character. However, failure is more socially acceptable if it is due to the "unstable economy", or some other random or chaotic event that has nothing to do with us personally.
- If we feel bored with life or if we feel restrained or trapped, we might secretly desire chaos to reshuffle the deck so that we can feel free to do something else. In this case, chaos translates into freedom.
- If we have prophesied chaos, we will secretly desire that it come to pass to validate ourselves in the eyes of others. Having predicted chaos, the prophet will then (consciously or unconsciously hope that it comes.

Whatever the reason, the very fact that we secretly desire chaos makes us powerful instruments for bringing it on. For example, if I want to move my office to a different location, but am afraid of making a move, I might procrastinate indefinitely. However, if a flood destroys my office (which it did), I am pushed to do the thing that I was afraid to do on my own initiative. I secretly welcome the random or chaotic event.

On the other hand, if we recognize the hidden desire for change, we can simply do it intentionally. We can consciously initiate change, rather than unconsciously wishing that a random or chaotic events forces change.

CHAPTER 57

Choice & Destiny

If we are inclined toward materialism, the universe is seen as chaotic. We might recognize laws of physics and chemistry that establish order, but we see those laws as operating against a background of random events and mindless chance.

If we believe that chaos doesn't tell the whole story, we are implying there is a fundamental order beyond the laws of physics and chemistry. If so, we are faced with a question: Who, or what, is establishing the order? Invariably, the order is attributed to *choice* or *destiny.*

Choice means *we* create order based on the decisions we make moment by moment. *Destiny* implies that order is established through a pre-set pattern, somewhat like the water of a river is destined to flow a certain way due to the pre-existing contours of the land. Destiny implies the existence of hidden "contours" in time and space that influence how our lives unfold.

Choice implies that we are each independent individuals acting on our own, creating our own lives as we interact freely with the world around us. On the other hand, destiny implies there is just one life. The one life has a plan that contains many smaller plans.

From a materialistic standpoint, we might say that we are born into a certain family by chance. Neither choice nor destiny play into it. However, if we believe there is an underlying order, we might say that it was our choice or our destiny to be born into a certain family.

Shopping for Parents

One of my patients had a young daughter who was bright and precocious, and learned to talk at a very young age. At age two, she reported the following to her mother: "Mommy, I picked you and Daddy."

"When did you do that?" asked the mother, rather surprised.

"When I was with God."

The mother was astonished because neither she nor her husband were religious, and had no interest in metaphysics. Later, when the child was four years of age, her mother asked her, "Do you remember when you were little and you said you chose Daddy and me?"

"Yes, I remember."

"Can you tell me anything more about that?"

"Yes. I was in heaven and God was busy, so Jesus helped me. He said, 'Hurry up, you have to be born soon.' So, I looked in a big book of pictures, like the police have."

"You mean, mug shots?" asked the mother, wondering how the little girl knew about such things.

"Yes," answered the child, "except that it was a book of pictures of mommies and daddies. I looked at the pictures and I saw yours and Daddy's pictures, and I said, 'I want them to be my Mommy and Daddy.' And then I was born."

The child's story, whether it is interpreted as fact or fantasy or a combination of the two, has the element of destiny (It is time to be born) and choice (I must choose my parents). Either way, her birth was not random; there was an ordering principle.

Incidentally, the child's story is not uncommon. Another one of my patients, a four-year-old girl, said to her mother, "Last time, *I* was mom." She didn't stop there. During one angry moment, when she was being disciplined by her mother, the child said, "I *let* you be mom this time."

Managing Choice and Destiny

It is relatively easy for choice and destiny to co-exist in the mind, as long as the two concepts are viewed separately. For any given event, we give the credit to either choice or destiny. If we like the outcome, we might be inclined to declare that it was our choice. If the event doesn't look very nice, we might be inclined to call it destiny (beyond our control). Quite often, we strike a compromise by saying that our choices can change the flow of destiny, or vice versa.

Quite often, however, the two concepts appear to be mutually exclusive. If we look deep enough, their dance defies logic and baffles the rational mind. Therefore, we typically don't look very deeply.

Will and Feeling Revisited

We can begin to understand the deeper mysteries of choice and destiny by considering the will and the feeling nature (chapter 20). The will and feeling nature are the two primary expressions of our human awareness. The will takes the initiative, while the feeling nature simply flows with life. The will makes choices, while the feeling nature yields to the flow of destiny.

To the extent that the will and feeling nature are balanced and integrated in the mind, so are choice and destiny. The will simply makes choices that reflect the feeling nature's vision of destiny, which ultimately has to do with freedom, relationship, family and fairness. When the will and feeling nature are not balanced, our choices seem to be in conflict with the flow of destiny. If the will and feeling nature are *very* dissociated, choice and destiny appear to be mutually exclusive.

Unity of Choice and Destiny

The deeper the communion between the will and feeling nature, the more deeply we sense the harmony between choice and destiny. If the will and feeling nature are integrated deeply enough, they merge into one – as do choice and destiny. When this happens, reality just isn't the same anymore. We can no longer say that our choices create destiny, or that our choices are in response to the flow destiny. Every choice we make is *indistinguishable* from the flow of destiny.

As suggested earlier, there are two ways we can describe the harmonious interaction of choice and destiny. We can say that the will's power of choice or intention sets the course of our destiny. Or, we can say that destiny compels us to choose as we do. From the latter perspective, destiny may be likened to invisible furrows in the field of space and time that silently compel us to follow a certain course.

Cause & Effect

Whether our choices create destiny or simply respond to destiny, one thing is clear: when we make choices, we do so within the context of linear time. This is such a fundamental part of our reality that we generally do not stop to think about it. To us, making a choice means there is a cause and an effect. To have cause and effect (as *we* understand them), we must live in linear time. For example, we choose to turn on the stove (cause), and the water boils several minutes later (effect).

Does this mean that choice does not exist beyond linear time? Not necessarily. It simply means that if we consider the possibility of making choices beyond linear time, things get really interesting! For example, we can no longer say that turning on the stove causes the water to boil. The two events, in one sense, simply co-exist.

(This is a good time to remember that beyond the familiar boundaries of linear time, the logic that we take for granted melts like iron in a furnace. When we speak of realms beyond linear time, our words and ideas seem to serve us best when we do not take them too seriously.)

Flatland

As an analogy, if we attempt to describe a cube to someone who lives entirely in two dimensions, we would describe it as a "square". It is not entirely accurate, but a square is what a cube looks like if we squash it down into two dimensions. Likewise, if we see that same cube beyond three dimensions, it would not be cube any more. We would see its past and future, and it would take on qualities that we could not describe in terms of size, shape, texture or color.

As long as our vision is limited to three dimensions and linear time, these multidimensional qualities are invisible to us, and we see just a cube. In a similar manner, to say that we create our lives through choice or destiny is a "flattened", three-dimensional explanation of a multidimensional phenomenon. From that "higher" perspective, choice and destiny are more organic and unified.

The Great Amoeba

If I am contemplating a move to the seashore, I might approach my decision in one of two ways. I might say to myself, "I choose the seashore." Or I might say, "I'm supposed to go to the seashore." The will says, "I choose the seashore." The feeling nature says, "I am drawn to the seashore; I feel destined to be there."

These two options are not paradoxical if the will and feeling nature are well integrated. In fact, when the will and feeling nature are deeply united, we begin to see beyond linear time, therefore, we might say, "I choose the seashore because, in one sense, I'm already there."

Choice implies that we are each independent individuals, creating our lives as we freely interact with the world. Destiny implies there is just one life dancing and flowing and wiggling like a giant amoeba. When one part wiggles, all the other parts wiggle. Every movement of every particle within the great amoeba affects every other particle. We feel destined to go this way or that way in accordance to the overall movement of the giant amoeba of which we are part. And, since this great organism exists simultaneously in the past and future, every step of its dance, in one sense, has already occurred.

As intelligent particles within this giant amoeba, we make choices. Our choices are expressions of the dance of destiny. And, simultaneously, our choices create that dance.

CHAPTER 58

Choice, Destiny and Prophecy

The dance of choices and destiny may be seen in precognitive events such as prophetic dreams, visions and clairvoyant seeing. Ethical psychics remind us they are looking into the *probable* future. They remind us that the actual events that transpire depend on the choices we make, individually and collectively.

Furthermore, the very act of looking into the probable future helps to bring that future into physical reality. Prophecy tends to be self-fulfilling. This does not invalidate the reality of precognitive seeing; we are simply looking into the detailed anatomy of destiny—which includes choice. When we receive a vision of the future, we are observing a probable future event and, simultaneously, we are helping to create it through the very act of seeing it. We are literally observing it into existence. The witness encourages the change through the act of witnessing. Therefore, if we receive images from the future and remember that it is not written in concrete, we can invoke the power of choice to change the events.

Prophecy and Sorcery

A prophet who uses the expectancy and belief of others to bring about a certain outcome is a sorcerer in disguise. The secret sorcerer simply "predicts" that such and such and event will happen as part of the natural flow of things.

The prophet/sorcerer makes sure there is an ample number of "witnesses" who believe the prediction or, at least, fear the outcome. In other words, the sorcerer, disguised as the prophet, harnesses the mental power of those around him like a farmer harnesses mules to plow a field.

This sort of manipulation does not have to be intentional. The prophet could very well be sincere in his intentions, which makes the prediction that much more convincing to the witnesses.

An individual with genuine clairvoyant abilities recognizes the element of sorcery within the prophecy, and is explicit about it, and is also explicit about the factor called free will or choice.

The Earthquake Prediction

A number of years ago, a psychic predicted a major earthquake in a certain area of the U.S. He published his prediction, and even insisted that the event was unalterable and would definitely occur at a specified date and time. One of my patients expressed great concern about the prediction because she had family living in the area where the earthquake was predicted. Many other individuals became anxious, fearful or excited over the prediction.

My own response was anger. Granted, the psychic may have had honorable intentions and felt he was doing a public service. He certainly had a right to publish his ideas. I was irritated, however, because he insisted that the event was immutable. (I didn't trust male psychics anyway, which may have added to my anger just a tad). I took every opportunity to voice my opinion to everyone who seemed interested in the earthquake prediction.

My reaction was so exaggerated that, eventually, I felt compelled to examine it. I even involved myself in earnest prayer and meditation to speed things up a bit. This apparently unleashed even stronger emotions, including remorse about my own past irresponsible use of knowledge and power. (No wonder I didn't trust male psychics!)

Anyway, the earthquake didn't happen – except inside the minds of many individuals, like myself, who paid attention to the prediction.

The Final Days Are Here Again

At this juncture, we can also address the plethora of doomsday predictions and other major prophecies that have flooded society in recent years. Whether or not the predictions are valid, they tend to have an emotional impact on us, and should therefore be given thoughtful consideration. When we do so, we notice several patterns:

- Historically, predictions of world-wide catastrophes and Armageddon have been more the rule than the exception. The anticipation of such events have motivated people to join various religions and mystery schools.

- The emotional impact is primarily fear. Typically, such fear has to do with loss of physical possessions, namely our bodies, houses and lifestyles, as well as our loved ones. Therefore, the degree to which we are influenced by doomsday predictions is directly proportional to how deeply identified we are with our bodies and other aspects of our physical existence. Fear diminishes as we methodically cultivate awareness of our non-physical identity. The more we contact our essential self and observe principles that feel right to us, the less vulnerable we are to fear and manipulation through doomsday predictions and other threats. In other words, the more we cultivate spiritual values, the less afraid we are of physical threats. Our spiritual values, even if we do not recognize them as such, show up as personal integrity, allowing us to face external changes with a measure of calmness and dignity.

- Some prophecies have the added twist of including eternal damnation or some sort of punishment or threat on a soul level. We are warned that if we do not conform to a given doctrine or join a certain group, we will suffer on a soul level. This warning seems particularly ridiculous when we commune with our own conscience. The deeper our sense of personal integrity, the less likely that we can be cheated, intimidated or deceived.

- It is interesting to note that over-concern with doomsday predictions – which implies strong identification with the body – has been the domain of religions and schools of thought that profess to hold the keys to spiritual salvation and liberation. On the other hand, many individuals that are openly materialistic tend to be less concerned about end-of-the-world prediction, even though it theoretically signals the end of their existence! This isn't as paradoxical as it may seem. Individuals who cling to the idea of an afterlife often do so because they have poor contact with their essence or spirit, and, therefore, are secretly afraid of losing the body and the things of the body. On the other hand, many atheists and materialists have, by necessity, developed a deep and silent contact with their own essence, which they express as a solid sense of self and a willingness to be personally responsible for their lives.

- Another common method of controlling people through doomsday predictions is by invoking the fear of "missing the boat". The message says, "If you don't join our group, you will be left behind – you will be part of the dross that is cleared away when God purifies the Earth with His flames of righteousness. Such a prediction would scare most anyone! Even those who practice healthy skepticism might feel a hint of fear because such a prediction taps into the fear of the toddler who sees mother going out and interprets it as abandonment. Playing on such infantile fears can induce compliance of the masses as effectively as a cattle prod.

A Time and a Season

Prophets sometime invoke the force of destiny by pointing to the great hypothetical cycles and seasons of life. They imply the existence of a natural order and rhythms that determine what will happen and when. Such an idea can liberate or entrap, depending on the intention. It is liberating when we use it to help ourselves relax into the flow of life, and do our best. The same idea, however, can be used to trick people into turning over their power of choice to whoever is clever and charismatic enough to convince others that such and such an event is part of the natural order of things. When the prophet dramatically proclaims that the time has arrived for a given event to occur, they are telling us to yield to the force of destiny – as they perceive it.

The individual with the gift of extended perception who has a knack for reading the book of destiny, also recognizes the power of choice. Such an individual can say, "The time is now...", while also understanding that the time has *always* been now. In a thousand years, the time will *still* be now. The ethical prophet or honest sorcerer understands that personal choice, made with sincerity and calmness, *is* the force of destiny.

Alternative Prediction

One possibility is that the many predicted earth-shaking changes are metaphors of inner events. In other words, the predicted physical changes may simply be symbolic of changes in the collective consciousness of humanity.

Perhaps the predicted great conflagration symbolizes the burning of sacred cows. Perhaps the predicted two hundred m.p.h winds will turn out to be new ideas that sweep through our lives and blow away the house-of-cards of our current political, religious, scientific and moral views. Perhaps the final battle will destroy nothing except our recurring need to have a final battle. Perhaps the great tidal waves will turn out to be great emotional upheavals that come crashing in from the ocean of the collective unconscious, changing the shoreline of our minds. Perhaps the melting of the polar ice caps is really a melting of long repressed feelings in the consciousness of humanity. Perhaps the worlds in collision represent a collision of conflicting beliefs.

It is even possible that the prophesized changes, whether they are inner or outer, won't significantly disrupt our lives as individuals, but rather reflect changes that occur gradually over a number of years or generations. Perhaps the outer changes that have been slated to occur in the blink of an eye, will, indeed, occur. But, how long is *the blink of an eye?* Whose eye is the prophet referring to?

The blink of an eye in one frame of reference could be a thousand years in another. The supposed reduction of the world's human population might be viewed as occurring in the blink of eye – in one frame of reference. In another frame of reference, it might be viewed as the product of many generations of intelligent living by a population of free and self-responsible people who are ruled by their own power of reason, and guided by their own conscience.

Perhaps the great tailed comet that we fear will strike the earth is actually "sperm consciousness" (chapter 38) – pure single-minded determination, working methodically year after year, generation after generation, penetrating the status quo, melting the polar icecaps of frozen feelings, thus establishing a new order of justice and fairness.

Admittedly, even if our collective psychodrama *is* the basis for some of the predicted outer events, this does not preclude the actual occurrence of the latter. However, since outer chaos often does result from unresolved inner conflict, some of the external calamities might be rendered unnecessary if their internal causes are addressed. For example, it is not unreasonable to suggest that the unfolding of destiny is very much influenced by the emotional biases that play into it. Consider your own emotional reaction to the idea that the predictions of outer changes are mere metaphors for psychological changes; changes that might possibility occur very gradually over many generations. Do you emotionally embrace this idea, or do you feel somehow threatened by it?

It doesn't matter what our emotional bias happens to be. What matters is that we are aware of it. As mentioned earlier, fear of conflict often hides a deeper fear of no conflict. We might be secretly uncomfortable with the idea of no future chaos or final battles to look forward to. On the personal level, we might want things to break down so we won't have to face our self-esteem issues or clean up the messes we have made. On a grander scale, periodic conflict and crisis are simply what we are used to. We might get bored without them.

The prophecies regarding physical changes to our world will either come about or they won't. Either way, the question is, W*hat do we believe?* Two other equally important questions are, *What are we afraid of?* And, *What do we want?* These are important questions because our own beliefs, amplified by our secret fears and desires, are among the great architects of destiny. When we thus recognize these inner architects of outer reality, Sir Choice and Lady Destiny can synergistically unite in the dance of creation.

CHAPTER 59

Known & Unknown

If we believe that we create our lives entirely by choice against a background of random events, the future is unknown, though we can sometimes make fairly accurate predictions based on available data. If the idea of destiny is real to us, the future can be known through some form of intuition. Either way, knowledge is power. Knowing the possible future, through intuitive seeing or rational thinking, means that we can change the future.

Since knowledge allows us to be somewhat in control of our future, most of us prefer knowledge over ignorance. Occasionally, however, we turn our eyes away from knowledge that is available to us. The same fear that usually causes us to grasp excessively for knowledge can also cause us to push it away. This is a major reason why the future often does not unfold as smoothly as we would like. We are fearfully preoccupied with gathering too much knowledge so we can anticipate every possibility, or we are afraid of looking at the facts. The balance point is where we allow the known and unknown to dance harmoniously within us – accepting the knowledge that is available, while trusting ourselves in the presence of the unknown.

Our preference for known over unknown often shows up as pretending to know in order to hide our discomfort or embarrassment with not knowing. Such pretending, when practiced habitually, contributes to emotional unrest and mental fogginess. An alternative to pretending to know is to allow ourselves to admit that we sincerely do not know. Or, we may give our ignorance a bit of pizzazz by asking the question, "What value am I getting from withholding this knowledge from myself?"

To Love is to Know

To love completely requires that we know completely. The reverse is also true. Total knowledge of a thing becomes available only if we are willing to love it totally. We see a version of this in interpersonal relationships. If we profess to love a person totally (unconditionally), the implication is that we know the person totally. If we withhold love from any part of the individual, our knowledge is incomplete.

The unity of knowledge and love also applies to oneself. To love ourselves is to know ourselves. The more we know ourselves, the more we can love ourselves—and vice versa.

Some schools of thought regard self love as a vice. Others regard it as a virtue. Both carry a measure of truth. Self-love is a vice if we attempt to love ourselves without knowing ourselves. Such an expression of self-love translates into self-deception, self-indulgence, avoidance of responsibilities and disregard for others. If self-love is understood to be synonymous with self-knowledge, self-love translates into loving relationship with others.

In other words, the key to loving ourselves is to remember that self-love and self-knowledge are inseparable. Loving ourselves more deeply is possible when we are willing to deepen our knowledge of ourselves. Likewise, we can deepen self-knowledge only if we have enough intrinsic self-love to see the hidden parts of ourselves with a spirit of acceptance and kindness.

Complete Knowledge

Fullness of knowledge or complete knowledge (which goes hand in hand with fullness of love or unconditional love) is not as difficult or unworldly as it might seem. It is possible to cultivate fullness of knowledge on the human level. The key is to remember that cultivating fullness of knowledge (in a stable form that doesn't overwhelm us), typically takes time. We might even say that cultivation of complete knowledge is what time is for.

The other key is to remember that fullness of knowledge is not just a mental thing. Since fullness of knowledge is synonymous with unconditional love, it must also include the feeling nature. Fullness of knowledge shows up as a mental perception and an emotional experience...and beyond.

Incomplete Knowledge

Incomplete knowledge is synonymous with judgment. Incomplete knowledge means we know less than we might think we know. Incomplete knowledge does not have to be false knowledge. False knowledge means that our perception is simply erroneous.

Most of our knowledge of ourselves and the world around us is incomplete. Nonetheless, incomplete knowledge (judgment) has value, provided we know that it is incomplete, or that, at the very least, we are open to the possibility that we are not seeing the entire picture.

Incomplete knowledge is false knowledge when we trick ourselves into believing that we are seeing the entire picture. When we mistake incomplete knowledge for complete knowledge, we are prejudging or misjudging something or someone.

In the presence of false knowledge, love is also false. We think we love someone when we might simply be infatuated with the false image we have of the person.

False knowledge occurs for one of two reasons:

- We have a hidden need to see the person or situation in a certain way. Therefore, we tend to block any information that doesn't fit our image.
- Defensiveness might prevent us from admitting our ignorance. Therefore, we make up things. We are tempted to cover the unknown with false or incomplete information.

If we pretend to know, there is no room for new information. The fullness of knowing is born in the place that is pristine and untarnished by the pretense of knowing. The purity of not knowing, free of the pretense of knowing, is, by definition, free of judgment. When the unknown is allowed to be itself rather than hiding behind false or incomplete knowledge, it becomes the empty vessel. It is a clear canvas for creation – which brings us to the next chapter.

CHAPTER 60

Darkness & Light

(Everything and Nothing)

To perceive light and darkness as separate is to be in duality. To see them as one is to experience singularity. The perception of their separateness is a thought. The experience of their unity is a feeling. When our thoughts and feelings are well integrated, we recognize the separate identities of light and darkness as well as their respective importance as partners in the dance of creation.

Light and darkness are often used to symbolize two fundamental aspects of our nature – which are otherwise difficult to verbalize without using a heavy dose of flowery metaphors and far flung teleological abstractions (which I will do in the next page). Such descriptions can become as far removed from our personal reality as the equations of a theoretical physicist. Yet, like those equation, they point to something fundamental to our existence. Not surprisingly, we have a strong emotional charge on light and darkness – as well as quite a bit of confusion.

Ultimately, that confusion and emotional charge stem from our deep cultural programming that places opposites as war with one another. Because of that tendency, the natural relationship of these two fundamental forces is torn asunder within us. That relationship is reestablished as we gradually cultivate an appreciation for the dance of opposites that makes life possible. In the meantime, we can begin to clear up some of the confusion clears up and tone down the emotional charge by first understanding light and darkness from a purely physical standpoint. In other words, let us first consider light and darkness as a scientist would.

The Physics of Light & Darkness

Light is a vibration of something. The exact nature of that something is open to interpretation. Whatever it is, however, it is definitely vibrating. We also know that light moves very fast. It travels through space at a velocity of about 186,000 miles per second, which is the fastest movement that physicists have been able to measure thus far. Furthermore, the vibrating and rapidly moving something that we call visible light is but one form of electromagnetism. Other forms include infrared waves, radio waves, microwaves, television waves, ultraviolet rays, x-rays and gamma rays.

Darkness is simply the absence of this vibrating and rapidly moving stuff. In that sense, darkness embodies absolute stillness and emptiness.

The difference between visible light and the other forms of electromagnetism is simply the rate of vibration or the frequency. Ultraviolet light, x-rays and gamma rays vibrate at higher frequencies than visible light. Likewise, visible light vibrates at higher frequencies than infrared waves, radio waves, TV waves and microwaves.

Higher frequency means higher energy. Large doses of ultraviolet light, x-rays and gamma rays are harmful to plants, animals and microbes because the high frequency translates into energy levels that are high enough to be harmful to living things.

The energy of visible light is low enough to be harmless to life. In fact, green plants use the energy of visible light to build the organic molecules that we consume as food. In one sense, our bodies consist of the energy of light (sunlight) stored within organic molecules.

Light as Information

With the invention of radio and TV, we learned that the same vibrating something (visible light, as well as other forms of electromagnetism) can be used to carry information. So, using a bit of poetic license, "light" becomes a metaphor for knowledge or meaningful information, while darkness is a metaphor for the absence of knowledge.

Our language reflects the fact that we equate light with knowledge, and darkness with the absence of knowledge. To "See the light" is to be in the known; to be in "the dark" is to be in the unknown. To become "illuminated" is to gain knowledge.

Preference for the Light

We prefer light over darkness because we prefer known over unknown. This is understandable. The desire for knowledge ("en*light*-enment") is instinctual. If that instinct is not expressed freely and naturally, it might show up a tendency to cling to light and reject darkness, or vice versa.

Fear of the unknown shows up as fear of darkness. The unspoken assumption is that light is good and darkness is bad. The light is perceived as something that dispels or banishes the darkness. This creates an insidious split in the mind. We prefer the light because it is visible and known and, therefore, predictable and safe. Yet, we also long for the stillness of darkness; for it is the domain of infinite possibilities, the womb that brings forth all things new and pristine. We yearn for it, but most us are also terrified of it – because of our tendency to place opposites are war with one another.

This inner split is so deeply repressed that it is barely noticed by most light-skinned people. However, it is much more real and much more personal for dark-skinned people living in a predominantly light-skinned society. This is especially true in an orthodox Judeo/Christian setting where light symbolizes good, and darkness symbolizes evil. In the presence of this deep cultural bias, a dark-skinned individual cannot help but feel uneasy, because a part of oneself is being rejected. The uneasiness, if it could speak, might say, "Society says light is good and dark is bad. I have dark skin. Hmmm..." Dark skinned people living in a predominantly light skinned society are uniquely qualified to see this preference for what it really is – a rejection of ones very soul.

The Metaphysics of Light & Darkness

As with other pairs of opposites, light and darkness have meaning only in the presence of each other. The light shines in the darkness because that is the only place it *can* shine. The light emerges from the darkness and maintains its identity by being nested in the darkness.

Darkness is synonymous with the unseen, unknown, unheard. It is silence, stillness, vacuum, the void. To our senses, darkness is simply *nothing*. In that sense, the idea of "casting out" or "banishing" darkness seems rather bizarre. How do we cast out emptiness? It is not a space-occupying lesion that we can just amputate. We do not "cast out" an emptiness. We fill it.

While darkness is emptiness and stillness, light is visible; it is seen; it can have shape, form, color, texture. It is forever moving, vibrating and expanding.

Light and darkness symbolize the two primordial forces that emerge from Unity and then give rise to everything else. This grand dance of creation, ultimately, defies description. We can, however, make it somewhat real to us by describing it in human terms. We might say that pure darkness gives birth to the fullness of light. And, thus, the darkness is able to look upon itself in the light of its own creation and it declares, *"I am!"* (unity is restored). In declaring *I am,* the fullness of light knows itself to be the purity of darkness made visible. It is simultaneously the purity of darkness and the fullness of light, eternally still and ever expanding, deeply mysterious and fully realized.

In other words, the relationship of primordial light and darkness may be likened to that of the womb and the baby. This analogy, however, doesn't quite tell the whole story. When light becomes "old enough" it unites with darkness in a different way. In this union, the light "cools down" a bit, allowing it to condense into tiny pellets of matter called protons, neutrons and electrons, which come together to form stars, planets, and sentient life forms. These created realities embody the infinite diversity and primordial wholeness of *I am.*

One variation on this creation myth shows light and darkness making war instead of love. Since this war takes place beyond linear time, we cannot speak of a "first cause". We might say that the darkness judges itself harshly and gives forth a blinding light. Why does the darkness judge itself harshly? Because it cannot see itself in the blinding light.

This confused combination of judging darkness and blinding light screams out, *"I am not!"* This is the scream of primal terror and shame. It is the terror of total annihilation; the shame of perceiving oneself as split from oneself. It is the ultimate accuser and accused rolled up in one. It is a dance of cosmic insanity, in which the angry accuser does not realize it is attacking itself, while the terrified accused does not know it is being attacked by itself. All other battles stem from this one.

The Psychology of Darkness & Light

"The light shines in the darkness, and the darkness comprehends it not." It does not comprehend that it is looking at itself made visible and tangible. In its panic, the darkness disowns its identity as darkness and projects itself entirely into the blinding light, becoming hardened intellect. Meanwhile, the darkness becomes a hurt and frightened corner of the human mind that feels unloved and cast out.

In everyday life, the judging darkness takes an identity called "evil" which tries to fill its emptiness with life stolen from others. Meanwhile, the blinding light creates its own identity called "good" which sustains itself on the self-worth acquired by defeating evil.

They do this over and over, until the two see each other as equal and perfectly symmetrical reflections of each other, at which point they speak with a single human voice that says, "I just want to know that I am loved." And, if we look deep enough into that call for love, we might another voice that says, "I just want to know that I am."

Many techniques have been devised to tap into the blissful state of inner integration, often called *I am.* In truth, we can't stop it from happening. The most effective way of expediting its emergence is to not rush it. We just do what comes naturally to us. We go about our lives; touching, giving, receiving, planting the tree, smiling at the cashier, etc. Light and darkness are at peace and at one within us when we are simply being human, doing the things that humans do, with honesty and dignity.

CHAPTER 61

Agnostic & Religious

I was driving along a country road on a clear summer day, when I passed by a church. Like other churches in that area, this one had a message board on the front lawn. The message board read, "God is love." I probably would have forgotten it completely if I hadn't walked into a bookstore shortly thereafter.

As I browsed among the shelves, I happened to pick up a very thick book on the principles and practice of Agnosticism. I thumbed through it briefly and flipped to a page that stated the basic credo of Agnosticism, which was, *There is no God – except love.* I remembered the sign next to the church, and I laughed.

To Join

The word "religion" comes from the Latin word "ligneous" which means "to link or join" and "re" which means "again". To practice *religion,* in the original sense of the word, means to practice the art of rejoining. The purpose of religion is to provide a framework for people to come together, rejoining with each other and with God.

The general consensus by individuals who claim to have tasted the fruit of God realization is that God is love. This realization is typically accompanied by the tendency to recognize God's signature in any religion. Thomas Merton, a Catholic monk, did a good bit of writing on this. After spending a number of years in quiet seclusion and contemplation, he received the pleasant realization that he loved everyone. Later, while traveling through Asia, he had a conversation with a Buddhist monk and they explained to each other the principles and methods of their respective systems. After a while, they looked at each other and chuckled when they realized that the surface differences concealed some deep similarities.

Merton's experience is not unique. Neither is it limited to those who live a monastic life. Religion is, literally, about joining. The more deeply and sincerely we delve into our own religious practice, the more we feel our commonality with others.

Jesus issued two commandments, to love God and to love one another. What he didn't say – not explicitly, anyway – was that the two are inseparable. The same religious practice that opens our hearts to God also opens our hearts to one another.

That sense of commonality does not wipe out our differences, nor does it invalidate or dilute our particular religious practice. On the contrary, that sense of commonality infuses our own religion with new life, allowing us to experience it in ways that are deeply meaningful to us and respectful of others.

The Bridge and the Trap

Every religion is potentially a bridge to realms of awareness that are beyond ordinary human understanding. Yet, that same bridge can become a trap. In order for religion to be a bridge between God and human, it must, of necessity, place itself between God and human. Therefore, in order for religion to fulfill its function, it must, at some point, step out of the way.

The use of symbols, stories or artifacts to guide us toward God must include the realization that God is not limited to those particular symbols, stories or artifacts. The conscientious shaman or priest is aware of this. They set the stage for the student to make contact with divinity, and then steps out of the way.

If the religious system and its leaders do not step out of the way, they become a replacement for God. The same principles that are designed to promote freedom, peace and kinship are used instead, to manipulate, entrap and provoke inner and outer conflict. How does the priest/shaman know when it's time to step out of the way? The answer is obvious if the teachings are used for spiritual communion. On the other hand, if they are used for political and economic power, the bridge becomes a trap, and the faithful become cattle.

However, before we shake our heads at the misuse of religion, let us remember that in order for this sort of thing to happen, all involved parties must (consciously or unconsciously) conspire with each other. One party wants to lead, and the other wants to be led. One party wants to seduce, and the other wants to be seduced. Each is driven by the secret belief that says, "I am too weak and insecure to live in a spirit of equality with my neighbors." Some people solve this problem by having a leader, while the others solve the problem by having followers. They come together and form a mutually-gratifying partnership, wherein each plays out its secret feelings of dependency on the other.

Agnostic

It is the clinging and exploitation aspect of religion that helps create a market for agnostic philosophies. Agnostic beliefs, like any religion, may be interpreted and shaped in various ways. For Example:

- The agnostic may simply question the existence of a supreme intelligence that created the universe.

- The agnostic may become the materialistic atheist who flatly denies there is any intelligence, supreme or otherwise, beyond the physical body. The atheist may assert that we are at the mercy of a universe that is run by blind chance.

- The agnostic may assert there is no supreme authority; that we are individually and collectively responsible for our actions. Therefore, our decision to treat our neighbors fairly comes from our genuine sense of ethics and caring, not from fear of being punished by an overseeing God. In order for life to be worth living, the agnostic must, of necessity, be devout in exercising personal integrity.

- The agnostic may go so far as to assert that we are individually and collectively responsible for *all conditions* of our lives. Even though there is no supreme intelligence, the physical universe is not ruled by blind chance but by the power of our own consciousness and our free will.

- In some belief systems, the latter philosophy is taken to extreme, in which case our only limitations are those we consciously or unconsciously impose on ourselves. Therefore, each of us is potentially omnipotent. In other words, the agnostic philosophy, placing itself in opposition to religion, can very well evolve in such as way as to conclude that *we are* the very thing that religion promotes.

War or Worship

When we simultaneously fear and desire something, we are likely to do one of two things: attack it or worship it. The typical act of worship consists of an attempt to establish contact with the Supreme Beloved who seems so far beyond our reach that we fear Him/Her. We want Him/Her so much, but feel unworthy and incapable of being worthy.

Those who don't worship might express cynicism or contempt toward those who worship. Yet, such contempt is just the buried pain of one whose spirit has been broken. The secret feeling is, "How dare they try to commune with the Beloved who is not available to me?"

On the other hand, if the individual has given up all worship simply because he/she is happy without it, there is no cynicism or contempt, just a quiet serenity – an acceptance of life as it is, and an acceptance of people as they are.

Such an attitude is not exclusive to even-minded agnostics. It is shared by those who engage in worship that is internally motivated and tempered with a warrior-like focus that is capable of independent thought and self-examination.

CHAPTER 62

God

In talking about God, we must bear mind that we are talking about the Absolute. To be absolute is to have no opposite. To have no opposite is to be beyond ordinary human understanding.

God the Absolute

Though the Absolute can have no opposite, we can get a limited understanding of God by comparing some of His/Her qualities with qualities that are familiar to us. This is, in fact, precisely what we do. We perceive God as *infinite* through contrast with our own finite nature. We understand God as the supreme *Creator* through contrast with those things that have been *created* (us). We understand that God is *timeless* through contrast with our own time-bound physical existence. We understand God as the supreme Mother or Father, by regarding ourselves as Her/His children

Our perceptions of God are useful as long as we are aware of their limitations. Fortunately, there is a built-in barometer that tells us when we are squeezing too hard on our ideas about God. That barometer is humor. As you may recall, humor goes hand in hand with humility. Humor helps us to loosen our grip on our ideas of God, so we don't squeeze the life out of them or have them slip through our fingers like watermelon seeds.

Actually, our concepts of God will eventually slip through our fingers anyway. However, by remembering not to take them too seriously, they don't slip away as fast; and when they do, we are less likely to get upset. We might even laugh about it. When we remember to apply humor and humility to our beliefs about God, we are blessed with ideas and concepts that can truly guide us in understanding ourselves and relating respectfully to others.

God the Self

A common distinction made about God is the one between God the self and God the other. God the other is the supreme being who is separate and distinct from us humans, and far superior. The other perspective declares that God is simply our deepest identity, the very core of who we are.

When we equate God with s*elf,* we must first make a distinction between *lower self* and *higher self.* The lower self is the personality that laughs, cries, gets angry, does goofy things and then gets embarrassed about it. The higher self is not really clearly defined, but it's in the same ballpark as "soul" or "spirit". It's our identity beyond the body and beyond our everyday thoughts and emotions. From this perspective, the supreme God is simply the highest (or deepest) expression of the higher self.

When we speak of higher self and lower self, we usually assume that the higher self is better than the lower self. We typically try to bring the lower self in harmony with our idea of the higher self. This is entirely appropriate because it reflects the evolutionary imperative to know oneself on deeper and deeper levels. However, when we have our own unique experience of the "higher self", we are treated to a big joke. To be in the pure experience of higher self is to make no distinction between lower self and higher self. There is just a wordless sense of wholeness.

The harmonious blending of the higher self and lower self may be described as follows: *I see the lower self that I am, playing in duality, and the higher self that I am, embracing it all and loving it all.*

God the Other

The idea of God within, liberating though it may be, can easily become encrusted with dogma that uses the bold declaration, "I am God" as a shield to conceal a mire of confusion, guilt or shame. The idea of "I am God" loses its potency when we deny the validity of what appears to be the opposite idea, which, in its purity, addresses God as would a young child looking up to its parents.

In other words, *I Am God* has meaning when it is experienced with the innocence of a baby suckling on mother's breast. Likewise, the act of praying to an external Supreme God has meaning only when it gradually leads us to the realization that says, "I am the thing that I have been praying to." The fullness of that realization is not arrogance. In fact, it is humbling. It is contact with the inner truth that compels us to feel our equality with those who walk the earth with us.

Our ability to commune with God depends on our capacity to be genuine. This is why little children have no problem entering the kingdom of heaven. If we try to enter the kingdom while harboring a basement full of deception, our efforts land us in hell.

When we are benevolent, God is benevolent. When we are compassionate, God is compassionate. When we are jealous and angry, God is jealous and angry. When we are treacherous, God is treacherous. For sure, if God is God, His will is capable of acting independently from ours, and His love is ever present, regardless of what we do. However, our sincerity has a profound effect on how *we* experience God. For all practical purposes, God is as present with us as we are honest with ourselves.

It doesn't matter whether we view God as our deepest identity or the Supreme Being who created us. Either one will do, provided that the God to whom we relate is truly the God of *our* understanding, rather than the God of someone else's understanding. Within or without, God seems to be a stickler for truth.

The Principle and the Person

God can also take the form of the Principle or the Person. God the Principle is the impersonal and supreme law that governs all other laws. God the person is an intelligent being with whom we can relate.

God the Principle might work for someone who tends to be very intellectual. God the person is important for those who are more emotional and therefore feel a need to have a *relationship* with God. The more emotional we are, the greater is our need for relationship. We cannot have a relationship with a principle. We can have a relationship only with another sentient being who is responsive to us on a personal level.

Mother God & Father God

To the extent that we are emotional, we will tend to desire a personal relationship with God. Our first and most emotionally significant relationships are with our parents. Not surprisingly, when we put all pretence aside and commune with God in a way that is deeply meaningful for us, we typically relate to God in a way that resembles a young child relating to mother or father.

With regard to the gender issue, God the He and God the She are one and the same, for the simple reason that God is, by definition, One. We make a distinction between Mother God and Father God simply because we find it useful. And, God doesn't seem to mind.

God the Mother

Mother God is the container that is big enough to contain everything else. She embraces all there is, making no distinction between the worthy and the unworthy. Mother God is the presence that allows all things to *be*; every rock, every flower, every child, every soldier, every monk, every thought, every feeling, every deed. She is the presence that allows us to be as we are, and to develop in a way that is natural for us. She endows our emotional nature with an intrinsic sense of self-worth, thus conferring on us the *will to live*. In so doing, She prepares us to receive the teachings of Father God.

God the Father

We receive from Father God the ability to create. Mother God allows us to *be,* while Father God shows us what to *do.* When we avail ourselves of Mother God's love, we become capable of doing Father God's work. Likewise, tending to the Father's work translates into the manifestation of Mother's love in a physical and tangible way. In truth, Mother's love and Father's work are one and the same, simply because Mother God and Father God are one and the same. At any given time, we might find value in giving greater attention to one, but the other is still invisibly present, silently supporting the one that is actively expressed.

Communing with Father and Mother God

We commune with Mother God when we feel the need for Her soothing touch. We commune with Mother God when we have a wound in the heart that seems beyond repair. We commune with Her when we feel a need for nourishment in places where we feel incapable or unworthy of receiving nourishment. She embraces those hidden places where we feel too dirty or ashamed to be embraced. If we listen deeply, we might hear Her whispering, "I will never forsake you, I will never forget you."

We commune with Mother God when the thought of communing with Father God is too threatening to us. When we feel Her quiet presence, we relax and melt. We become aware that She does not put us on a schedule or push us to develop. She simply nourishes and heals, and then allows us to emerge from the nest when our wings spontaneously start to flutter.

When we commune with Mother God, we cannot help but receive the teachings of Father God. We commune with Father God when we are ready to reach out to others. We commune with Father God when we feel the urge to build and to create. We commune with Father God when we seek the power and the wisdom to sing our personal song, and to give the gifts that we yearn to give. We commune with Father God when we are ready to receive the understanding that allows us to relate respectfully and effectively with those around us. If we listen deeply to Father God, we might hear Him say, "Honor your Mother in all that you do."

Higher Power

The term *Higher Power* is, perhaps, the most generic name for God. By referring to the supreme creative force as *Higher Power*, we avoid the distinction between God the self and God the other, God the principle and God the person, God the Mother, God the Father. These distinctions are left entirely up to the individual. This way, no one is excluded, and no one is compelled to conform to any particular image of God.

Regardless of how we experience our Higher Power, we avail ourselves to a power that is beyond duality and, therefore, beyond weakness and conflict. Such a Higher Power is available to all because it does not require knowledge of metaphysics, initiation into any mystery school, or the schooling of any particular religion. We simply relate to It in a way that is consistent with our human understanding of It. We may speak to It, listen to It, believe in It, get angry at It, or even feel Its presence within us and around us.

Our sincerity alone invokes the power that can gracefully guide us in finding the courage to change whatever needs to change, the serenity to accept whatever we cannot change, and the wisdom to distinguish between the two. When our prayers and communion are done in a way that is simple and natural to us, our Higher Power becomes more and more real to us; we draw closer and closer to It – until we become It.

CHAPTER 63

Christian & Pagan

(Natural Friends Forced to Fight)

Christian and Pagan are opposites only in the sense that they embody *monotheism and pantheism.* Monotheism embraces purity; the purity of the one God. Pantheism embraces fullness; the fullness that includes all possible expressions of God.

Historically, the two have been at odds with one another. This may be attributed to the fact that both have been used as means of getting power over others; political power and economic power.

When the two "opposing" systems are simply regarded as methods for the individual to commune with the creative power of the universe, there is no cause for conflict between them. When conflict does arise, it can be quickly resolved by remembering the primary purpose of the teachings.

Monotheism and Pantheism

Monotheism, in its purest form, recognizes the one God in all things. Pantheism, practiced in fullness, recognizes that everything is God because everything pulsates with the life of the one God. Conflict between pantheism and monotheism arises when we look only at the surface of each—which is what we tend to do when we use any religion as a sword and shield. On the other hand, when we use either pantheism or monotheism as a means for cultivating self-knowledge and inner peace, we naturally plunge deeply and sincerely into our practice. When we look deeply enough inside one, we see the other.

The pantheism of the Pagan is often personified as the deity called *Pan,* which literally means *everything.* Likewise, in the Bible, when Moses asked God to identify Himself, God responds, "I Am." Apparently, *I Am,* is just a rough translation. Hebrew scholars say that a more accurate translation is, *I Am all there is.* The Christian and the

Pagan who are at odds with each other have both forgotten something. Each side struggles against the other; struggling against the hidden truth that brings their respective belief to life.

To the Christian, God often becomes a projection of the omnipotent parent who rewards good behavior and punishes bad behavior. Forgotten is the truth that God is, by definition, everywhere and resides in everything. To the Pagan, there are either many gods to solicit and placate, or there are no gods at all, but just "energy" to be harnessed as a means of acquiring power. Forgotten is the truth that this "energy" is intelligent, creative, and has a life of its own.

When each perspective loses sight of the truth contained in the other, it limits its own teachings. This can only lead to the placing of great importance on the preservation of laws, doctrines and customs, while the dignity of the individual human is sacrificed.

Likewise, the pure Christian and pure Pagan both understand the same thing:

- The Energy/God that fills the universe is omnipotent, benevolent and intelligent beyond anything we can comprehend with the rational mind.
- This Energy/God is, in a very real sense, the first cause of all creation; the Father and Mother of all that there is.
- The same infinite intelligence that created the universe resides in every corner of creation, and is at the disposal of our human calling. It beckons us, *"Command Ye Me!"*
- When we call upon this Energy/God to effect a change anywhere in the physical universe, it will effect the same change in the one who makes the call, because this Energy/God makes no distinction between "self" and "other", "us" and "them", "friend" and "enemy". Whether we are casting a spell or praying, the one who makes the call is affected in the same manner as the recipient.

God and Real Estate

I was once in a Mexican restaurant having dinner with my friend "Allen". Allen's primary focus for most of his adult life has been the deepening of his relationship with God. Over the years, he would occasionally report to me, with deep earnestness, that he had experienced a new level of connection with Source.

For example, on one occasion, he came to my office looking especially happy. I mentioned this to him. I also pointed out that, in recent months, he had been rather joyful and carefree. When I asked him why, he just laughed and threw his arms in the air. There was no specific external blessing to which he could point. It was all coming from the inside. Shortly after that, his business started booming.

As we sat in the restaurant, sipping margaritas and munching on chips and salsa, he informed me that several months earlier he had experienced yet another new level of connection with Source. He said that in the past he would sit in meditation and, eventually, experience the inner door opening a bit. This time, however, the walls had come down – and they stayed down. The occasional trickle in the cosmic faucet had become an open fire hydrant gushing freely.

For Allen, sitting in prayer and meditation had become virtually irrelevant. He did not feel inclined to use his deep sense of connection to Source to make changes in his physical life. Neither did he feel inclined to use his newfound awareness to preach or teach.

Did Allen lose all interest in Earthly life? Did he feel inclined to retreat to the mountains and become a hermit? Not at all. In fact, his prolonged time of God communion coincided with a tremendous newfound passion for *real estate!* In addition to his regular profession, he was putting in many hours a week negotiating deals, tracking interest rates, wrestling with tenants, hiring and firing contractors, etc. He didn't feel inclined to ask God to make his business or anything else in life smooth and easy. He simply had an easy willingness to participate in the adventures that every new day had to offer. He seemed perfectly content not knowing what tomorrow would bring. In fact, I specifically asked Allen if he felt at all tempted to use this sense of God connection to do "magic" or get a sneak-preview of the future. He basically said, "No, that would be boring."

Interestingly enough, Allen also found that he had more sexual energy than usual. As we sat in the restaurant, he would occasionally stop talking as an attractive woman passed by. He would remain discreet and proper as his face quietly took on the aura of a snorting bull-just for a moment— then he would resume talking passionately about God – or real estate.

Heaven & Earth

Monotheism, when practiced with purity, tends to create earthly peace and prosperity. How much peace? A lot! How much prosperity? Enough prosperity so that the individual is more than content. In other words, when we sincerely say, *Thy will be done*, our earthly existence is infused with new life. Awareness of the One Life gives birth to new life. When we really *do* seek first the kingdom of God, all else really *is* provided, and all things are made new again. If our surrender to the one God is profound enough, we might feel as if we have been reborn. In practical terms, this means we experience newfound enthusiasm for Earthly life. We want to relish our relationships and joyfully plunge into our work, whether we drive a bus, program computers, or sell real estate.

Pantheism, when practiced in fullness, results in an overpowering desire to seek the one God. This might seem strange if we have only a superficial understanding of pantheism and Paganism. Nonetheless, the inevitable result of communing deeply enough with any of the many gods is awareness of the one God, because they are all expressions of the one God. Furthermore, if we really *do* master the Pagan art of manifestation through rituals and the power of the mind, the result is, again, a pure desire for God realization; a desire that emerges organically and silently from within.

When monotheism is *not* practiced with purity, the result is a rejection or denial of the things of the earth. In essence, we are saying "no" to God's creation. Likewise, when pantheism or any Earth-based religion is not practiced in fullness, the result is rejection or denial of the one God. In essence, we are cutting ourselves off from the source of all our power and earthly riches.

The *pure* practice of monotheism must give birth to the fullness and richness of earthly life, with all of its diversity and sensuality. Likewise, when pantheism—and Earth religions in general—are practiced in *fullness*, they awaken within us a pure and spontaneous remembrance of the one God, and the yearning to simply return home.

CHAPTER 64

Remembering & Forgetting

One quiet summer afternoon, while I was home, I got down on the floor and started breathing deeply and rapidly while evocative music was blasting out of my boom-box. Prolonged deep breathing – preferably under skilled supervision – can reveal troublesome issues hidden just beneath conscious awareness.

On that afternoon, however, I was not burdened by any specific troublesome thoughts or emotions. I just felt a little "antsy". After I breathed deeply and rapidly for about 20 minutes, I commenced releasing deep sobs, which was interesting since I wasn't feeling particularly sad when I started. I was just feeling...antsy.

Bringing In the Sheep

At first, I did not understand why I was sobbing. I just felt like sobbing, so I did. Eventually, however, I became aware of the various persons and situations that I was having issues with. The issues did not seem very serious. Each one was small enough that it was easy to ignore. However, I could see how the silent accumulation of these little issues might cause me to feel "antsy".

As the sobbing subsided, I had the strong impression that parts of me had been scattered around, clinging onto those various persons and situations that I was having issues with. In the stillness, I felt as if those parts of me were "returning", like so many lost sheep. The feeling was one of great relief. My body relaxed and my mind became calm. For a while, I bathed in a sublime sense of wholeness.

A Time to Remember

As I lay quietly on the floor, I spontaneously started thinking about the act of remembering. I was already familiar with the idea that we are much more than we think we are. As the story goes, we are im-mortal beings who decided to forget who we are, so we could spend some time pretending we are weak and vulnerable humans. Philoso-phically, I was inclined to agree with that idea, though, if pressed for an honest answer, I would have to say that I was pretty much identified with my physical form.

That day, however, something was different. As I mentally mulled over the hypothetical cosmic remembering of ourselves, I was still emotionally experiencing the "returning" of the lost parts of me that had been scattered about. At that moment, an interesting merger oc-curred in my mind. The word *remembering* took on a whole new meaning. Remembering became synonymous with *unifying*. In other words, the "members" of myself were coming together again. I was *re-membering* myself. At that point, my sobbing resumed and became so deep, I felt like I was going to physically explode.

This business of remembering ourselves, as I experienced it, isn't merely the recalling of thoughts and images from the past, like re-membering a trip to the zoo at age four. The capacity to re-member who we are, depends on our capacity to *feel*. The feeling is one of wholeness—of bringing the pieces of oneself back together. When they return, there is no mistaking the feeling. The experience is not unlike re-uniting with a long lost loved one.

In that moment of re-membering myself, I was gladly willing to give up all my worldly possessions, ambitions and all my accumulated perceptions and beliefs about myself and others. The re-membering of myself felt more important than any of the details of my life, because, such re-membering is what gives meaning to the rest of my existence.

The next day, as I was driving to the mountains, I realized that a synonym for *remember* is *recollect*, which literally means *bringing together again pieces that were once united*. As I stopped my car along a mountain road to purchase a jar of homemade honey from a roadside vendor, I realized that the hidden meaning of the words *re-member* and *recollect* is not just a quirk of the English language. In Italian, the word for remember is *recordo*, which has the same origin as the word *accordo* which means *together* or *in agreement*. A similar tendency exists in a number of other languages. There seems to be a general recognition that the act of remembering is synonymous with the act of re-joining what had previously been torn asunder.

And a Time to Forget

If remembering is the mental equivalent of achieving wholeness or unity, forgetting is the equivalent of *separation*. Since remembering of oneself involves the capacity to feel, forgetting entails suppression of the capacity to feel.

To remember too much, too soon could be psychologically damaging. Therefore, the brain forgets anything we cannot safely address on a conscious level.

Forgetting things does not mean that the information is destroyed. The brain has seemingly "dispersed" the memory into many separate bits of data, and prevents them from coming together into a hologram of conscious awareness. Physiologically, this simply means that the involved brain cells don't communicate.

The time of forgetting is a time of rest, when we prepare ourselves for the time when the brain can allow formerly unbearable memories to surface into conscious awareness. These memories may be traumatic childhood experiences or the awareness of who we are beyond our mundane human awareness. Either can be damaging if done carelessly or prematurely. Either can be tremendously healing if done with care.

As mentioned earlier, the urge to know oneself is an evolutionary imperative that eventually asserts itself no matter how much we try to restrain it. We may experience this urge as the simple desire to reclaim an emotionally shattered past, or a desire to commune more deeply with the God of our understanding. The urge cannot be long denied, for it is essential for our health and well being. If we resist this urge, it creates a condition that some would describe as "hell" – a painful, burning combination of remembering and forgetting. It is the full-blown awareness of how we are inwardly torn asunder, and feeling helpless to do anything about it.

Nonetheless, at some point in our personal journey through life, this hellish condition is more acceptable than the pseudo-peace of repressed inner turmoil – that familiar state of dullness or boredom, the "robotic" behavior that covers low-grade anxiety and depression, or the unfulfilled desires that just won't go away.

A Time and a Season

The remembrance of oneself occurs naturally when it is neither suppressed nor forced open. Our inner wisdom knows there that is a time of remembering and a time of forgetting. The time of forgetting is a time of sleep and rest, when the subconscious mind gathers energy and prepares the conscious mind for a time of deeper remembering.

The time of remembering is a time of self-discovery. It is a time when the warring parts of oneself are brought together. It is a time when the members that had been cast out are welcomed home. It is a time when we instinctively gravitate toward truthfulness, stillness and loving touch; for these are the three great healers; the three keys by which we unlock the silent integrative power with. When we practice truthfulness, stillness and loving touch, we begin to recognize that life is a dance of opposites, and we gradually and organically awaken ourselves to the unity beyond opposites.

REFERENCES

Ageless Body, Timeless Mind—by Depak Chopra
Birth Without Violence—by Robert LeBoyer
Children of the Future—by Wilhelm Reich
Dracula, Prince of Many Faces—by R. Florescu & R. MacNally
Fear of Life—by Alexander Lowen
Gilgamesh—by Herbert Mason
God's Fool—by Julien Green
Gods of Eden—by William Brambly
Kundalini—by Gopi Krishna
Man and His Symbols—by Carl Gustav Jung
Plain Talk About Depression—by Marilyn Sargent
The Power of the Subconscious Mind—by Joseph Murphy
Rebels & Devils—edited by Christopher S. Hyatt
Taoist Secrets of Love—by Montak Chia
Touching—by Ashley Montague

Book Purchasing Information

This book may be purchased directly from the author by visiting **Innerintegration.com,** or by calling **404-315-0394**.

- Volume discounts available.
- Signed copies are provided on request.